Eating People Is Wrong

Eating People Is Wrong,

and Other Essays on Famine, Its Past, and Its Future

Cormac Ó Gráda

PRINCETON UNIVERSITY PRESS

PRINCETON AND OXFORD

Copyright © 2015 by Princeton University Press
Published by Princeton University Press, 41 William Street, Princeton, New Jersey 08540
In the United Kingdom: Princeton University Press, 6 Oxford Street, Woodstock,
Oxfordshire OX20 1TR

press.princeton.edu

Cover image © Anna Jurkovska/Shutterstock, jacket design by Leslie Flis

First paperback printing, 2020
Paperback ISBN 978-0-691-21031-5

The Library of Congress has cataloged the cloth edition as follows:

Ó Gráda, Cormac.
    Eating people is wrong, and other essays on famine, its past, and its future / Cormac
Ó Gráda.
        pages cm
    Includes bibliographical references and index.
    ISBN 978-0-691-16535-6 (hardback : alk. paper) 1. Famines—History. I. Title.

    HC79.F3O567 2015
    363.809—dc23
                            2014037905

British Library Cataloging-in-Publication Data is available

This book has been composed in Sabon Next Pro with Adobe Garamond display

Printed in the United States of America

Do Dhiarmuid,
do Mháire,
agus d'Fhionn

Contents

Eating People Is Wrong

Introduction

No two famines are the same, yet, superficially at least, most have a lot in common. The usual symptoms might include high food prices beyond the reach of the poor; increases in evictions, and in crime and antisocial behavior; vagrancy and migration in search of employment and charity; rising unemployment; hunger-induced reductions in the birth and marriage rates; protests and resistance that give way to apathy and hopelessness as the crisis worsens; early philanthropic efforts that, in the more protracted crises, give way to donor fatigue; fear of, and lack of compassion towards, the victims; and, above all, increases in mortality from disease and starvation. There has probably never been a famine where a more caring ruling elite could not have saved more lives. But there are differences too. The context may be economic backwardness and crop failure, but the shortages of food or purchasing power that can lead to famine need not require a big harvest shortfall: war (Sancerre in central France in 1572–73, Leningrad in 1941–44, the western Netherlands in 1944–45) or human agency (the Soviet Union in 1931–33, North Korea in the mid-1990s) may be enough. Moreover, some famines last only a few months (Somalia in 2011–12, the Dutch Hongerwinter of 1944–45), while others straddle several years (Ireland in the late 1840s, China in 1959–61).

All famines bring out the best and the worst in people, and generate attitudes and actions that are difficult to pass judgment on. As the Russian literary scholar Dmitri Likhachov, who survived the blockade-famine of Leningrad during World War II, put it so eloquently: "In the time of famine people revealed themselves, stripped themselves, freed themselves of all trumpery. Some turned out to be marvelous, incomparable heroes, others—scoundrels, villains, murderers, cannibals.... The heavens were unfurled and in them God was seen."[1] Another Leningrad survivor confided in her diary that only those who had not experienced hunger were capable of heroism and self-sacrifice. Hunger had "degraded and crushed" her and her husband. They had been both the victims and perpetrators of food theft.[2] Famines always create their own versions of what Auschwitz survivor Primo Levi[3] called "grey zones," where the survivors are more likely to be the stronger and the savvier, the less scrupulous, and the more ruthless and vicious. In Xiakou in China's Sichuan province during the Great Leap Forward Famine of 1959–61, to survive one had to be "tricky" and willing to steal. Those who died were of the wrong class background, or else "those without guts, and the stupid."[4] But the grey zone was an area where, as Levi insisted, "one must beware of the error that consists in judging distant epochs and places with the yardstick that prevails in the here and now."[5]

In societies the world over, famines have laid bare the dark, ordinarily hidden side of human nature. In a Ukrainian village in 1933, children trying to survive on "cookies" made of frozen potatoes and on wild birds and their eggs dismissed their incapacitated and dying father's pleas for food: "Go and find potatoes for yourself." That evening the poor man was "already in the cemetery."[6] In Mirganj in the Indian state of Bihar in 1897 a group of starving children followed a compassionate American visitor around their orphanage, "and when we came to a stand they would collect about us, staring at us with dull looks . . . and putting their claw-like little hands on our boots." It made the visitor shudder, but not the native overseers, who had been depriving these children of their food.[7] In Mainpuri, Uttar Pradesh, during another Indian famine in 1837, when parents were selling their daughters for a few rupees, the local police merely cautioned them against certain women "of ill fame" who would sell the chil-

---

[1] Likhachov, as cited in Reid 2011: 194.
[2] Kochina 1990: 84.
[3] Levi 1988. Thanks to Breandán Mac Suibhne for this reference.
[4] Flower and Leonard 2006.
[5] Levi 1988: 165.
[6] Harvard Project on the Soviet Social System, Schedule A, vol. 36, Case 333/(NY)1582 (interviewer J.F., type A4), p. 25 (http://pds.lib.harvard.edu/pds/view/5608007?n=25&imagesize =1200&jp2Res=.25&printThumbnails=no).
[7] Cited in Merewether 1985: 174–75.

dren on as prostitutes.[8] The chaotic scene at a soup kitchen in County Donegal during the Great Irish Famine was recalled in folklore a century later:

> It was in the second year of the famine that a soup cauldron arrived in this place. Bones were boiled in it to make the broth. Two local women looked after the big pot and distributed the soup. It is said that they gave the first and thinnest part of the gruel to the people, while they kept the thicker part at the bottom of the pot for themselves.
>
> That soup pot saw many rough days. The people were so famished that their compassion and consideration had left them. Healthy men used their strength to muscle past women, children, and the weak. They trampled on top of one another, everybody trying to get close to the soup pot.
>
> One day a poor man, a stranger, approached the pot. When he reached the front he stood aside from those next to him for a while; the pushing and shoving was so violent that a woman fainted. Room was made for two men to carry her away from the pot, and they threw her on the ground, leaving her for dead. When they returned they found the poor man next to the pot where the woman was. One of the men caught him by the back of the neck and flung him back on the stony ground. "It wouldn't take much," he said to the poor man, "for me to dump you in the cauldron. And you daring to come here to drink some of our broth when it is so scarce and not enough for our own needs." The poor man got up and left without saying anything. A man named Eoghan Thuathail was standing next to the pot and what had happened to the stranger upset him. He called him back and gave him half of his own broth.[9]

The folk memory of famine recalls many such incidents, in Ireland, in China, in Greece, in Malawi, and elsewhere.[10]

Gloomy predictions from demographers and scientists about the imminent threats of overpopulation and famine were commonplace in the 1960s and 1970s. The alarm bells go back further; in 1948 William Vogt and Fairfield Osborn had led the way with *Road to Survival*

---

[8] Sharma 2001: 115.

[9] Póirtéir 1996: 69 (my translation); Mac Suibhne 2013; Ó Gráda 1994.

[10] Zhou 2013; Hionidou 2011; Ó Ciosáin 2004; Vaughan 2007.

and *Our Plundered Planet*, and a decade later French demographer Alfred Sauvy had sounded another warning in his *De Malthus à Mao-Tsé-Toung*.[11] Paul Ehrlich's best-selling *Population Bomb* (1968), which was inspired by that earlier literature, began with the statement that "the battle to feed all of humanity is over. In the 1970s hundreds of millions of people will starve to death in spite of any crash programs embarked upon now." Drought-induced famine in the Sahel—that vast semi-arid area south of the Sahara, stretching from Somalia to Sudan—in the early 1970s, followed by more severe famines in Ethiopia in 1973–74 and 1983–85, in Bangladesh in 1974, in western Sudan in 1985, and in Somalia in 1992 may have seemed to confirm these predictions. Today, however, earthquakes and tsunamis are more likely to make the front pages than famines. And while the famines of the last decade or two share many of the characteristics mentioned above with earlier famines, they do pale in terms of severity or intensity.

The territory of the famine historian cuts across those of demographers and economists, historians and political scientists, literary critics, anthropologists, and folklorists.[12] This volume accordingly addresses the topic from a variety of disciplinary, chronological, and geographical perspectives. All essays except the first, which sets out to highlight the repulsiveness of famines, build on some elementary economic concepts.[13] They cover case studies ranging from *ancien régime* France to India during World War II and from Ireland in the 1840s to Somalia in the 2010s, but their main focus is on some of the twentieth century's most notorious famines. Learning from those famines and placing them in broader historical context guides our assessment, in the concluding essay, of the prospects for a future free of famine.

The horrors of famine include child abandonment, voluntary enslavement, increasing resort to prostitution, and the rupture of communal and neighborly loyalties. But perhaps the greatest horror of

---

[11] "World Famine by 1980 Scientist Warns," *Irish Times*, 2 September 1964; Mathieu Gilbert, "Le Monde échappera-t-il à la famine?," *Le Monde*, 11 November 1958; Sauvy 1958. Compare Lam 2011.

[12] Compare Ravallion 1997; Dyson and Ó Gráda 2002; Póirtéir 1995, 1996; Mac Suibhne 2013; Lynch 1992: 67 (on interdisciplinarity in historical demography).

[13] Only in Essay 3 does the economics become a bit more complex.

all is being the victim (or even worse, perpetrator) of cannibalism. Essay 1, "Eating People Is Wrong," is about this disturbing feature of famine. Homophagy is so universally frowned on that in the past reports of it during famines have often been dismissed as a dramatic motif or trope not intended to be taken literally. But cannibalistic acts have been highlighted—and some perpetrators and victims identified—in several recent accounts of the Chinese Great Leap Forward Famine. Both Frank Dikötter's *Mao's Famine* (2010) and Zhou Xun's *The Great Famine in China, 1958–1962: A Documentary History* (2012) devote chapters to the topic, and they do not spare the reader the gory details. The rhetorical impact is powerful.

Famine cannibalism has a long history, however, and instances linked to earlier famines in China, and in the Soviet Union in the early 1920s, the early 1930s, and the early and mid-1940s were based on more than hearsay. Less convincing, perhaps, were rumors in May 1946 that in the famished suburbs of Budapest "children had been killed and sold for meat," or the claim in June 1979 by one of Vietnam's boat people that "those on his boat were reduced to cannibalism," or recurrent reports in the 1990s and 2000s of famine-induced cannibalism in North Korea.[14] On the other hand, in September 1969 the only remaining Western correspondent in war-torn Biafra was anxious to deny any return to cannibalism there, although it had been "once widespread."[15] Such reports highlight the difficulties of separating fact from fiction and the silences and taboos surrounding famine cannibalism. The first essay nevertheless makes the case for cannibalism as one of the horrors, if not one of the defining characteristics, of severe famine, and suggests that the lack of evidence for it during recent food crises may merely indicate that they were "minor" by historical standards. The essay devotes special attention to the case of Ireland and, in particular, to claims of cannibalism during the famine of the 1840s.

[14] "Cannibalism Rumour Sweeps Budapest," *Irish Times*, 13 May 1946; "Refugee Crisis a Global Concern," *Irish Times*, 20 June 1979 (referring to Vietnam); Mark Nicol, "Famine-struck North Koreans 'Eating Children.'" *The Telegraph*, 8 June 2003. Further details are provided in Essays 1 and 5.

[15] "Biafran Morale Is Slumping After Two Years of War and Starvation," *Irish Times*, 16 September 1969.

Essay 2, "'Sufficiency and Sufficiency and Sufficiency,'" revisits the Great Bengal Famine of 1943–44. That famine, which caused the deaths of over two million people, achieved paradigmatic status in the wake of Amartya Sen's classic *Poverty and Famines* (1981). The timing and context of this horrendous crisis—on the eve of Indian independence and after several decades when India was free of famine—had already guaranteed it a prominent place in post-colonial historiography. My essay, based in large part on contemporary press and archival sources, reassesses the role of politics, market failure, and food supply in India's last major famine. It also offers a fresh perspective on the political economy of public action in a context dominated by wartime priorities, colonial rule, and communal tensions.

Essay 3, "Markets and Famines," focuses on an issue that also resonated in Bengal, the role of food markets during famines. In the wake of a minor famine in the west of Ireland in 1822, novelist Maria Edgeworth consulted her friend, the famous economist David Ricardo, on the merits of the potato as the staple of the Irish poor. At that time about one-third of Ireland's population relied almost exclusively on a food from which there was no trading down, because the potato was "*an bia ba shaoire ag síol Éabha* [the cheapest food available to man]."[16] Ricardo in reply insisted that much depended on whether the crop was storable from one year to the next—as Edgeworth (incorrectly) claimed it was—and on the presence of merchants who would store the potatoes. The skeptical economist (who represented the Irish borough of Portarlington in Parliament at the time) required "some proof that there were among you some of those patient, plodding, calculating merchants who would be contented to enter into a speculation on a prospect of its success in four, five, or ten years."[17] For Ricardo such merchants mitigated the risk of famine.

But in *The Black Prophet*, which appeared in 1847, at the height of the Great Irish Famine, Irish novelist William Carleton wrote of "a

---

[16] Austin Bourke 1993: 52–73; Ó Gráda and Ó Muirithe 2010: 56.
[17] Ricardo to Edgeworth, 13 December 1822 (in Ricardo 1951: letter 511).

class of hardened wretches, who look forward to a period of dearth as to one of great gain and advantage, and who contrive ... to make ... sickness, famine, and general desolation ... sources of successful extortion and rapacity, and consequently of gain to themselves."[18] Throughout history those threatened by famine—and sympathizers such as Carleton—singled out for opprobrium traders who "gambled on hunger." The hungry, convinced that they were victims of an artificial scarcity, demanded a "moral economy" that delivered food to all at a fair price. Supporters of unfettered markets argued, on the contrary, that traders should not be impeded, and that their actions minimized the damage caused by famines.

The same contrasting views on the role of food markets in alleviating or exacerbating food shortages crop up repeatedly in discussions of famine. They have a huge resonance for Bengal in 1943–44. After a review of the economic-historical debate on markets and famines, which goes back to the eighteenth-century Enlightenment, Essay 3 turns first to a series of historical case studies: famines in nineteenth-century India, in *ancien régime* France, in Ireland in the late 1840s, and in Finland in the 1860s. Its strategy is to compare spatial and intertemporal arbitrage in crisis and non-crisis situations. It also assesses evidence on how markets functioned during some recent famines and near-famines. It ends up arguing that while, by and large, market forces may have done little to mitigate famine mortality, they usually did not exacerbate it either.

The Chinese Great Leap Famine of 1959–61 was undoubtedly the greatest modern famine ever in terms of lives lost. It is still among the most controversial, not least in China, where some neo-Maoists are now denying even the lower-bound estimates of excess mortality proposed by demographers.[19] Is it enough to declare the famine "Mao's Famine" (as, say, Frank Dikötter or Jasper Becker would); or should it be considered instead as an ill-conceived and reckless at-

---

[18] Carleton 1979: 48.

[19] Chris Buckley, "Milder Accounts of Hardships under Mao Arise As His Birthday Nears," *New York Times*, 16 October 2013; "New (Approved) Assessments: the Great Famine," *The Economist* 9 September 2013 (http://www.economist.com/blogs/analects/2013/09/new -approved-assessments).

tempt at making a desperately backward economy catch up (as, say, Felix Wemheuer or Stephen Wheatcroft would argue)? What role did economic conditions before the Great Leap Forward play? Is there any resolution to the controversy about excess mortality? Long "hidden," the famine has recently been the subject of several high-profile books aimed at a broad market, including Dikötter's *Mao's Famine* (2010), Yang Jisheng's *Tombstone* (2012), Zhou Xun's *Forgotten Voices of Mao's Great Famine* (2013), and Felix Wemheuer's *Famine Politics in Maoist China and the Soviet Union* (2014).[20] Essay 4, "Great Leap into Great Famine," addresses this largely man-made catastrophe as described in these works in broader historiographical perspective. Such a perspective would include—of course—comparing China in the 1950s with the Soviet Union in the 1920s and 1930s; but it would also include looking back to the 1920s, when Walter Mallory, secretary of the China International Famine Relief Commission, dubbed China "the land of famine," and to the 1930s, when English economic historian R. H. Tawney likened the position of the rural population in parts of China to "that of a man standing up to his neck in water, so that even a ripple is sufficient to drown him," and focusing more on the huge regional inequalities in famine mortality.[21]

By historical standards, what have passed for famines in the new millennium (so far) have been "small." They have killed very few—with the exception of Somalia in 2011–12, a very special case—and have not lasted long. Nowadays the closest countries outside parts of sub-Saharan Africa come to famine is what the Food and Agricultural Organization dubs "severe localized food insecurity," and that hardly ever culminates in famine. Insofar as recent history is any guide, it indicates that famines in peacetime are no longer the looming threat they have been throughout history. "In peacetime" is the crucial qualifier. The globalization of disaster relief and increasing global food output are responsible for this. Is it time, then, to turn those apocalyptic forecasts of the 1960s and 1970s on their head?

---

[20] See also Zhou 2012; Manning and Wemheuer 2011; Wemheuer 2011; Garnaut 2013a, 2014b.
[21] Mallory 1926; Tawney 1966: 77.

At the same time, malnutrition remains a more intractable and pressing problem: while the proportion of the world's poor that is malnourished continues to decline, the food situation facing a billion or so people condemns them to ill health and premature death. These contrasting signals are not lost on international nongovernmental organizations (NGOs), since they have important implications for the nature of relief work and the future of humanitarian aid. Essay 5, "Famine Is Not the Problem—For Now," explores how recent famine history intersects with the role of NGOs and global malnutrition. It also assesses the challenge posed by the prospect of global warming.

An earlier version of "Eating People Is Wrong" was presented at the annual meeting of the American Conference for Irish Studies (New Orleans, March 2012). "Sufficiency and Sufficiency and Sufficiency" began as a paper presented to a workshop on twentieth-century famines in Melbourne University in June 2010, and "Famine Is Not the Problem" grew out of an invited lecture to the 82nd Anglo-American Conference of Historians (Institute of Historical Research, London, July 2013). Essays 3 and 4 build on and considerably extend material previously published in the *Journal of Interdisciplinary History* and *Population and Development Review*, respectively.[22]

In writing this book, I have relied greatly on help and feedback from friends near and far over an extended period. They include Bob Allen, Tom Arnold, Lance Brennan, Neil Buttimer, Perry Curtis, David Dickson, Maureen Egan, Michael Edelstein, Melissa Fegan, Anthony Garnaut, Sheldon Garon, Rachel Herrmann, Mary Healy, Andreas Hess, Violetta Hionidou, Paul Holliday, Morgan Kelly, Liam Kennedy, Breandán Mac Suibhne, Stephen Mennell, Joel Mokyr, Michaël Neuman, Maire Ní Chiosáin, Niall Ó Ciosáin, Diarmuid Ó Gráda, Fionn Ó Gráda, Kevin O'Neill, the late Barry Quest, Karl-Gunnar Persson, David Rieff, Carl Riskin, John Rundell, Peter Solar, Felix Wemheuer, and Stephen Wheatcroft. The book reached close to its final shape at the end of a stay at Les Treilles in the south of

---

[22] Ó Gráda 2005, 2011, 2013a.

France in September-October 2013. I am very grateful to the Fondation des Treilles and its staff for their help and warm hospitality. Finally, where would I be without Princeton University Press? My special thanks to its busy director, Peter Dougherty, for guidance and support, and to his team, including Jodi Beder, copy editor *par excellence*, for bringing the book to fruition.

1

Eating People Is Wrong

FAMINE'S DARKEST SECRET?

The act of cannibalism symbolizes how far human beings are willing to let themselves fall.

Kon Ichikawa, Japanese filmmaker

On looking around I noticed a woman lying on her face. She was dead and perfectly naked ... and the side of her face and breast were gnawed away. Two famished-looking men and a woman were seated a few yards aft glaring at the body with wolfish eyes. Could famine have driven them to this horrible repast? I would not believe, and yet I could not doubt it, so hungry and ravenous were their looks....

William Brittlebank (1873: 180–81)

There was also of course a great deal of psychic decomposition, even right down to some cases of cannibalism, even, or especially, cannibalism in one's own family. It was, as far as we can tell, of the deranged, of those who were themselves victims, driven mad by hunger.

Joseph Lee, Irish historian[1]

John Post's *The Last Great Subsistence Crisis in the Western World* (1977) is a classic work of famine history. Its title refers to the famine that followed the dark and cold European summer of 1816, when (in Lord Byron's words) "The bright sun was extinguish'd,

The late Barry Quest suggested this title.
[1] Lee 1997: 168.

and the stars did wander darkling in the eternal space, rayless, and pathless, and the icy earth swung blind and blackening in the moonless air." Post's title was a misnomer, an exercise in historic license. True, by the 1810s famine in England and France was already history. England had not experienced a truly "biblical" famine since before the Black Death, and France's last such famine had occurred during the devastating winter of 1709. But in the Western world as a whole, the era of famine—and famine is defined here as "a shortage of food or purchasing power that leads directly to excess mortality from starvation or hunger-induced diseases"[2]—would not end for another 130 years. The famines linked to the failure of the potato in the 1840s, including the Great Irish Famine but lesser famines too in the Low Countries and in parts of what is now Germany, were still to come[3], as was the Finnish famine of 1867–68 (on which more in Essay 3). So was the famine that resulted from the Allied blockade of Germany in 1918–19, the massive Soviet famines of 1920–22 and 1931–33, and the several war famines of World War II. But the dubious distinction of "last subsistence crisis in the western world"[4] belongs to Moldova and adjoining parts of the Soviet Union in 1946–47.

Moldova's was no small famine, relatively speaking; in the Soviet Union, as in Ireland and in Finland, the era of famines came to an end with a bang, not a whimper. As many as 0.2 million[5] Moldovans out of a population of 2.5 million may have perished. Yet little has been written about the famine, and what has been written has been colored by the Cold War and the post-Soviet legacy. The Romanian-speaking core of Bessarabia, henceforth the Moldavian Soviet Socialist Republic, had been annexed by the Soviet Union as recently as 1940 as a by-product of the Nazi-Soviet pact. For Russian historian V. F. Zima, its famine was the product of excessive grain procurements by Moscow.[6] For Soviet specialist Stephen Wheatcroft,

---

[2] Ó Gráda 2009: 4. There is more on defining famine in Essay 5 below.

[3] On which see Ó Gráda, Paping, and Vanhaute 2007.

[4] Post 1977.

[5] This number may be on the high side. It is based on the monthly numbers of deaths in 1946 and 1947 given in Council of Europe Parliamentary Assembly, Document 12173, 1 March 2010 (http://assembly.coe.int/ASP/Doc/XrefViewHTML.asp?FileID=12386&Language =EN).

[6] Zima 1999.

by contrast, the famine must be analyzed against the backdrop of a critical food supply situation in the Soviet Union and elsewhere at the time.[7] And there is no denying the role of food supply: in 1945 in Russia, less affected than the famine zones elsewhere in the Soviet Union, grain output was less than half the prewar norm (25.4 versus 51.9 million tons), and in the following year it was lower still (21.2 million tons).[8] Wheatcroft provocatively claims that the Stalinist regime, faced with a severe shortfall in output, coupled with no prospect of outside aid and with "dangerously low" stock levels, pressed workers in rural areas harder than the peasantry.[9]

Two generations on, the Moldovan famine remains a highly contentious and emotional issue in Moldova itself. As recently as 2006, the Moldovan legislature rejected an attempt to provide "a political and legal appreciation" of the 1946–47 Moldovan famine. Opposition deputies described the famine as "premeditated," but the official line—from a pro-Moscow administration—was that while there was no denying that there had been a famine, it had "a pragmatic explanation historically demonstrated: the difficult post-war period, the poor crops, and the drought." And so communal tensions in present-day Moldova drive one side to absolve Stalin of all responsibility for the famine. The same tensions also drive discussions of famine in Ukraine in 1932–33.

One aspect of the Moldovan famine that makes its memory more fraught is the gruesome suggestion that "the eating of corpses took place on a large scale."[10] The authorities were aware of the practice and sought to stamp it out. They even showed Alexei Kosygin, soon to become a member of the Politburo, who had been sent from Moscow to investigate in February 1947, a corpse that had been prepared for consumption. There were stories both of survivors living off the corpses of those who had perished and the murder of people for the purpose of consumption:

> [I]n June 1946, there were a number of cases in the villages of Alexandreşti, Recea-Slobozia and Sturzeni in Râşcani district.... On 8

[7] Wheatcroft 2012.

[8] Dronin and Bellinger 2005: 158.

[9] Wheatcroft 2012: 1005.

[10] Ellman 2000: 617fn1; "The 1946–1947 Famine in Bessarabia" (http://assembly.coe.int /Main.asp?link=/Documents/WorkingDocs/Doc10/EDOC12173.htm); see also Caşu 2010: 45.

September 1947, the District Committee of the Communist Party of Cahul, where 10 cases of cannibalism were officially recorded between February 1946 and February 1947, prepared a document advising secretaries of district party committees on how to prevent cannibalism. According to the document, the district leadership had information on cannibalism and the use of human bodies as food in certain villages in the districts of Vulcănești, Taraclia, Ciadâr-Lunga, Baimaclia and, particularly, Congaz. An official told party and state leaders that on 7 and 8 February 1947 in the village of Baurci in Congaz district (currently in the Gagauz Autonomous Territorial Unit of the Republic of Moldova), he had recorded four killings for the purposes of cannibalism. According to this source, the consumption of bodies had become a frequent occurrence. There were cases of stolen bodies that had been taken to the cemetery and not buried. The muscles and limbs of several bodies found at various places in the village had been removed. In the village of Beșalma the situation was even more serious. The consumption of bodies was also common in other villages, he concluded. In January 1947, a peasant woman from the village of Tambula, in Bălți district, killed two of her four children, a girl of six and a boy of five, with a view to eating them. A peasant in Glinjeni, in Chișcăreni district, invited a female neighbour into his house then strangled and ate her. Another peasant from the village of Cajba in Glodeni district killed his 12-year-old grandson who had come to visit and ate him. Some 39 cases of cannibalism were recorded in Moldova during the 1946–47 famine.[11]

Cannibalism is famine's darkest secret, a taboo topic. How common was it in the past? I am not referring here to what scientist and historian Jared Diamond has dubbed "customary cannibalism,"[12] i.e., the ceremonial or ritual consumption of human flesh in nonemergency situations. Our focus is on famine cannibalism, that is, cases of cannibalism during life-threatening food shortages.

Of all the horrors of famine, cannibalism may be the most unsettling. Sociologist Pitirim Sorokin, writing against the background of the Russian famine of 1921–22, which cost millions of lives and during which he claimed cannibalism was "an ordinary occurrence,"

[11] Council of Europe, "Commemorating the Victims of the Great Famine (Holodomor) in the Former USSR," Doc. 12173 (1 March 2010) (http://assembly.coe.int/ASP/Doc/XrefView HTML.asp?FileID=12386&Language=EN); Cașu 2010.

[12] Diamond 2000.

pointed out that the practice entailed the suppression not only of religious, moral, legal, and aesthetic reflexes, but also those related to group preservation.[13] Much in the same vein, Danish anthropologist Kirsten Hastrup has argued that when famine results in cannibalism it has gone "far beyond mensurational reach" to a level of "hardship so extreme that humanity itself seems at stake."[14]

Hastrup did not distinguish between "survivor cannibalism"— survivors consuming the corpses of those who have already died— and what might be called "murder cannibalism," that is, murdering people for meat. But during the Great North China Famine of 1876– 78, in a widely reproduced letter the Catholic bishop of Shanxi reported that "until lately the starving people were content to feed on the dead; but now they are slaughtering the living for food."[15] Kathryn Edgerton-Tarpley refers to three stock phrases regarding cannibalism which recur in gazetteers' accounts of the 1876–78 North China famine: "people ate each other," "exchanging children and eating them," and variants of "people ate each other to the point that close kin destroyed each other." In Russian, too, there are different words to describe murdering for food (*lyudoedstvo*) and corpse consumption (*trupoedstvo*).[16]

The record on famine cannibalism, like that of ritual cannibalism, is contested. William Chester Jordan, historian of the Great Northern European Famine of the early fourteenth century, notes that references to famine cannibalism may act as a form of cliché to convey the "stark horror" of famine conditions: "to make a famine real, one had to include cannibalism in the story." And famine historian David Arnold dismisses most of the evidence for it as "second-hand and hearsay."[17] Stories of famine cannibalism have also been invoked for pejorative purposes, as part of a narrative that demonizes enemies or "outsiders."[18] Recurrent references to old women or "hags" devour-

---

[13] Sorokin 1975: 136. For background see Charnock 1866; Tannehill 1975; Vandenberg 2008; Macbeth, Schiefenhövel, and Collinson 2007.

[14] Hastrup 1973: 730.

[15] "The Famine in China," *Irish Times*, 13 July 1878; "The Famine in the North of China is Happily Decreasing," *Otago Times (New Zealand)*, 5 October 1878; see also "Horrors of the Chinese Famine," *Red Bank Register (New Jersey)*, 25 July 1878.

[16] Edgerton-Tarpley 2008: 223; Davies and Wheatcroft 2004: 421.

[17] Jordan 1996:149; Arnold 1988: 19.

[18] E.g., Taithe 2009: 149.

ing children recall sinister narratives of witchcraft: and who believes in witches anymore?

Yet several well-known and well-documented historical episodes highlight how desperate people can be driven to cannibalism during life-threatening food emergencies. Examples include the following (in chronological order):

- Survivors of the wreck of the French naval frigate *Méduse* off the west coast of Africa in July 1816. The victims were immortalized in Théodore Géricault's famous oil painting, *The Raft of the Medusa*.
- Much in the same vein, the surviving crew of the Nantucket whaling ship *Essex*, sunk by a sperm whale in the South Atlantic in 1820; they followed the "custom of the sea" whereby shipwrecked survivors drew lots to see who would be killed and eaten to enable the others survive.[19]
- The California-bound Donner party of American pioneers, led by brothers George and Jacob Donner, some of whom resorted to cannibalism when stranded high in California's Sierra Nevada during the winter of 1846–47.[20]
- The British explorer Sir John Franklin and his crew, who met their deaths in attempting to find the Northwest Passage, also in 1847, and some of whom, according to contemporaneous accounts now supported by recent archaeological research, engaged in cannibalism.[21]
- Tom Dudley and Edwin Stephens, survivors of yet another South Atlantic shipwreck in 1884, who murdered 17-year-old cabin boy Richard Parker on the principle of "death for all or cannibalism for some." Their trial gave rise to a celebrated judicial verdict rejecting the "custom of the sea" as described above and denying, in effect, that necessity knew no law.[22]

[19] Philbrick 2001.
[20] Grayson 1990. See also Kristin Johnson's "Donner Blog" (http://donnerblog.blogspot.ie/2013/10/donner-party-cannibalism-article.html) and the sources mentioned there.
[21] "The American Franklin Search Expedition," *Irish Times*, 9 October 1880; Keenleyside, Bertully, and Fricke 1997.
[22] Simpson 1984; "The Sea," *Irish Times*, 29 December 1888. Resort in the past to cannibalism in the wake of shipwrecks seems not to have been so unusual (see Fabel 1990: 9–10). I am grateful to Kevin O'Neill of Boston College for this reference.

- Another, less well-known instance of cannibalism at sea concerned the mainly Irish crew of the barque *Maria* of Belfast, dismasted in rough seas off the coast of west Africa in December 1876. The sole survivor, twenty-year-old James McLinden of Kilkeel in County Down, explained how the last to die had attempted to survive on the bodies of comrades who predeceased them.[23]

- Nicholas Werth's *Cannibal Island* describes how Stalin's policy of cleansing Moscow and Leningrad of "outdated elements" in 1933 by dumping them on the remote island of Nazino in western Siberia culminated in many instances of cannibalism. Werth reckons that the number of cannibals was low, and profiles them as young males from rural backgrounds who had previously served time for criminal activity. He notes that those eating human flesh "were well aware that they could do so with impunity so long as it had not been proven that they had previously murdered the victim."[24]

- Japanese troops in New Guinea towards the end of World War II, as described in Kazuo Hara's disturbing 1987 documentary, *The Emperor's Naked Army Marches On*. Prohibited from surrendering and cut off from food supply chains, some resorted to cannibalism. Several Japanese military were found guilty of sanctioning or engaging in cannibalism against civilian populations and enemy soldiers by the U.S. and Australian war crimes tribunals and executed for their crimes.[25] Survivor cannibalism also features in *Fires on the Plain*, the 1951 novel by Oaka Shohei about a lone soldier in the Philippines at the end of World War II.

- In Bergen-Belsen concentration camp in 1943–45 evidence of cannibalism compounded, if that were possible, the horrors of the Holocaust. Prison doctors told a British medical officer of fleshless bodies, with "the liver, kidneys, and heart . . . knifed out."[26]

[23] "Horrible Story of Cannibalism at Sea," *Irish Times*, 3 March 1877. See also "A Terrible Story of the Sea: Shipwreck and Cannibalism," *Irish Times*, 19 November 1888; "Shocking Story of Cannibalism at Sea," *Irish Times*, 9 September 1899.

[24] Werth 2007: 132–45.

[25] Stephens 2007; "Death for Jap Who Practiced Cannibalism," *Canberra Times*, 17 April 1946; "Jap Officers to Hang for Cannibalism," *Canberra Times*, 5 October 1946.

[26] "Cannibalism in Prison Camp: British Medical Officer's Visit to 'Most Horrible Place,'" *The Guardian*, 19 April 1945; "Says Cannibalism Rampant at Belsen, Saw 300 Cases," *Toronto Daily Star*, 27 September 1945; "Cannibalism at Belsen Described," *Daytona Beach Morning Journal*, 29 September 1945.

- The survivors of the crash of Uruguayan Air Force Flight 571 in the high Andes in 1973. Some initially refused to resort to cannibalism, but relented after a few days when all other food supplies were exhausted.[27]

More controversial is the case of recently arrived colonists in Jamestown, Virginia who—so it was claimed—"driven thru insufferable hunger to eat those things which nature most abhorred," resorted to cannibalism during the winter of 1609–10. Historian Rachel Herrmann has contested the documentary evidence for this particular instance, long accepted, but archaeological analysis of the remains of a teenage girl in 2012 implies postmortem cut-marks consistent with the butchering of human flesh.[28] I exclude the famous literary example (based on a real-life thirteenth-century character) of Count Ugolino della Gherardesca, whom the poet Dante consigned to hell for having eaten his own children and other crimes, but whom recent forensic DNA analysis absolves of cannibalism.[29] I also exclude an account from Athens during the famine of 1941–42, where survivor cannibalism is a plausible inference, but unproven.[30] And there are more.[31]

---

[27] Read 1974.

[28] Zinn 2003: 24; Herrmann 2011; Stromberg 2013.

[29] Dante, *Inferno*, Canto 33; "Experts Dig Up Count to Solve Mystery," 7 February 2001 (http://rodin-web.org/works/ugolino_no_cannibal.htm).

[30] Skouras et al. 1947: 348:

> And it is certain that if private initiative had not reached the extent it did with the popular soup kitchens and the fight for survival, the problem of hunger would have taken such dimensions of primitiveness and barbarity, that even cannibalism would end up being a common phenomenon.... The horrific picture of the corpse of a girl whose left thigh was missing made an impression on E. E., who writes, "It was cut so smoothly that someone must have cut it with a knife. The thought made me feel sick. That is what made the biggest impression on me during the Occupation/famine."

I am grateful to Violetta Hionidou for the reference and the translation.

I also exclude instances such as the arrest, as recently as 2001, of two men in Moldova for selling human flesh as meat. A customer had become suspicious at the taste of the meat, which sold for $2 per kilo, and it emerged that poorly paid workers in a cancer hospital had sold human body parts, including breasts, legs, and arms, to the arrested men. The men were fined for selling meat without a license (Kate Connolly, "Cannibalism Is Symbol of Moldova's Decline," *The Guardian*, 5 April 2001).

[31] E.g., "Cannibal Tales," *Shipping News*, posted 18 May 2013 (http://marinelives -theshippingnews.org/blog/2013/05/18/cannibal-tales/).

These cameos and anecdotes cover quite a range of circumstances; most suggest that "normal" people could be reduced to cannibalism in extreme situations, and that survivor cannibalism was by no means the preserve of the psychopathic or the psychologically unstable. Note too that in most accounts the perpetrators were Europeans or of European origin, not some alien, primitive "savages." The evidence on whether those who engaged in murder cannibalism during famines were also "normal" is scarce and more ambivalent, however.

While famine cannibalism has never been widespread or responsible for more than a miniscule fraction of famine deaths, references to the practice recur throughout history.[32] Like much else about famine, it is mentioned in the Old Testament. Conditions during the Syrian siege of Samaria in the ninth century BCE were so severe that "a donkey's head was sold for eighty pieces of silver, and the fourth part of a *kab* [pint] of wild onions for five pieces of silver."[33] And 2 Kings 6 continues:

> And as the king of Israel was passing by on the wall, a woman cried to him, saying, "Help, my lord, O king." And he said, "If the Lord doesn't help you, how can I help you? Out of the barn floor, or out of the winepress?" And the king said to her, "What ails you?" And she answered, "This woman said to me, 'Give your son, so that we may eat him today, and we'll eat my son tomorrow.' So we boiled my son, and ate him: and I said to her on the next day, 'Give your son, so that we may eat him': and she has hid her son."[34]

The reluctance of mothers to kill their own children in such circumstances is a theme that recurs in later accounts and is echoed in one of the Chinese depictions mentioned above of people "exchanging children and eating them."

References to famine cannibalism thereafter range from an account from Edessa (present-day Şanliurfa in southeastern Turkey) in

---

[32] Ó Gráda 2009: 63–68.

[33] 2 Kings 6:25–28.

[34] There is more along the same lines in Deuteronomy 28:53–57, describing the effects of another siege in the seventh century BCE. Interestingly, the account in Kings informs the Gaelic text from the 1830s edited by Buttimer (1997: 60–61, 63–64).

503–4 CE, where the local general executed those guilty of murdering for food but gave leave to eat the corpses of the dead "and this they did openly, eating the flesh of dead men,"[35] to an account describing Egypt in the early 1200s, when at first it "formed the subject of every conversation" but "eventually people grew accustomed, and [made] these detestable meats . . . their ordinary provender";[36] from a report that in Poland in 1315 "men did not abstain from the corpses, or even from dung" to claims that famine reduced some Italians to cannibalism in 567, 890, 1359, and 1396 CE;[37] and from stories of mothers eating their own children during the apocalyptic Ethiopian famine of 1889–91[38] to a case in war-torn Scotland in 1341 when "the starving sufferers were compelled to feed on substances most abhorrent to human appetite; and one wretch called Christian Cleik, with his wife, subsisted on the flesh of children whom they caught in traps and devoured. These wretched cannibals were detected, condemned, and burned to death."[39]

Two recent monographs on crises in early modern Europe focus particularly on evidence of famine cannibalism in time of war. Guido Alfani invokes Jean de Léry's *L'Histoire mémorable du siège de Sancerre* (1574), which describes in gruesome detail a case involving three adults during an eight-month-long siege in 1572.[40] Lauro Martines explains how during the siege of Augsburg (1634–35), after all the city's pets and pack animals had been killed and eaten, resort to cannibalism was "inevitable."[41] Reports of famine-induced cannibalism feature in siege narratives from places as far apart in time and space as Numantia (Spain, 133 BCE), Maarat (Syria, 1098 CE), Jerusalem (70 CE), and Leningrad during World War II.[42] Defenders of the Irish city of Derry barely escaped the same fate in 1689: a "corpulent gentleman," who "conceiving that some of the garrison in the

---

[35] Wright 1882: 62. See also Stathakopoulos 2004; Ó Gráda 2009: 63–68; Marvin 1998.
[36] Tannehill 1975 (citing an Egyptian source).
[37] Camporesi 1989: 87.
[38] Pankhurst 1986: 84–85.
[39] Scott 1830: 121.
[40] Alfani 2013; Nakam 1975 (on war and famine in sixteenth-century France); Martines 2013: 118–19, 128 (on the siege-related famines during the Thirty Years War).
[41] Martines 2013: 137–38, 140.
[42] On siege-famine in late Roman Empire, see Stathakopoulos 2004: 46–47.

extremity of their hunger looked at him with rather a longing eye, hid himself for three days, till the cannibal desire might have time to subside."[43]

A striking feature of several accounts of famine cannibalism is their rather nonjudgmental tone. Some display an understanding, if not outright empathy, towards the perpetrators. In Hara's 1987 documentary former soldier Kenzo Okuzaki more than once states that he did not condemn the cannibals, but "those who put them in that situation." A former production team leader remembered that during the Great Leap Forward Famine in Henan "people had no choice." There was no note of condemnation.[44] Again, the contemporaneous commentary accompanying a Chinese woodblock of 1878 describes "bodies ly[ing] dead on the road, and the living striv[ing] together for their flesh."

> The superior man in ordinary times, while he eats cooked flesh, has his shambles and kitchen away from his hall. But in this year of famine, men eat one another. Letters from the country tell us that if a body lies unburied, the starving surround it, ready to rush on it with their knives, and eat off the flesh for food. The dead died because they could get no food, and the living now seek to prolong their lives by eating the dead. *Would you have them die rather?* What will famine not compel men to do? [45]

The woodblock appeared in a pamphlet addressed to an English readership highlighting the urgency of sending aid to China.

The vignettes of cannibalism described above refer to localized crises: what of recent famines? At the height of the Soviet famine of 1920–22 cases of both survivor cannibalism and murder cannibalism were well documented;[46] an officially sanctioned exhibition held in a room in the Kremlin highlighted the urgency of the situation with gruesome images provided by the Cheka (Soviet secret police). Communist Party newspapers carried reports of cannibalism for

---

[43] Witherow 1879: 184 (http://www.archive.org/stream/derryenniskillen00withrich/derry enniskillen00withrich_djvu.txt).

[44] Wemheuer 2010: 191.

[45] Legge 1978: 22–23, emphasis added.

[46] Sorokin 1975: 136; Patenaude 2002: 262–70, 332; Tahk 2013.

their shock value, and a billboard on display in Moscow read: "These people who eat their dead because they are hungry are not cannibals; the cannibals are those who do not give their surplus to the hungry." Indeed, Lenin sought to exploit the descent into cannibalism as an excuse for expropriation of ecclesiastical property.[47] French journalist Paul Erio's account, relayed by the *New York Times*, carried a racist edge, noting that the images and documents in the Kremlin "show that cannibalism occurred most commonly among the Tartars, Tchouwaches and Kirghizes." However, Erio added, the prevalence of women in the photographs did not imply that they were "more addicted to cannibalism than men," only that they were less afraid of the Cheka.[48]

A decade later, during Stalin's collectivization famine, there were reports of murder cannibalism too, though this time hidden from the public eye:

> Every day there were cases of cannibalism. Mothers killed their children and ate them up. In such villages as Kordyshivka, Soshenske, [and] Pytiiv, cannibalism was very widespread. It was awfully dangerous for a person who looked good to go there. I don't know why people change so much. Ukrainians are very generous and very kind people, but during that hunger they looked like wolves.[49]

In a March 1933 survey of forty-two districts in Ukraine in which starvation was rife, the Kiev secret police listed seventy-two cases of *lyudoedstvo* (murder cannibalism) and sixty-five of *trupoedstvo* (corpse consumption). Gruesome accounts of cannibalism also survive from the Kazakh famine of 1932–33, which followed a Soviet campaign to "sedentarize" and collectivize a largely nomadic population. In Kazakhstan the fear of murder cannibalism, "an omnipresent threat," added to the horror of famine.[50]

---

[47] Avramescu 2009: 232.

[48] "Cannibalism Still Prevails in Volga Famine Districts," *New York Times*, 29 May 1922.

[49] Harvard Project on the Soviet Social System, Case 333 (http://pds.lib.harvard.edu/pds/view/5608007?n=25). See also "American Talks with Convicted Cannibals: Relief Worker in Russia Reports that He Found a Dozen Undoubted Cases," *New York Times*, 28 February 1922 (report by Walter Duranty); "Starving Eat Dead, Soviet Told," *New York Times*, 29 December 1921. On 1932–33, see Davies and Wheatcroft 2004: 422.

[50] Kindler 2011: 22–23; 2014: chap. 4; on the background to the famine see Piancola 2004; Ohayon 2013; Kindler 2014.

Evidence for cannibalism during the blockade-famine of Leningrad during World War II is also plentiful. At the height of the crisis,
between early December 1941 and mid-February 1942, nearly nine
hundred people were arrested for unspecified crimes relating to cannibalism. Harsh repression and an attenuation of the crisis reduced
its incidence thereafter.[51]

Finally, turning to the very recent past, histories of the Chinese
Great Leap Forward Famine of 1959–61 have highlighted incidents
of cannibalism and, indeed, have gone so far as to reveal the names
of victims and perpetrators (see Essay 4). Frank Dikötter claims that
"in the midst of state-sponsored violence ... necrophagy was neither
the most common nor the most widespread way of degrading a
human being."[52] But famine cannibalism was nothing new in China
in 1959–61. Instances were reported in Henan in 1942, in Sichuan in
1936, in Gansu in 1929, in Shanxi during the Boxer Rebellion in
1900, during the Great North China Famine of 1876–78, and in
Nanking in 1861.[53] How ironic, then, that in 1981 a Chinese scholar
should blame cannibalism during Great North China Famine of the
1870s on "a man-eating social system [that had created] a man-eating
social disaster."[54]

And yet, although cannibalism is a recurring feature of accounts
of famine, by no means all famines led to it. Thierry Brun guards
against lumping all famines together in a quest for universal patterns, and notes in particular that the atmosphere of despair and cruelty which was linked to cannibalism during the Soviet famine of
1920–22 is absent in the Biafra famine of the late 1960s and also the
Sahel famine of 1972–73.[55] There is no evidence for it during the
Great Bengal Famine of 1943–44, for example, but it seems that not
all nineteenth-century Indian famines were free of it.[56]

More recent famines in sub-Saharan Africa have yielded little evidence of cannibalism either. True, the official responsible for relief

[51] Belozerov 2005: 223–24.

[52] Dikötter 2010: 323.

[53] "Cannibalism in China," *Irish Times*, 20 April 1929; Li 2007: 304; "Human Flesh Sold in
Chinese Markets," *Los Angeles Times*, 19 December 1900; Edgerton-Tarpley 2008; "The Famine
in China," *Irish Times*, 29 June 1878; "War and Famine," *Times of India*, 8 October 1861.

[54] As cited in Edgerton-Tarpley 2008: 214.

[55] Keys et al. 1950; Brun 1980.

[56] "The Indian Famine: An Alleged Case of Cannibalism," *Irish Times*, 30 August 1877.

during the Ethiopian famine of 1984–85 told Australian novelist Thomas Keneally that he had witnessed cannibalism "in an inadequate feeding centre in the Ethiopian highlands," for which (according to his informant) "these people were not to blame."[57] But cannibalism does not feature in accounts of major famines in the Sahel, in Biafra, and elsewhere.[58]

Occasional claims of famine cannibalism from North Korea since the late 1990s, if substantiated, would constitute a shocking indictment of its despotic leadership. Médecins Sans Frontières were the first to highlight such claims, based on interviews with refugees, in 1998, but the executive director of the World Food Programme denied the claims at the time.[59] More reports emerged in 2003 and in 2012–13. Most referred to isolated cases involving individuals or very small groups, but a few to cannibalism as the "new norm" or as "rampant" in North Korea.[60] It must be noted that hard evidence is still lacking. Whether the severe famine conditions usually associated with famine cannibalism truly existed in North Korea in 2012–13 remains moot. Recent scholarship, discussed in Essay 5, suggests that *engagé* scholars bent on "regime change" in the 1990s and 2000s greatly exaggerated excess mortality from famine in North Korea.

Lucht Feola Daoine d'Ithe, Consumers of Human Meat

What evidence is there for famine cannibalism in Ireland? As Nicholas Canny[61] noted long ago, dubbing the native Irish "canyballs" was

---

[57] Keneally 2010.

[58] Ó Gráda 2009: 67–68; Rahmato 1991.

[59] Associated Press, "Cannibalism Reported in North Korea," 15 April 1998 (http://www .apnewsarchive.com/1998/Cannibalism-Reported-in-North-Korea/id-91eb6e8608b6112 887f498d971dde245); "Famine Turning North Koreans into Cannibals," *Independent* (Dublin), 13 April 1998.

[60] "North Korea 'Executes Three People Found Guilty of Cannibalism,'" *The Telegraph*, 11 May 2012; "North Korean Cannibalism Fears amid Claims Starving People Forced to Desperate Measures," *The Independent*, 28 January 2013; Nicol 2003; Becker 2005: 213; Williams 2013.

[61] Canny 1973: 587; compare Ó Drisceoil 2001; Hulme 1986.

a feature of early English colonialist rhetoric. The allegation has a much older history, however: in *Foras Feasa ar Éirinn* ("The Basis of Knowledge about Ireland") poet-historian Seathrún Céitinn (c. 1569–c. 1644) traced it back to the Greek geographer Strabo (63 BCE–24 CE). Strabo was an unreliable witness: in his famous *Geography* he admitted to knowing little about Ireland "except that the inhabitants are more savage than the Britons, since they are man-eaters as well as heavy eaters," and that they "count it as an honourable thing, when their fathers die, to devour them." However, he confessed to writing this "on the understanding that I have no trustworthy witnesses for it."[62] Elizabethan poet Edmund Spenser was present at the horrific execution of the "notable traitor" Murrough O'Brien in Limerick in 1577, where he saw O'Brien's foster-mother "take up his head whilst he was quartered and suck . . . up all the blood running thereout, saying the earth was not worthy to drink it."[63] But Spenser's depiction of this as an example of ritualistic Irish savagery hardly carries conviction.[64]

Céitinn based his rejection of Strabo's accusation that the Irish were cannibals ("*gurab lucht feola daoine d'ithe na h-Éireannaigh*") on the lack of references to cannibalism in the old Gaelic sources.[65] Our concern here is not human sacrifice[66] but famine cannibalism. And if references to the latter are evidence, then Céitinn was clearly incorrect.

The earliest Irish mention of famine cannibalism refers to 698–700 CE, when, according to the medieval *Chronicon Scotorum*, "*fames et pestilentia iii annis in Hibernia facta est, ut homo hominem comederet*" ("famine and disease raged for three years in Ireland so that

[62] As cited in Killeen 1976: 209; see also O'Brien 2001; John Connolly, "An Irishman's Diary," *Irish Times*, 23 September 1997.

[63] O'Brien 2001: 37.

[64] If this was ritual cannibalism, then Eibhlín Dhubh Ní Chonaill's instinctive reaction on finding her murdered husband's bloodied body on the roadside in Carraig an Ime (Cork) in 1773—"*níor fhanas le hí ghlanadh ach í ól suas lem basaibh*" ("I didn't wait to wipe off the blood but drank it up in with my cupped hands")—made her a cannibal too. Eibhlín composed a famous lament, which includes this line, in her husband's memory (compare Angela Bourke 1993: 166).

[65] http://www.ucc.ie/celt/online/G100054/, chap. 2. He cites one scandalous exception, which related to 'the pagan era.'

[66] On which see Robinson 1913; Borsje 2007.

man ate man"). There is a hint of cannibalism too in the *Fragmentary Annals of Ireland*'s entry for 700 CE, which refers to "the greatest famine, in which men were reduced to unmentionable foods."[67]

The *Chronicon Scotorum*'s entry for 1116 notes that in the wake of an attack on Thomond by Connacht warlord Toirdhealbach Ó Conchubhair, "There was great famine in the spring so that a man would sell his son and his daughter for food and men would even eat one another, and dogs. All Leinster was *almost* emptied, and scattered throughout Ireland on account of the famine."[68] The sale of children is a recurrent theme of famine history, but the reference to cannibalism here does not imply that children were being sold for consumption: more often they were sold as slaves or concubines. Cannibalism was also recorded in the mid-1310s during Robert the Bruce's Irish campaign: "*do ithdais na daine cin amuras a cheli ar fod Erenn* (and undoubtedly men ate each other throughout Ireland),"[69] when warfare exacerbated the impact of dismal harvests.

Edmund Spenser's *View of the Present State of Ireland*, describing Munster in the 1580s, reported that the surrendering Irish rebels "looked like anatomyes of death, they spake like ghostes crying out of theyr graves; they did eat of the dead carrions, happy were they yf they could finde them, yea, and one another soone after."[70] Admittedly, Spenser's claim may have been based on hearsay, although he was in Ireland at the time. Less than two decades later Fynes Moryson wrote of war-induced famine in County Down towards the end of the Nine Years' War:

> Captain Trevor and many honest gentlemen lying in the Newry can witness, that some old women of those parts used to make a fire in the fields, and divers little children driving out the cattle in cold mornings, and coming thither to warm them, were by them surprised, killed and eaten, which at last was discovered by a great girl breaking from them by strength of her body, and Captain Trevor sending out soldiers to

---

[67] Gearóid Mac Niocaill, ed., *Chronicon Scotorum* (http://www.ucc.ie/celt/published /G100016/index.html); *Fragmentary Annals of Ireland* (http://www.ucc.ie/celt/online/T100017 .html).

[68] http://www.ucc.ie/celt/published/G100016/index.html.

[69] *Freeman* 1944: 252–53; Sayles 1956: 95.

[70] Spenser 1970: 104.

know the truth, they found the children's skulls and bones, and apprehended the old women, who were executed for the fact.[71]

Shades of Hansel and Gretel, perhaps! A later commentator, more sympathetic to the old women, did not deny their deed, but added: "The authors of the famine were the authors of cannibalism, not the unfortunate hags, who were driven by the extremity of hunger to that shocking sustenance."[72] In a reversal of the "hags" motif, Moryson also wrote of "a most horrible Spectacle of three Children (whereof the eldest was not above ten Years old,) all eating and gnawing with their Teeth the Entrails of their dead Mother, upon whose Flesh they had fed 20 Days past."[73] Again, a little skepticism seems appropriate here; surely it would have taken less than twenty days for flesh to rot?

Nor was the discourse purely a colonialist one directed at indigenous savages. Tarlach Ó Mealláin, a Franciscan friar, kept a diary while on the run during the early stages of the Confederate Wars in Ulster in 1643. This was a time of widespread famine in Ireland; Sir William Petty, the founder of political arithmetic, who knew the place well, reckoned that between 1641 and 1652, 87,000 had died "of Famine and Cold, Transportation to the Barbadoes, &c." Petty's demographic estimates were cavalier and imprecise, but his figure tallies with Pádraig Lenihan's suggestion that Ireland's population declined by 0.2–0.3 million (or by 15–20 percent of a population of about 1.5 million) between 1649 and 1652, since Lenihan's figures combine deaths from plague and famine.[74] Ó Mealláin's reference to cannibalism is probably to corpse consumption:[75]

It was also resolved that whoever should steal a cow or horse, steed or gelding, sheep or goat or the value of any of these, would have a like amount confiscated from him, if he were a man of means; or hanged, if he were a man of no means.... Many other fine decisions were made. There are people in the country, Ó Catháins, O'Devlins, O'Haras, and

[71] Fynes Moryson, widely cited, e.g., in Taaffe (1801: vol. 2, 100–101). See also Quinn 1966: 139–40.

[72] Taaffe 1801: II, 101.

[73] As cited in Wittkowsky 1943: 93.

[74] Smith 2006: 161; Petty 1899: 151; Lenihan 1997.

[75] Dillon 2000: 350.

the people of Iveagh, all of Clandeboy and the Route [reduced to] eating horses and steeds; the end of spring; stealing; carrying off cats; dogs; eating humans [corpses?]; rotten leather; and undressed leather.[76]

The following excerpt from the May 1645 deposition by one Peter Hill, landlord and High Sheriff of County Down, recalls Fynes Moryson's account of the same county some four decades earlier:

> The Rebellion began but especially for a year and above now last past it hath been a very common & ordinary thing for the Irish to murder, devour, and eat the persons of such English as they could light upon, and when they could light upon none of them then to kill devour and eat one another. And about one year now since there *was* brought to this deponent at his house called Ballyhornan an Irish woman for wounding & attempting to kill another Irish woman and her child which woman so accused & brought before him upon her examination confessed that she had hurt (but had an intent to have killed) the other woman and her child, and to have eaten the child, whereupon & because he was credibly informed that such a like fat woman had killed and devoured divers others, he this deponent caused her to be hanged.... About the time aforesaid viz. a year since three troopers under the Lord Conway's command going out for Lisnegarvie over the River into the County of Down with their horses about 2 miles off to fetch home grass were suddenly surprised by some of the Irish together with their horses which three troopers were then and there murdered, and afterwards their flesh eaten and devoured by divers barbarous Irish women that lay in the woods. And the very bones of those men were afterwards found in the woods clean picked and the flesh (first *as was conceived* boiled) eaten quite off the same.[77]

Even after discounting for its strong sectarian tone—and it has been claimed that "no story about the Irish could be too gross, too wildly improbable, for [Hill's] acceptance,"[78] the account—a formal legal statement—is persuasive enough.

[76] For the original, see Ó Donnchadha (1931), who remarks that the cryptic nature of the text may imply that Ó Mealláin intended to build on it at a later stage.

[77] http://1641.tcd.ie/deposition.php?depID=837030r020, spelling modernized.

[78] Fitzpatrick 1904: 73. On interpreting the depositions, see Fennell (2011); on the famine context, see Lenihan (1997).

There is a claim that people also resorted to cannibalism in 1652–53, again a time of severe famine: Richard Lawrence was "credibly informed that they digged Corps out of the Grave to eat," and described an eyewitness account of old women and children eating such a corpse.[79] Again, what credence do we place in second-hand accounts and in being "credibly informed"? Note that all the above instances except (perhaps) the first occurred during periods of civil war or colonial conquest.

There is no evidence for cannibalism during the famine of 1728–30[80] nor, interestingly, during the much more serious famine of 1740–41.[81] Our next mention of cannibalism in Ireland turns out to have been bogus, but is worth describing as an example of how elusive evidence for cannibalism can be. It relates to an incident in Wexford in the wake of the United Irish Rising of 1798 as described in Sir Jonah Barrington's *Personal Sketches*:

> During the rebellion ... Mr. Waddy, a violent loyalist, ... fled to a castle at a considerable distance from the town of Wexford.... Here [he] concealed himself, and everybody was for a long time utterly ignorant as to his fate.... At length, it occurred to certain of his friends, to seek him through the country.... Their search was in vain, until approaching by chance the old castle, they became aware of a stench, which the seekers conjectured to proceed from the putrid corpse of murdered Waddy. On getting nearer this opinion was confirmed, for a dead body lay half within and half without the castle, which the descent of the portcullis had cut nearly into equal portions.... [T]o their infinite astonishment, they perceived it was *not* Waddy, but a neighbouring priest who had been so expertly cut in two; how the accident had happened nobody could surmise.... [T]he other half of the priest was discovered immediately within the entrance, but by no means in equally good condition with that outside; inasmuch as it appeared that numerous collops and

---

[79] Lawrence 1682: pt. 2, 86–87. I am grateful to Breandán Mac Suibhne for this reference.

[80] This crisis may have prompted Jonathan Swift's *A Modest Proposal for Preventing the Children of Poor People in Ireland From Being a Burden to Their Parents or Country, and for Making Them Beneficial to the Public*. However, Swift is more likely to have been inspired by Fynes Moryson's depiction of the horrors of the Nine Years' War than by events in his own day (Wittkowsky 1943: 92–93).

[81] On which the best source is Dickson 1997.

rump-steaks had been cut off the reverend gentleman's hindquarters by Waddy who early one morning had found the priest thus divided; and being alike unable to raise the portcullis or get out to look for food, certain indeed, in the latter ease, of being piked by any of the rebels who knew him, he thought it better to feed on the priest, and remain in the castle till fortune smiled, than run a risk of breaking all his bones by dropping from the battlements, his only alternative.[82]

It turns out, however, that Barrington, writing two decades after the event, was being his usual unreliable self. Contemporary accounts[83] make it clear that there was no cannibalism involved. The castle at Clough East to which ultra-loyalist Richard Waddy, a prosecution witness in the trial of executed rebel leader Bagenal Harvey, fled was his own home. He was not starving. The priest was John Byrne, a Carmelite friar from Goff's Bridge near Taghmon who had been "a very zealous and active rebel" in 1798. "A drinking, giddy man," during the Rising Byrne had been asked by his bishop to leave Ferns diocese and threatened with suspension. How come in December 1799 he found himself at Waddy's table remains a mystery. An altercation between the two men followed an alcohol-fueled dinner. It was said that Byrne, believing that he had killed his host, was trying to escape when Waddy let the portcullis that shielded him from intruders drop, virtually severing the friar's body. Next morning Waddy's servants found the corpse, and a few days later an inquest jury returned a verdict of "accidental" on Byrne's death. So, for whatever reason, Barrington invented Richard Waddy's cannibalism.

What of the Great Famine of the 1840s? In an unpublished paper Perry Curtis has commented that "the silences surrounding cannibalism are almost deafening enough to arouse suspicion."[84] Metaphorical references, such as Thomas Carlyle's account of a gombeen man (village shopkeeper-cum-moneylender) who had "prospered … by workhouse grocery-and-meal trade, by secret pawnbroking—by eating the slain," or John Mitchel's gothic depiction of the workhouse in Glenties as "the fortress of Giant Despair, whereinto he

---

[82] Barrington (1827: vol. 1, 162–63).
[83] *Freeman's Journal*, 31 December 1799, p. 3; Whelan 1987.
[84] Curtis 1999: 14.

draws them one by one, and devours them there,"[85] capture the horrors of the famine but prove nothing about cannibalism.

But Mitchel's reference to "insane mothers [who] began to eat their young children, who died of famine before them" is in a different league. So too is the reference in John de Jean Frazer's obscure poem, "The Three Angels," first published in *The Cork Magazine* in August 1848 and reprinted in Chris Morash's *The Hungry Voice*:

> Some gathered their kith to a distant land;
> Themselves, and their kindred, thro' sheer despair,
> Some slew, in belief that *to slay* was *to spare*!
> A cannibal fierceness but ill-suppressed
> In many—made some—we must veil the rest![86]

William Carleton's *Red Hall*[87] (later reissued as *The Black Baronet*) and *The Squanders of Castle Squander*,[88] both novels written during the Great Famine, also refer to literal cannibalism:

> Fathers have been known to make a wolfish meal upon the dead bodies of their own offspring. We might, therefore, be carried on our own description up to the very highest point of imaginable horror, without going beyond the truth.
>
> On Saturday, the 25th inst., a tender and affectionate father, stuffed by so many cubic feet of cold wind, foul air, all resulting from extermination and the benevolence of a humane landlord, will, in the very wantonness of repletion, feed upon the dead body of his own child—for which entertaining performance he will have the satisfaction, subsequently, of enacting with the success the interesting character of a felon, and be benevolently lodged in the gaol of the county.

The Squanders of Castle Squander devotes a few pages to describing a father who made a meal of his dead son. It is likely, as Melissa Fegan notes,[89] that this account (and possibly also Mitchel's claim) were

[85] Carlyle 1882: 160; Mitchel 1873: 212.

[86] Morash 1989: 181–87, lines 252–57. I am very grateful to Melissa Fegan for alerting me to this reference and to the account in William Carleton's *Castle Squander* (see below).

[87] Carleton 1852a: II, 34–35, 51.

[88] Ibid., II, 265–69.

[89] Ibid., II, 265–69; Fegan 2002: 152–53.

inspired by press reports of one of two incidents involving corpse consumption in Galway a few years earlier, to which I now turn.

In May 1849 Rev. James Anderson, rector of Ballinrobe in County Mayo, wrote a long open letter to Prime Minister Lord John Russell, in the course of which he described a starving man who had extracted the heart and liver from a shipwrecked corpse "and *that* was the maddening feast on which he regaled himself and his family." Anderson's letter was widely reported in the press and raised in the House of Commons by Henry Arthur Herbert, MP for Kerry.[90] In a subsequent public letter to Russell, Anderson added some further detail, stating that he had first heard of the incident from a vice-guardian of Clifden Union, Mr. Scrope, who stated that "it been proved before Mr. Briscoe . . . , who had been vice-guardian here, but a short time since." On hearing the report of a relieving officer, Briscoe

> proceeded to the investigation at Claggan near Clifden, and it was then and there proved on oath that an unfortunate man named Diamond had cut up a shipwrecked human body—had thus exposed the heart and liver—had laid aside on the rock the fleshy parts of the thighs, and in furtherance of his intention to make use of the same for food—had returned for a basket, in which to carry home all those parts, but that being watched by some of his neighbours to discover what he wanted with the basket, was subsequently surprised by them and hindered from his purpose, on their seeing, to their horror, that the body was that of a human being! The wretched man did not actually eat it, simply by reason of the prevention, but he deliberately and manifestly intended doing so.[91]

Russell felt compelled to reply in some detail to the charge of famine-induced cannibalism.[92] In his statement to the House of Commons he revealed that the alleged incident had occurred the previous November in Clifden Poor Law Union and claimed that the culprit was a well-fed laborer "of singularly voracious appetite . . .

[90] H.C. Debates, 25 May 1849, vol. 105, col. 978.

[91] "State of the Country," *The Tablet*, 16 June 1849, http://archive.thetablet.co.uk/article/16th-june-1849/5/lambs-hotel-drummond-street-london-june-12–1849.

[92] H.C. Debates, 1 June 1849, vol. 105, cols. 1033–34.

not at all suffering from distress himself" (although two of his sisters were on relief). Initially, according to Russell, the "cannibal" did not identify the corpse as human, but on being apprised of this by neighbours, "it does not appear that he ate any portion of the flesh, whatever his original intention might have been." Russell's disingenuous statement was widely reported,[93] and was the focus of a long rebuttal in the *Freeman's Journal* and a further letter from Rev. Anderson. The *Freeman's* protested that the only detail on which Anderson had erred was on "the eating of the putrid heart," and took particular exception to Russell's assertion that "the Clifden cannibal," one Patrick Diamond,[94] was well fed or, as claimed by the London *Times*, "a fat man":[95]

> Patrick Diamond, the fat labourer, must be as great a curiosity as the extinct *Dodo*. We believe he is the only man of his race on whom a pound of Indian meal per diem has raised the thick coat of fat which gives the *Times* the power of triumphant refutation. Such miraculous obesity cut away the ground from the Rev. Mr. Anderson, and raises the presumption that all the Irish are shamming. . . . But, after all, it did appear that Diamond did cut out the heart—nay more, that this "fat and well-fed labourer" did meditate the eating thereof until he was told, what his eyes must plainly have told him before, that the trunk was that of a human body! This could not well be got over, and how is it explained? Well, by another fact of equal singularity with the fabulous fatness—that Diamond had a most voracious appetite, and of such abnormal irregularity, that he would devour rank weeds or green grass to satisfy its enormous cravings! We leave this satisfactory explanation untouched. Is there a human being, Lord John and the *Times* inclusive, who believes it?

Neither Patrick Diamond's girth nor his failure to distinguish the corpse as human is very plausible. James Anderson was firmly con-

---

[93] E.g., *Trewman's Exeter Flying Post or Plymouth and Cornish Advertiser* (Exeter, England), 7 June 1849; *Scotsman*, 2 June 1849.

[94] Might this have been Patrick Diamond (born Rusheen, County Galway, 1814; died Fountainhill, Co. Galway, 1894; http://www.mcdade.bravepages.com/i77.html#i27617)?

[95] "Distress in Ireland," *Freeman's Journal*, 4 July 1849; *Anglo-Celt*, letter from Rev Anderson to Lord John Russell, 8 June 1849; *Nenagh Guardian*, letter from Rev Anderson to Lord John Russell, 13 June 1849.

vinced that Diamond knew what he was doing, and Rev. James Me-
credy, curate of Spiddal, reassured Anderson that he had told "a tale,
alas, too familiar here." But what actually transpired is rather lost in
the "spin" of the different reports. "Sometime afterwards," Anderson
relates," Diamond sought admission to Clifden workhouse "in a very
emaciated state, and the vice-guardians, finding that he was seriously
declining in health, permitted him to leave the house for out-door
relief."[96]

Another instance, the likely inspiration for Carleton's account, is
harder to discredit. It refers to another Connemara man, one John
Connelly, who had been convicted of stealing sheep and sentenced
to three months' hard labor, since "an end should be put to such
practices or that no man's property could be safe." The sentence
prompted a resident magistrate to intervene:

> Mr. Dopping, Resident magistrate, stood up and addressing the Court
> said, that he felt bound to explain to the Court that he knew of this case.
> He had been told that the prisoner and his family were starving when
> this offence had been committed. One of his children had died and he
> had been credibly informed that the mother ate part of its legs and feet
> after its death. He had the body exhumed and found that nothing but
> the bones remained of its legs and feet. A thrill of horror pervaded the
> court at this announcement. There was deep silence for several minutes,
> during which time many a tear trickled down the cheeks of those pres-
> ent. Even the court wept. The prisoner was instantly discharged.[97]

---

[96] "The Clifden Tragedy," *Freeman's Journal*, 5 June 1849.

[97] *Galway Vindicator*, 1 April 1848, as cited in Langan-Egan (1999: 127). Also *Ballina Chronicle*, "Condition of the Poor," 6 June 1849. The case is also mentioned in *Census of Ireland for the
Year 1851* (vol. 5[1], Tables of Death, pp. 243, 310) and in Keneally (2010). In a later letter on
the Diamond case (*Anglo-Celt*, 8 June 1849; *Liverpool Mercury*, 8 June 1849) Anderson also referred to this episode. He reported Dopping as having informed the court that

> four of the poor man's children had died of starvation, that the husband and wife had
> been brought from Kilkerrin to Clifden, upwards of twenty miles; that the wife, on
> being conveyed from the car to the Bridewell, was found to be dead, through the ex-
> haustion of famine, and that they had both (a short time before her death) declared
> that such were the extremities to which they had been reduced, that they had abso-
> lutely eaten a portion of the legs of one of their children; that in order to come at the
> truth, if possible, the bodies of the said children were exhumed, and that the appear-
> ance of mutilation, as stated, was visible.

The sympathy shown for the accused recalls references above to China in the 1870s and the Soviet Union in the 1920s. It suggests that anthropologist Jared Diamond's sweeping claim that—unlike some non-Caucasians—"Westerners abhor cannibalism" is misconceived.[98]

I noted earlier the difficulties posed by references to cannibalism in accounts of famine in the past. On the one hand, it is not always easy to distinguish between what can be attested and what seems plausible. Legal and standard documentary sources may sway us more readily than folk memory or biblical narratives. But is it fair to dismiss the latter as mere rhetorical devices? On the other hand, the relative "silence" on cannibalism in Ireland during the 1840s is no proof that it did not happen. The taboo against cannibalism meant that, if it occurred, it would have been furtive, all traces hidden by the perpetrators. And the same taboo would have inhibited others from recalling it. William Carleton's expressed unease about portraying cannibalism in *Castle Squander*, even though "six or seven such scenes occurred in Ireland during the last four years,"[99] is interesting

---

Anderson stated also that Baron Lefroy was the judge, and the sentence was one year for stealing a calf.

[98] Again there is some ambiguity about this case. Kathleen Villiers-Tuthill suggests that the *Vindicator* may have been referring to an earlier story concerning one Bart Flaherty from Cill Chiaráin, who had claimed that his wife out of desperation had consumed parts of their two dead children. Their bodies were in too advanced a state of decomposition when exhumed to provide conclusive evidence of cannibalism (Villiers-Tuthill 1997: 127–29).

What seems to be a recycled version of the same episode is given by Thomas Gallagher (1982: 112–13), and invoked in turn by Smart and Hutcheson (2007) and by Smart (2010):

> In Belmullet, County Cork (*sic*), a starving woman lay in her hovel next to her dead three-year-old son, waiting for her husband to return from begging food. When night fell and his failure to return led her to imagine him dead in a ditch, she lay there in the faint light of the fire's dying embers, caressing with her eyes her dead son's face and his tiny fists, clenched as if for a fight to get into heaven. Then slowly, with death searching her, and now with her own fists clenched, she made one last effort to remain alive. Crawling as far away from her son's face as she could, as if to preserve his personality or least her memory of it, she came to his bare feet and proceeded to eat them.
>
> When her husband returned and saw what had happened, he buried the child, went out, and was caught trying to steal food. At his trial, the magistrate from his immediate district intervened on his behalf, citing the wife's act as a circumstance deserving special consideration. The baby's body was exhumed, the flesh of both its feet and legs were found to have been gnawed to the bone, and the husband released and allowed to return to his wife.

[99] Carleton 1852b: II, 265.

in this respect. Folklore about the Great Famine contains no evidence or even hints of it, although it is rife with mentions of famine foods, familiar and unfamiliar—the list includes sycamore seeds, watercress, horsemeat, dog-meat and dog soup, laurel berries, red clover, heather blossoms, dandelions, nettles, donkey's milk, silverweed, goose grass, and much else.[100] But perhaps folk memory's silence on human meat as famine food reflected twentieth-century sensitivities rather than nineteenth-century realities?

Seathrún Céitinn had his own reasons for treating cannibalism as a libel against the Irish race. His elision of awkward references in Gaelic annalistic sources to cannibalism might be excused on the grounds that the contestability of some historical references is plain. Yet the hard evidence for both corpse consumption and murder cannibalism in conditions of extreme famine in both twentieth-century Russia and China, and in the micro-historic anecdotes outlined at the outset of this essay, lend more credence to earlier less well-documented assertions. And, in fairness to Céitinn, they also rather undermine anthropologist Jared Diamond's assertion that "Westerners abhor cannibalism."[101]

This essay has been about one of the human race's darkest secrets. For reasons stated above, in this context empirical history must inevitably take a back seat to speculative inference. Given the truly massive scale of the Great Irish Famine by world-historical standards, it is the paucity of hard evidence for famine cannibalism in the 1840s that is surprising. By then a horrific practice long associated with extreme famine in Ireland had apparently become rare. Had it become taboo? Can we assume that some silent cultural shift or civilizing process[102] was at work? We may never know, given that

---

[100] Póirtéir 1995: 61, 64; 1996: 31–39, 46, 47.

[101] Diamond 2000. Similarly, Brittlebank (1873: 95) referred to "famine such as can be witnessed in Eastern lands."

[102] In "Involvement and Detachment" Norbert Elias (2007: 175) writes: "It is true that people no longer hunt each other for food. Cannibalism, as well as slavery, has become rarer. But the way in which people kill, maim and torture each other in the course of their power struggles, their wars, revolutions and other violent conflicts, is different mainly in terms of the techniques used and the numbers of people concerned." I am grateful to Stephen Mennell for this reference.

a shock like the Great Irish Famine is unlikely to recur. But the ghosts of those Irish members of the Donner party who engaged in cannibalism in the Sierra Nevada precisely at the time when the Great Famine was raging in Ireland, and of the mainly Irish crew of the dismasted barque *Maria*, who tried in vain in 1876 to survive on the corpses of those who had died before them, argue against complacency.

2

"Sufficiency and Sufficiency and Sufficiency"

REVISITING THE GREAT BENGAL FAMINE OF 1943–44

> Mindful or our difficulties about food I told [Fazlul Huq] that he simply must produce more rice out of Bengal for Ceylon even if Bengal itself went short!
>> Lord Linlithgow to Leo Amery, 26 January 1943

> The doctrine of sufficiency and sufficiency and sufficiency must be preached ad nauseam.
>> H. S. Suhrawardy, May 1943

> The dead body of a ... boy was found floating in a ditch near the Adamdighi railway station. ... [T]he deceased along with his brother was coming towards Adamdighi to get "Prasad" from the local "Puja Baris." In the midway the younger brother was staggering and fell down unconscious. Seeing him on the verge of death the elder brother, to get rid of him, pushed him into the ditch and then hastened to the "Puja Bari" and partook of the "Prasad."
>> Kali Charan Ghosh, *Famine in Bengal 1770–1943*

Establishing the incidence, spread, and severity of famines in the past has never been easy. The infrequency of famines in India before the mid-eighteenth century relative to the nineteenth century[1] may be more apparent than real, since it rests on the dubious presumption that no documentary evidence means no famine. Nineteenth-century Indian famines are well documented, however, as are the signs that the Third Horseman was retreating from the subcontinent in the following century. The first four decades of the new century was largely famine-free, and just a few years before the Great Bengal Famine of 1943–44 a retired colonial civil servant might be forgiven for confidently declaring that, insofar as the Indian subcontinent was concerned, "the old famine of history, with its dreadful death toll, is not likely to recur." It was not to be: the Bengal famine would prove a major blot on the final decades of the British Raj.

The broad chronological and demographic contours of the famine of 1943–44 are well known,[2] but its underlying causes are still debated. The authorities at the time blamed the unfolding crisis on undue war-induced hoarding by merchants, producers, and consumers alike, and public policy was based on that premise. This interpretation was repeated in the officially appointed Famine Inquiry Commission's *Report on Bengal*, which also accused local politicians and bureaucrats of incompetence while absolving the imperial government in London of all blame. Not surprisingly, Bengali historians have been much more critical of Bengal's imperial masters.

In the 1970s and 1980s Nobel Laureate Amartya Sen popularized the view that the famine was due mainly to market failure in a wartime context, rather than to adverse food supply shocks. Sen's now-classic account (Sen 1981) not only began a long academic debate about the Bengal famine; it also switched the analysis of famines generally away from food availability decline (FAD) *per se* to the distribution of, or entitlements to, what food was available. Bengal, Sen

---

An earlier version of this essay was presented in June 2010 at a conference at the University of Melbourne organized by Stephen Wheatcroft. Thanks to Stephen Hannon for drawing the maps. It complements an earlier account in Ó Gráda 2009: 159–94.

[1] Bhatia 1967: 7–8.

[2] Blunt 1937: 184. Accounts of the famine include Das 1949; Sen 1981; Greenough 1982; Bowbrick 1986; Brennan 1988; Law-Smith 1989; Goswami 1990; Dyson 1991; Dyson and Maharatna 1991; Maharatna 1996; Weigold 1999; Bayley and Harper 2004: 281–91, 295–98; Batabyal 2005; Mukerjee 2010; Mukerjee 2014.

argued, contained enough food to feed everybody in 1943, but massive speculation, prompted in large part by wartime conditions, converted a minor shortfall in food availability into a disastrous reduction in marketed supply. Sen's analysis has been enormously influential, so while his interpretation of the Bengal famine continues to be focus of specialist debate,[3] for specialist and nonspecialist alike that famine has achieved paradigmatic status in the broader literature on famines.

Crucially, the famine was a war famine. The Burmese capital Rangoon had fallen to Japanese forces in March 1942. In the following months the Japanese air force sank a destroyer and several merchantmen in the Bay of Bengal, and engaged in the sporadic bombing of Bengali cities; an air raid on Calcutta in December 1942 caused considerable panic and the displacement to the countryside of thousands of civilians. Although Japanese forces were too thinly spread to risk an invasion, Bengal remained exposed and vulnerable. Its usual supplies of Burmese rice, albeit a small proportion of aggregate consumption, were cut off. On military advice, officials removed rice and paddy (rough, unhusked rice) deemed surplus to the requirements of the local population from coastal districts such as Midnapur, Bakerganj, and Khulna. They also requisitioned and destroyed boats capable of carrying ten or more passengers to prevent their use by any invading Japanese soldiers. This "boat denial policy" compromised the livelihoods of two of the most vulnerable groups—fishermen and boatmen—and increased transport costs. Moreover, the authorities prioritized the city of Calcutta, where many workers were engaged in war-related production, over the rest of the province. More than half of India's war-related output was produced in Calcutta by an army of workers numbering up to one million, "made up to a considerable extent of a volatile class recruited from outside Bengal."[4] Concern for the city's "priority classes" accounted for the forcible requisition of rice from mills and warehouses in and around the city in late December 1942.[5]

[3] Most recently in Tauger 2004, 2009; De 2006; Islam 2007; Ó Gráda 2008; Das 2008; Mukerjee 2010.

[4] Braund 1944: 25.

[5] Greenough 1982: 108–11.

Sen has also made the more general point that famines are unlikely in democracies, since free assembly, a free press, and the threat
of electoral redress force elites to intervene.[6] Research by economists Tim Besley and Robin Burgess, using state-level evidence from
post-independence India, supports Sen's hypothesis. They find that
greater newspaper circulation and electoral accountability prompted
more generous and effective public disaster relief. Development
economist Dan Banik corroborates, also on the basis of recent Indian data, although he also finds that elites are less concerned with
non-crisis starvation and malnutrition than with the threat of
famine.[7]

The role of the local press during the Bengal famine is interesting
in this respect. On the one hand, wartime censorship limited the
freedom of the press to criticize or, indeed, to publish news deemed
damaging to the war effort. A good case in point is the devastating
cyclone that struck Midnapore (now Medinipur or Midnapur) in
the west of the province on 16 October 1942, news of which took
nearly a fortnight to reach a senior minister in the Bengal government. Only in January 1943 was the real scale of the damage revealed,
because of fears that news of the calamity would play into the hands
of the Japanese.[8] Opposition spokesmen claimed that the severity
of the impending famine was being kept from the people because
"the government has gagged the press and forbidden public meetings where food problems are likely to be discussed."[9] Newspapers
supporting the nationalist, anti-British Quit India movement were
censored or shut down at this time and their editors fined or im-
prisoned.[10] A clandestine press and an underground opposition op-
erated, but these were poor substitutes for the genuine article. The
case of Bengal suggests that Sen's hypothesis might thus be extended
to democracies or semi-democracies during wartime.

---

[6] Sen (1999: 16, 178, 184) cites India in 1973, and Zimbabwe and Botswana in the early
1980s, as cases in which responsive governments took remedial action. See also Sen 2009:
338–48.

[7] Banik 2002; Besley and Burgess 2002. See also Bhattacharya 1995, 1997.

[8] Das 2000: 57; Greenough 1982: 98.

[9] "Bengal Assembly Meets," *Statesman*, 6 July 1943 (reporting a speech by Huq in the provincial assembly).

[10] E.g., "Editor and Printer Tried," *Statesman*, 23 January 1944.

On the other hand, the government did not ban press reports of the famine, nor did it ban newspapers not deemed directly subversive. *Amrita Bazar Patrika* and the *Hindustan Times*, for example, continued to appear,[11] although they presumably engaged in some self-censorship, as did pro-government newspapers. Ministers also expected the press to propagandize on their behalf. In Bengal in 1943 this meant helping to calm public fears about the food supply and to counter the "psychological factors" responsible for food shortages and price rises.[12] Here the case of Bengal's most influential English-language daily, the Calcutta *Statesman*, is of particular interest. The *Statesman* won accolades for publicizing the famine through a series of graphic photographs published in August 1943.[13] Late in the following month, it bravely pointed to the uncanny similarity between official reactions to incipient famine in Bihar and Orissa in 1866 and Bengal in 1943. In both cases the authorities denied that there was a genuine dearth, "large stores being in the hands of dealers who are keeping back stocks out of greed"; in both they refused to recognize "advancing calamity"; in both cases disaster followed.[14] Yet for months beforehand, the *Statesman* had toed the official line, berating local traders and producers, and praising ministerial efforts.

Occasionally, there was evidence of direct interference even with the likes of *The Statesman*. In early September 1943 that newspaper was asked to cease publishing figures "showing the number of people nearly moribund from starvation" admitted to Calcutta's hospitals. It was "coolly informed" that the authorities were "considering" the publication weekly of cases of death by starvation, but that "no special advantage" was to be gained from publishing daily press reports and that it could find better use for the column inches saved

[11] Some their reports were reprinted in book form; see T. Ghosh 1944; Santhanam 1944.

[12] "Food Situation in Bengal," *Statesman*, 14 May 1943; "Bengal Food Drive (editorial)," *Statesman*, 9 June 1943; Greenough 1982: 122.

[13] An in-house history (*Brief History* 1948: 40) claimed that its reports had focused 'world's humanitarian gaze upon a great calamity.' Note to be outdone, perhaps, *Amrita Bazar Patrika* (*ABP* hereafter) also published a series of graphic photographs of the famine in late August 1943. See also the selection reproduced in Santhanam 1944: 85–96.

[14] "Reflections on a Disaster," *Statesman*, 23 Sept 1943. According to Chakrabarti 2004, "The 1866 famine was prompted by 'an extensive crop failure for two successive years'" (p. 203).

thereby. However, this piece of censorship was short-lived.[15] Be that as it may, the *Statesman* and Calcutta's other leading English-language newspaper, *Amrita Bazar Patrika*, published a lot of useful information on assembly debates, policy shifts, price movements, and local conditions throughout 1943 and 1944.[16] Information culled from these newspapers informs much of what is argued in this essay, the sections of which address how those in authority—the British, local administrators, Hindu and Muslim politicians—interpreted and reacted to the unfolding crisis; evidence on prices, hoarding, and land sales during and in the wake of the crisis; and the regional dimensions of the famine.

The Unfolding Crisis

> Famine conditions of 1770 are already upon us.
> *Amrita Bazar Patrika* editorial, August 1943

Even before the end of 1942 Bengal's prospects were causing disquiet in London, Delhi, and Calcutta.[17] The weather was not propitious, with much more rain than normal in the west of the province in October and November. Meteorological data indicate that rainfall had been above average across much of west Bengal, although only six out of ninety-one weather stations—Berhampore (Murshidabad district), Sonamukhi (Bankura district), Midnapur (Midnapur), Contai (Midnapur), and Gopiballabhpur (Midnapur), and Ulumberia (Howrah)—recorded precipitation of more than two standard deviations above the average.[18] In early December 1942 a memorandum from the Delhi government's Food Department informed the secre-

---

[15] "Lessons in Secrecy," *Statesman*, 14 September 1943.

[16] Here I would disagree with later claims by the *Statesman*'s editor that it had been sounding the alarm bells since March 1943. See Stephens 1966: 169–97; Greenough 1982: 122.

[17] "Rice Position in Bengal," *Statesman*, 3 January 1943; "Rice and Dal Prices in Calcutta: Government Order," *Statesman*, 4 January 1943.

[18] Data from several weather stations in west Bengal, especially in Midnapur, Hooghly, Bankura, 24-Parganas, and Burdwan divisions (http://dss.ucar.edu/datasets/ds575.0/data /part5of5), show rainfall of one or more standard deviations above the mean in October to November. Compare Padmanabhan 1973: 13–17. The details on rainfall are given in Ó Gráda 2010: table A1.

tary of state in London of an impending crisis due to "loss of Burma rice, floods in Sind, cyclones in rice growing areas of Bengal and Orissa, and an indifferent rice crop generally in Bengal which is the main rice producing province."[19]

In January 1943 a committee appointed by Calcutta's municipal council suggested the need for food rationing.[20] By March–April the situation was already critical both in coastal sections of Midnapur in western Bengal, where the cyclone had struck, and in eastern Bengal. Relief works began, albeit on a small scale, in villages near Dacca in March, and food rations were supplied to government employees at controlled prices. In early April a deputation from Chittagong, next to Japanese-occupied Burma, prompted an assurance from a senior official that rice and paddy supplies would be provided "immediately" and food rationing introduced there shortly. In Patgram in the extreme north, in "very many cases" barley chaff was being substituted for rice. There was severe hardship too in the area hit by the cyclone in mid-October and in the east of Bengal.[21]

An outbreak of cholera in Calcutta in May 1943 drew media attention to the growing influx of destitutes from the surrounding countryside.[22] The migrants' habit of queuing for hours for food in front of controlled shops led them to "indulge in unhygienic practices and create unhealthy conditions in the localities where shops are located." This prompted the call from a corporation health official for the establishment of controlled shops in the areas when the migrants came.[23] The poor were also blamed for the appalling state of the city's trash cans.[24] Meanwhile the Ministry of Civil Supplies announced that laborers' food rations in Calcutta in future would

[19] Memorandum from the Delhi government's Food Department, 9 December 1942 (published in Mansergh 1971: 357).

[20] "Food Rationing: Corporation Committee's Suggestions," *Statesman*, 28 January 1943; "Measures for Food Rationing," *Statesman*, 2 February 1943. As it turned out, rationing would not begin in Calcutta until February 1944. The measures then came as a shock to the well-to-do, who were initially innocent of the sacrifices called for; some applied for extra rations for their pets and to hold parties.

[21] "Rationing of Rice: Chittagong Measure," *ABP*, 2 April 1943; "In the Cyclone Area," *Statesman*, 28 March 1943; Sen 1981: 55; Greenough 1982: 98–99.

[22] "Cholera Raging Unabated," *ABP*, 2 May 1943.

[23] "Setback in City's Health," *Statesman*, 16 May 1943.

[24] "Appalling Condition of Calcutta's Dustbins," *Statesman*, 3 June 1943; "Calcutta's Dust Bins," 24 June 1943.

consist of equal shares of *atta* (a kind of wheat flour) and rice, in order to release rice for the rural areas. Urban workers were expected to "cheerfully bear this sacrifice" for the sake of others who required assistance "very badly."[25] In early July the government opened its first food shop in Calcutta, selling rice at 6 annas[26] per seer (about 2 lbs.) to the very poor. Huseyn Shaheed Suhrawardy of the Muslim League, as the minister responsible for civilian food supplies during the famine, made the first sale.[27] Meanwhile "growing economic distress" in the city was producing a considerable increase in petty crime.[28] Classic symptoms of famine, such as the sales of girls and women, mass migrations into the towns and cities, and the consumption of "unedibles and meat from dead cows,"[29] were widespread by July.

The travails of an ordinary male worker in Calcutta seeking provisions in price-controlled shops at the height of the crisis are worth recording in full:

> 2 a.m. joined rice queue—no sleep, no shelter from rain.
>
> 6.30 a.m. arrival of control clerk to give tickets. Crowd disorderly, clerk angry, refused to sign my ticket. I got no rice.
>
> 9 a.m. joined sugar queue. 10 a.m. tickets distributed to everyone whether there is sugar or not. 11 a.m. received one seer sugar. I had stood two previous mornings without receiving any. One day my ticket was signed 'empty' and as I do not read well I waited thinking it was signed.
>
> 11.30 a.m. joined kerosene queue. 2.30 p.m. received one bottle kerosene. 3 as (annas).
>
> Thus apart from any other bazar, I spent from 2 a.m. to 3 p.m. getting these few necessities. A woman from my street did the same: on her return she collapsed.
>
> The atta queue is at the same time as the sugar, so if I go for the one I cannot get the other. The ration card has to be shown for both rice

---

[25] "'Atta' to Replace Rice Rations," *Statesman*, 15 May 1943.

[26] Before decimalization in 1957 the Indian rupee was worth 12 annas, and 1 anna was equivalent to 12 pies. A pound sterling was worth 13.33 rupees.

[27] "Food Shop Opened," *Statesman*, 2 July 1943.

[28] "Crime Increase in City," *Statesman*, 11 July 1943.

[29] *ABP*, 15 May 1943.

and coal. I have to get rice each day except Sunday so I can only wait for coal on Sunday. I then receive 5 seers for 3 as.

Besides, discrimination in giving rations is evident. Friends of the shopkeeper come before the public. Bribes are taken. Uniformed volunteers are necessary to keep order in queues, to see justice done: also to keep a check on those known to frequent queues for re-selling supplies.[30]

The regional incidence of the famine may be inferred from maps 2.1 and 2.2. Map 2.1, based on the classification adopted by the government's revenue department, was criticized for omitting subdivisions found to be "appreciably or even severely affected" in an ambitious survey organized by statistician P. C. Mahalanobis for the Indian Statistical Institute.[31] Map 2.2, based on an alternative classification and deemed more reliable by Mahalanobis,[32] highlights two clusters of "very severely affected" subdivisions. The first, in the coastal west, includes two subdivisions in Midnapur (Contai and Tamluk) and one (Diamond Harbour) in 24-Parganas. The second much larger cluster contains twelve subdivisions straddling the eastern divisions of Noakhali, Tippera, Dacca, and Faridpur. In addition, eight subdivisions to the north of the second cluster and twelve to its west were "severely affected." Both maps imply that the western half of the province, apart from the three subdivisions in the first cluster and "severely affected" Howrah (area 34 in maps 2.1 and 2.2), escaped relatively lightly.

At the outset the official stance was that there would be no problem as long as "consumers do not rush to lay in stocks at once for a long period ahead."[33] As the crisis intensified the focus shifted to hoarding, whether out of fear or greed, which the authorities blamed

---

[30] "Food Queue Ordeals," *Statesman*, 4 September 1943.

[31] Maps 2.1 and 2.2 are derived from Mahalanobis, Mukherjea, and Ghose 1946: 5–10 and Greenough 1982: 144. Maps 2.4 and 2.5 are derived from data in Maharatna 1996: 179–80, 200–201. Maps 2.3 and 2.8 are derived from data in the 1941 population census. The data in map 2.6 come from the Pinnell Papers (India Office Library [IOL], Ms. Eur. 911/8), while those for map 2.7 refer to 1951 and are taken from Boyce 1981: 140–41.

[32] Mahalanobis, Mukherjea, and Ghose 1946: 14; Greenough 1982: 139–47 (a discussion of the regional dimensions of the famine); Chattopadhyay and Mukerjee 1946: 2.

[33] "Rice Position in Bengal: Minister's Appeal," *Statesman*, 3 January 1943.

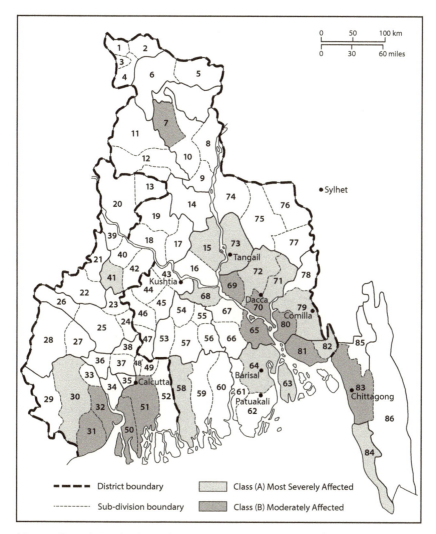

Map 2.1 Bengal: Famine intensity, Revenue Department Classification. Sources: Mahalanobis, Mukherjea, and Ghose 1946: 5–10, and Greenough 1982: 144.

for the "maldistribution" of available rice supplies. Until the crisis degenerated into out-and-out famine, the policy mantra—as articulated by Secretary of State for India Leo Amery in London,[34] Viceroy Lord Linlithgow in Delhi, and H. S. Suhrawardy in Calcutta—was

[34] On Amery's career, see Lavin 2004.

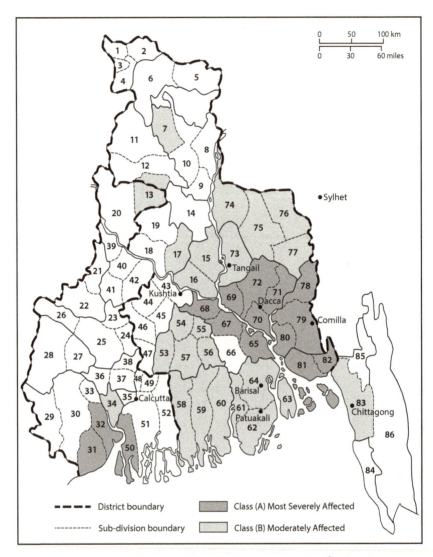

Map 2.2 Bengal: Famine intensity, Industries Department Classification. Sources: Mahalanobis, Mukherjea, and Ghose 1946: 5–10, and Greenough 1982: 144.

that "grave maldistribution" was the problem. And it was not the producer who suffered as a result, since he could keep part of his crop; nor was it the rich consumer, who bought more than he needed; nor was it profiteers and hoarders, who should be dealt with ruthlessly: the victims were the poor consumers who lived precariously on a few annas. The press published regular pleas from the authorities to "outcast the hoarder."[35]

The extremely awkward timing of the Bengal crisis from a British military standpoint helps explain why Secretary of State Amery acted as if he believed that denying the true extent of the problem would make it go away. During the first half of 1943 Amery repeatedly downplayed the gravity of the crisis in the House of Commons. On 28 January he repeated a statement from the Indian government that "there is no famine and no widespread prevalence of acute shortage." On 5 May he noted that Bengal's problem was "primarily one for the Ministry of that self-governing province," and when Labour MP Reginald Sorensen, a critic of British rule in India, asked him whether famine conditions had not reduced people to "eating new grass," he replied that he had "not been informed of that." At the beginning of July Amery was still holding to the mantra that there was "no overall shortage of foodgrains," while conceding that the "plans elaborated by the Food Department of the Government of India earlier in the year [had] been less successful than was hoped." A fortnight later he attributed "the present difficult situation" to "a widespread tendency of cultivators to withhold foodgrains from the market, to larger consumption per head as the result of increased family income, to hoarding by consumers and others," and to the lack of interprovincial grain movements. In a short statement on 23 September he conceded the role of "a poor rice crop in Bengal"; but in reply to Sorensen's insistence that "until recently an impression was given to the general public that the shortage in India was not so severe as obviously had been the case and [that] it was largely if not entirely due to hoarding," Amery, by now clearly unconvinced of his stance, still held that "the problem is undoubtedly, in the main, one of distribution." At which point another Labour member, Emmanuel Shinwell, exclaimed, "could there be anything worse than disclaiming responsibility?"[36]

A key witness and actor in the early stages was Leonard Pinnell, Director of Civil Supplies in Bengal until April 1943. Pinnell was

---

[35] Sen 1944: 20.

[36] *Parliamentary Debates*, Commons, 5th series, vol. 389, cols. 597, 2440–41; vol. 390, col. 1774; vol. 391, cols. 216, 392–99.

privy to reports in late 1942 and early 1943 that the *aman* (autumn rice) harvest was poor.[37] According to his colleague Henry Braund, in February 1943 Pinnell had "openly asserted" before a conference on the food situation in Delhi that "there was a twenty per cent failure of the rice crop in Bengal, with crop disease even more disastrous than the [Midnapore] cyclone." The combined effect of the cyclone and the crop failure—the result of crop disease—was a shortfall of two million tons, as admitted in private by the central government in mid-March. From then on censored reports from East Bengal described a situation of impending famine. In a memorandum dated April 9 and forwarded to Delhi by the Bengal government, local officials reported that "the villagers, cultivators, traders, and jotedars [a Hindi word signifying rich peasants who often combined commercial farming and moneylending] were all predicting shortage." Yet Braund admitted that when he arrived in Calcutta in March 1943 "the conviction of shortage had not spread to the official classes and most business men." Nor did the truth dawn on him. The tendency was rather to dismiss the whole thing as the result of panic and "hoarding."[38]

Pinnell knew better, but at first he supported—as "any officer with a sense of responsibility to India as well as to his Province in a common danger"[39] would do—the official line from Delhi and London that there was no deficit, and employed an ineffective combination of compulsion and moral suasion to keep prices down. Tensions between him and the coalition led by first minister Abul Kasem Fazlul Huq coalition were high, with ministers accusing Pinnell of being more concerned with the war effort than with the plight of the Bengali people.

By spring 1943, Pinnell realized that his anti-hoarding campaign was tilting at windmills and that the damage to the 1942 crop was significant.[40] His public stance remained as before, though. Ian Stephens, editor of the Calcutta *Statesman*, described Pinnell and

---

[37] India Office Library (hereafter IOL), Mss. Eur D911/8, chronological table appended to "Memorandum on the Famine of 1943 and the Measures taken in relation thereto."

[38] Braund 1944: 30. See also Mukerjee 2010: 129–30.

[39] IOL, Eur. Mss. D911/8, "Memorandum on the economic condition of Bengal prior to the famine of 1943."

[40] Amery 1988: 954.

Braund as "two unhappy but not dishonest men working to a brief they didn't believe," whose inept performance convinced Stephens that a catastrophe was inevitable. The tension proved too much for Pinnell, who suffered a nervous breakdown in April 1943 and resigned.[41] Braund succeeded him as commissioner for food supplies. In material prepared for the Famine Inquiry Commission in the following year, however, Pinnell vehemently contested the charge that "Bengal itself is to blame for the trouble owing to the failure to deal with a ring of speculators and hoarders who conspired to hold the Province to ransom."

In a candid unpublished account written in the famine's wake, Braund conceded that he had been initially convinced that hoarding was the root problem and that the authorities in Delhi were particularly insistent on denying an "intrinsic shortage." And although Suhrawardy warned his audience at an important official conference about food supply in Delhi in early July that Bengal was "in the grip of a very great famine," even at that juncture representatives of other Indian provinces ignored him and applauded instead the suggestion that "the only reason why people are starving in Bengal is that there is hoarding." But Braund also conceded that even in March some brave officials—and he named two—were predicting famine. [42]

Bengal governor Sir John Herbert began to sound the alarm in private in early July, pleading with the viceroy:

> I must invoke all my powers of description and persuasion to convey to you the seriousness of the food situation in Bengal. Hitherto I have studiously avoided overstating the case and I have faithfully reported any day-to-day alleviation of the situation: I am now in some doubt as to whether I have not erred in the direction of understatement.[43]

However, Linlithgow interpreted Herbert's report that the food drive had located only 100,000 tons (equivalent to only about one

---

[41] Stephens 1966: 176; Pinnell 2002. Pinnell's memoir does not refer to his breakdown, but it is mentioned in Mookerjee1993: 89, and in Weigold 1999: 69fn26 (citing an official source).

[42] Braund 1944: 30.

[43] Sir John Herbert to Lord Linlithgow, cited in Batabyal 2005, p. 90. Herbert died of cancer at the height of the famine. His widow worried that his attempts to raise the alarm, which were ignored by Linlithgow, would be forgotten. See British Library, India Office Library (IOL), Mss. Eur. D911/9, letter from Government House to L. Pinnell, 1 January 1944.

percent of annual production) in stocks of 400 maunds (1 maund = 82.3 lbs) or more as evidence of "how much is in fact available." Earlier, Suhrawardy had referred in the Bengal legislature to "seven to eight million maunds" (0.2 to 0.3 million tons) as "approximately ... the quantity that has been discovered in hoards."[44] Linlithgow's stance as the famine unfolded was appalling. He failed to divert supplies from other provinces to Bengal, and decided not to visit Bengal during the crisis. Indeed, he later feared that the Bengal Famine Inquiry would judge him harshly, and went so far as to get a senior India Office official to make representations on his behalf to Sir John Woodhead, the inquiry's head.[45] He need not have worried, since the *Report on Bengal* failed to point the finger at any representative of the British government.[46]

By mid-July, however, Linlithgow had changed his tune and was demanding food imports as a matter of extreme urgency, no matter "how unpalatable this demand must be to H.M.G." (His Majesty's Government) and realizing its "serious potential effect on military operations." His demand was made "after full reflection and with the conviction that it is wholly justified and in the best interest of the prosecution of the war."[47] Linlithgow wished to announce the imminent arrival of food shipments in his valedictory address to the New Delhi legislature.

Back in England, as noted above, for months Amery had been insisting that the problem was one of hoarding, and that there was "no overall shortage of foodgrains ... but a maldistribution for which responsibility is shared by all parties from the cultivator upwards."[48]

---

[44] Mansergh 1973: 44, 60; *Statesman*, "Bengal Assembly Meets," 6 July 1943.

[45] The details are described in Ó Gráda 2008; see, in particular, IOL, D714/67, letter from Woodhead to Sir David Monteath, Assistant Director, India Office, Whitehall, 10 July 1945; Aykroyd 1974: 70–1, 74.

[46] IOL, Mss. Eur. D714/67, draft of letter from Sir David Monteath to Sir John Woodhead, 10 August 1944; Linlithgow to Monteath, 12 August 1944. See also Bhatia 1967: 339; Glendevon 1971: 274; Bence Jones 1982: 287. On 8 June 1943 Herbert warned of an irreconcilable conflict between Bengal's needs and those of her neighbors. He sought to convince Linlithgow that the onus was on "the only authority to enforce its decision on the dissenting parties—the Central Government"—to act (cited in Mansergh 1971, 1050).

[47] Mansergh 1973: 77.

[48] *Parliamentary Debates*, Commons, 5th series, vol. 390, col. 343 (3 June 1943); vol. 390, col. 1174 (1 July 1943); vol. 391, col. 216 (14 July 1943).

But Amery now began to take Linlithgow's pleas seriously. He argued the case at a War Cabinet meeting on 31 July. His insistence that failure to help would seriously compromise India's role as a theatre of war fell on deaf ears, however. The War Cabinet now treated the demand for food "in the main as an anti-hoarder bluff," holding that "the shortage of grain in India was not the result of physical deficiency but of hoarding" and that grain imports would not solve the problem. [49] Against Amery's pleas, the War Cabinet supported the position of the Minister of War Transport, Lord Frederick Leathers, who was willing to offer "no more than 50,000 tons [of wheat from Australia] as a token shipment . . . to be ordered to Colombo [capital of Ceylon, now Sri Lanka] to await instructions there," and 100,000 tons of Iraqi barley.[50] On August 16 *Amrita Bazar Patrika* published a telling cartoon on its front page of emaciated people on a beach with ships carrying food in the distance, with the caption "A Mirage! A Mirage!"

In early September Amery was informed by Lord Leathers that he had "an actual deficiency of ships" for the operational plan prepared by the military and approved by cabinet. A few days later, General Claude Auchinleck, head of British forces in India, echoing Amery's request, pleaded with the chief of imperial general staff in London that "so far as shipping is concerned, the import of food is to my mind just as if not more important than the import of munitions."[51] The shifting stance of *The Economist* on this issue of shipping is also worth noting. At the end of January 1943 it had resisted demands to divert food and ships to India: "Clearly, the best way to end the famine is speedy victory, and, however hard the decision, food ships must come second to victory ships. . . . But once the 'unconditional surrender' of the Axis has been achieved, the food ships must be sent in with the least possible delay." However, at the end of October *The Economist*'s tune was a different one: "Mr Amery claims that 'substantial' quantities of shipping were allotted to take food to India early this year; but nothing that is known, by the

[49] Mansergh 1973: 139–41, 158.
[50] Ibid., 156, Braund 1944: 30; Amery 1988: 933 (entry for 4 August 1943).
[51] Amery 1988: 911–12 (3 September 1943); Mansergh 1973: 217 (Auchinleck citation, 8 September 1943).

Gregory Committee[52] or anyone else, about actual imports, bears this out; and there is no evidence that demands for tonnage, commensurate with the famine that was already spreading a year ago, have ever been made to the Allied shipping authorities in London or Washington."[53]

Later Amery repeated the general's argument: conditions in Bengal were becoming "a serious menace to supply operations and the movement of troops, and also very bad for troop morale." To no avail: on 24 September the War Cabinet decided that diverting ships to lifting grain for delivery in India before the next Indian harvest would not be possible. This prompted Amery to muse in his diary that "Winston [Churchill] may be right in saying that the starvation of anyhow under-fed Bengalis is less serious than sturdy Greeks, at any rate from the war point of view, but he makes no sufficient allowance for the sense of Empire responsibility in this country."[54] Although in mid-October Amery was still referring in public to only "scarcity verging on famine," in private he must have known that the game was up. His missive to Lord Wavell, who had just taken over as viceroy from a culpably ineffective Linlithgow, really explains it all. Amery recognized the "natural and widespread feeling here that somehow or other the ultimate responsibility rests with us and that this country could or should have done more." But

> As to that, you know as well as I do the military preoccupations of the War Cabinet and the difficulty of diverting shipping from the first duty of winning the war. As you will remember, the last War Cabinet decision was that the matter should be reviewed at the end of the year. I am not sure that that is not leaving things too late and, if you can manage at an early date to visit Bengal yourself, or, even apart from that, feel that you should weigh in with a strong demand for earlier consideration, I hope you will do so.

[52] A committee chaired by Sir Theodor Gregory, formed to review India's food problems: for more see Mukerjee 2010: 139–43.

[53] "Food for India," *The Economist*, 30 January 1943, p. 141; "Hungry Millions," *The Economist*, 30 October 1943, pp. 577–78.

[54] Amery 1988: 912, 943 (22 September 1943, 24 September 1943). On 10 November 1943 Amery noted that Churchill's dislike of India was a factor impeding relief (Amery 1988: 950). See also Bayley and Harper 2004: 286; Mukerjee 2014: 74.

Even then, Amery raised again the canard that London "will have to be convinced that everything has been done within India to extract hoarded supplies and get them to the starving districts."[55]

Suhrawardy, who was responsible for maintaining civilian food supplies, may well have been misled at first by the gospel of plenty propagated by the colonial authorities. His early pronouncements were based on the premise that there was "a sufficiency of foodgrains for the people of Bengal" and that "maldistribution was the real evil."[56] Herbert paid Suhrawardy's energy and enthusiasm "a high tribute."[57] An influential opposition spokesman, Syama Prasad Mookerjee, caricatured him as telling people, "Don't get panicky. I am sitting here as the civil supplies minister and telling you there is plenty of foodstuffs. We have statistics which we do not want to publish. Everything will be alright. Do not get panicky," and accused him of minimizing "the gravity of the situation."[58] A few months later, Mookerjee accused the ministry of doing the greatest "disservice to the people of Bengal by emphasizing that there was no shortage of foodstuffs in Bengal."[59]

In May 1943 Suhrawardy asked newspaper editors to preach the "doctrine of sufficiency and sufficiency and sufficiency ... *ad nauseam*" against the "psychological factors" of "greed and panic."[60] A propaganda campaign targeting hoarders was buttressed by an official determination to prove "statistically" that Bengal contained enough food. The propaganda, however, also described the government as "rushing grain ships to India, even from rationed Allies, even at the expense of munitions," an assertion that would have been more convincing had the public been given "some general idea of the quantum of supplies coming forward instead of an occasional photograph of the unloading of a wagon."[61]

---

[55] Amery to Wavell, 21 October 1943.

[56] "Sufficient Food in Bengal," *Statesman*, 13 May 1943.

[57] Herbert to Linlithgow, 2 July 1943.

[58] S. P. Mookerjee, as cited in Batabyal 2005: 108; Das 2000: 65.

[59] Mookerjee (1993: 89–91) highlighted the contrasting attitudes of the Huq and Nazimmudin administration to the supply situation. See also "Evidence of Krishak Praja Muslim Leaders," as reprinted in Gupta 1997, p. 2020.

[60] IOL, Mss. Eur. Pinnell 911/9.

[61] *Capital* (Calcutta financial weekly), 25 February, 4 March 1943.

Soon enough, Suhrawardy realized that Bengal was in serious trouble, although he was under pressure from Delhi and London to stress "sufficiency" and "hoarding."[62] There was little effective that he could do; he could not apply the Famine Codes[63] because the food required to sustain the prescribed rations was lacking and because doing so would be bad for wartime morale. In notes presented to the Famine Inquiry Commission Pinnell commented on the non-declaration of famine, claiming that before June 1943 non-declaration was based on the need to maintain morale and the conviction that large-scale imports would soon materialize. When they did not, implementing the Famine Codes thereafter would have been futile, since Bengal "had neither funds nor supplies to meet the distress in which nearly 10 percent of the people of the province were faced with starvation and 40 percent more with semi-starvation. It would have been useless to declare a famine in the circumstances and the only effect of such a declaration would have been to give a handle to the enemy to carry on pro-fascist propaganda." So the authorities "weighed the pros and cons very carefully and decided finally to take all possible measures to carry on relief operations on the basis of a famine without the formal declaration of a famine."[64]

An increasingly disillusioned Suhrawardy appointed an expert to devise a form of gruel that would contain as little rice as possible, and advised the poor to try substitute foods. He organized the food drives (described in the following section). He announced at the end of August that rationing would be introduced in Calcutta and the industrial areas (but only in October). He also claimed that the rest of India was gradually realizing Bengal's parlous state, and held to the hope that prices would soon fall.[65]

The *Statesman* changed its tune in early July, with an editorial on the province's need of "more and cheaper food." By mid-August it was adopting a much more critical stance, stating that the crisis menaced Bengal "in many ways ... apparently there are months of this

[62] T. Ghosh 1944: 18.

[63] On the scope of the codes, see Brennan 1984; Hall-Matthews 1998.

[64] IOL, Pinnell papers, Confidential. Government of Bengal. Revenue Dept. *Memorandum on the Famine of 1943 and the measures taken in relation thereto.*

[65] Brennan 1988. Lance Brennan (personal communication) suspects that the records of Suhrawardy's Department of Civil were destroyed after the famine.

penury and disintegration to come";[66] referring to the "growing annoyance" being caused by long speeches calling on public opinion to rally behind the official campaign against hoarding; and commenting acidly that "presumably these loud assertions about evildoers growing rich on the people's misery have their foundation in knowledge." "If there are large-scale culprits," the *Statesman* held, "they should be ruthlessly jumped on without further delay, and there will be applause for the jumper." [67] Thereafter, the *Statesman*—and *Amrita Bazar Patrika*—adopted a policy of reporting on the extent of starvation frequently and graphically. Its photographic images of the famine made world headlines.[68] On 5 October it editorialized:

> We have not liked all the comments lately transmitted from Britain about the Bengal famine. Some have looked neither tactful nor true.... There has been the further obscuring factor of war-time censorship which until a fortnight or so ago seems virtually to have withheld from the British public knowledge that there was famine in Bengal at all. But a proportion of the cabled comments seem to have been inspired (we choose this verb deliberately) by a wish to lay blame for catastrophe wholly on Indian shoulders.

By now, the *Statesman* doubted Suhrawardy's credibility, given his "earlier disingenuousness or ill-informed propagandistic optimism."[69] Later, it confessed that it too had been duped into false hopes. In a strongly worded editorial in mid-January 1944 the *Statesman* berated Amery for blaming the provincial authorities for the famine, and for claiming that "when it became necessary for the Government of India to act, it did so promptly." Part of the blame lay with "Mr. Amery's own important office in Whitehall":

> Throughout the months when disaster in Bengal approached, the authorities in London, as in New Delhi and Calcutta, were lavish in soothing assurances that no genuine or serious food-shortage existed in

---

[66] "Food and Society," *Statesman*, 13 August 1943.

[67] "Public Opinion," *Statesman*, 16 August 1943.

[68] "Bengal's Foodless," *Statesman*, 22 August 1943; "An All-India Disgrace," 29 August 1943; Aykroyd 1974: 69; Santhanam 1944: 85–96.

[69] "Consequences of Untruth," *Statesman*, 12 October 1943.

India, the perceptible signs of deaths being due merely to transient maladjustment originating mainly from defective transport. Conceivably (though we do not think so) officialdom's policy was to deliberately conceal from the Indian public ugly certainties then well known to themselves, in order that unavoidable factual dangers might not be worsened by others of a psychological sort. But in that case there is no particular reason for supposing that the realities of the situation are being candidly placed before the public now. Government cannot have it both ways.[70]

Later, when the worst was over, a public admission by Herbert's successor that the 1942 *aman* crop had indeed been a poor one prompted the Calcutta *Statesman* into editorializing:

Memories remain fresh of the long dismal period last year ... when Authority in Calcutta, in New Delhi, and in London was profuse in subsequently falsified assurances that no serious danger impended, that enough food for harassed and bewildered Bengal and for India existed, and that the only need was greater trustfulness on the public's part and minor redistribution of stocks of grain. Over-optimistic and provenly erroneous assertions such as these, from persons presumably in a position to know the truth, have their inevitable psychological sequel.[71]

Bengal's rice output in normal years was barely enough for bare-bones subsistence. An output of 9 million tons translates into one pound per day or less than 2,000 kcal per adult male. Even allowing for imports from neighboring provinces and Burma—and trade accounted for only a small fraction of supplies in 1942/3 (fig. 2.1)—the province's margin over subsistence on the eve of the famine was slender. It is hardly surprising, then, that almost from the outset there was controversy about an issue that has dominated the historiography on the Bengal famine: the extent of the *aman* harvest shortfall in late 1942 and of food availability in 1943.

Although the authorities in London and New Delhi expected political leaders in Bengal to argue the case for adequacy of food supplies, the weak coalition government that ruled until late March

[70] "Famine Retrospect," *Statesman*, 12 January 1944.
[71] "A Governor's Forecast," *Statesman*, 2 April 1944.

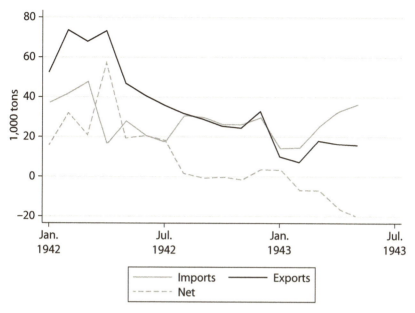

Figure 2.1 Bengal's rice trade, 1942–43. Source: India Office Library, Famine Inquiry Commission Papers.

1943 was ambiguous on the issue. In early January 1943 its agriculture and industries minister, the Nawab Bahadur of Dacca, sought to reassure consumers by claiming that although the 1942 *aman* crop was less than the previous year's, it was no worse than that of 1940. In February, however, the nawab announced that estimated rice production in 1942/3 (6.9 million tons) was far short of consumption requirements (9.3 million), an assessment that caused the price of rice to rise significantly. His statement, according to the Communist weekly newspaper *People's War*, "encouraged hoarding right and left."[72] In March the nawab revealed that Bengal was also short of other essential foodstuffs, "namely wheat, *dal* [dried legumes], mustard, sugar, and salt." As for rice, the loss of Burmese imports, military demands, the so-called "denial policy" which had led to the requisitioning of stocks in areas vulnerable to Japanese attack, and "hoarding on a fairly extensive scale" had produced local shortages.[73]

[72] *People's War*, 28 November 1943.
[73] "Bengal Council Debate on Food Situation in Province," *Statesman*, 10 March 1943.

In opposition, the Muslim League had accepted that Bengal was short of rice; its leader even warned that "the disaster of 1770 would be re-enacted" unless effective action was taken.[74] In power, Suhrawardy, its main spokesman, immediately linked the scarcity of food to "the evils of hoarding and profiteering" and hoped to lift the issue of supplies "above the level of party politics." On 11 May he announced his plan of opening hundreds of shops where necessities would be sold to the poor at controlled prices and of waging an aggressive campaign against hoarders, under the slogan "Do not Grind the Faces of the Poor." "Sufficiency" was the cornerstone of the Suhrawardy plan.[75]

As ministers and their supporters intensified their attacks on hoarders and speculators—in mid-April the *Statesman* called for tougher action against "the hoarder and speculator," and suggested special courts to bring the "evilly disposed" to book, while in mid-May a senior politician referred to them as "national enemies"[76]—opposition spokesmen blamed the authorities for "clouding issues on the assumption that there are hoards of foodstuffs in the rural areas of Bengal which, if made available, will solve the problem."

The numbers promised by Suhrawardy, buttressed by a "surmise" regarding the carry-over of rice stocks from the previous year, were immediately attacked as faulty and unreliable by two widely respected scholars at a meeting organized by the opposition in Howrah. Professor Radhakamal Mukherjee held that it was "not safe to take too optimistic a view of Bengal's food resources at this juncture and stress ... psychological factors ... rather than the economic factor of serious actual food shortage."[77] Henry Braund, who as regional food commissioner should have been in a position to know, claimed that at the end of 1942 the carry-over position was "precarious."[78] Less than a week later an opposition party working committee "express[ed] deep concern at the food situation [and] called on the authorities not to juggle with figures but to admit can-

[74] "Food Situation in Bengal: Council Debate," *Statesman*, 9 March 1943. Bengal suffered a massive famine in 1770.
[75] "Ministry Reviews Food Situation," *Statesman*, 3 May 1943.
[76] *Statesman*, 15 April 1943; "Sir A. Haque's Assurance," 16 May 1943.
[77] "Howrah Meeting," *Statesman*, 16 May 1943.
[78] Braund 1944: 19.

didly that Bengal was a deficit province and to deal with the situation with an appreciation of the stern realities."[79] In the course of a lengthy debate in the local assembly in mid-July, the opposition accused ministers of obfuscating reality by focusing on carry-over and hoarded stocks, and demanded that Bengal be declared a famine area. A prominent opposition leader noted that the previous ministry had at least "declared that there was shortage of food in Bengal and they made the Government of India accept that position," but that Suhrawardy had played a "colossal hoax" on the people by saying there was no rice shortage in Bengal.[80]

By early July Suhrawardy was conceding that there was a food availability problem:

> I have found criticisms made against me that I had stated that there was no shortage when actually there was serious shortage in the Province. I do not plead guilty to the charge. It appeared to me that insistence on shortages would only increase panic and stimulate hoarding and thereby aggravate the general food scarcity and push up prices.[81]

Later, his reply to the accusation that "for five months he had declared that there was no shortage of foodgrains" would be that "mere insistence on shortage would not help anyone."[82] Even in mid-October, when describing the crisis as "unprecedented famine," he still added a plea to cultivators and traders to release stocks for public consumption, prompting the *Statesman* to muse that "many will certainly disbelieve" his forecast that prices were bound to fall. The *Statesman* went on to criticize politicians for their "disgraceful" record of "false or ignorant prophecy," noting how Amery, Delhi, and Suhrawardy's "inept" predecessors had "proclaimed that food-shortage in India and Bengal was practically nonexistent."[83]

In Bengal, socioeconomic status broadly overlapped with religion, and preexisting religious tensions conditioned the positions adopted by various parties during the famine. Pre-partition Bengal

---

[79] *Statesman*, 22 May 1943.

[80] "Food Debate in Bengal Assembly," *Statesman*, 15 July 1943.

[81] "Bengal Assembly Meets," *Statesman*, 6 July 1943.

[82] *Statesman*, 28 September 1943.

[83] "Consequences of Untruth," *Statesman*, 12 October 1943.

had a Muslim majority. The Muslim share was highest in the east of the province (map 2.3). Where Muslims were in a minority, as in Calcutta, they tended to live in residentially segregated areas. Moreover, the sectarian divide was widening over time. In Calcutta, for example, the Muslim share of the population remained at about one-fourth between 1901 and 1941, but the coefficient of variation (i.e., the standard deviation divided by the average: a standardized measure of the dispersion of a variable such as, in this case, population share) in the Muslim share across the city's districts rose from 0.50 in 1901 to 0.65 in 1921 and 0.71 in 1941, evidence that they were living in increasingly segregated neighborhoods.

Bengali Muslims were poorer and less educated than Bengali Hindus, but they were well mobilized politically. The poorest strata among the peasantry were disproportionately Muslim, and Muslim leaders prominent in 1943 such as Fazlul Huq (first minister of Bengal from 1937 to 1943), Food Minister Suhrawardy, and Khawaja Nazimuddin (first minister during the famine) had cut their teeth on populist communal politics in the 1920s and 1930s, supporting pro-peasant land reforms and curbs on moneylending. Hindu politicians were more likely to represent landlord and trading interests, as well as the genteel, literate, and mainly upper-caste Hindu *bhadralok*.[84] Communal rioting took on an economic hue, with the wrath of Muslim peasants directed particularly against Hindu and Marwari traders and moneylenders.[85]

Communal tensions in Bengal had escalated in the twentieth century.[86] Muslims, broadly speaking, tended to side with the British authorities as the Hindu intelligentsia increasingly rejected the Raj and embraced nationalism. After 1939 the Muslim League, representing the majority of Muslims, supported the war effort, whereas Hindus were unenthusiastic at best. There were also divisions within the two main religious groups, however. Most Hindus supported the

[84] The following notice in *ABP* (29 August 1943) reflects its part-*bhadralok* constituency: "Cheap canteen for Middle Class People in Calcutta: Appeals for Running Free Kitchens in the City: It is time we should turn our attention to the poor middle class families whose womenfolk are the worst sufferers in this crisis. They cannot stand in a queue for foodstuff. Neither can they go to canteens for their meals."

[85] Compare Greenough 1982: 160.

[86] For background, see Chatterji 1994, 2001; Batabyal 2005.

Map 2.3 Bengal: Percentage Muslim in 1941, based on population census data.

nationalist Indian National Congress, but some went further, backing Syama Prasad Mookerjee's sectarian Hindu Mahasabha or Subhas Chandra Bose's pro-Axis Indian National Army.[87] Fazlul Huq was more willing to collaborate with Hindu politicians, and not trusted by the colonial authorities, who connived in the collapse of his weakening coalition in late March 1943 and its replacement by a more pliant Muslim League administration, headed by Khawaja Nazimuddin.

"The Hindu section of the traders is dominant in the internal economy of Bengal," noted P. C. Joshi, general secretary of the Communist Party of India, in the party organ *People's War*.[88] Moneylending was mainly in the hands of Hindu *banias* (traders), *mahajans* (usurers), and landowners, and the Bengal Moneylenders' Act of 1940 had hit them hard.[89] It follows that the hoarders targeted by the Muslim League during the famine were likely to be Hindus. While the League was criticized for giving contracts to the giant trading firm of Isphahani Brothers, prominent Muslim League supporters, the Hindu-nationalist Mahasabha movement attacked the government and "big firms, particularly non-Bengalis" (code for the Isphahanis) for holding on to excess stocks. The pro-*bhadralok* Mahasabha also claimed that repeated warnings against hoarding only served to create panic, especially among "the poor middle class people who were obliged to keep small stocks to meet the present abnormal situation."[90] Religious affiliation thus influenced the positions taken by leading actors during the famine, and also the attribution of blame, both in its wake and subsequently.

Markets, Phantom Hoards, and Land Sales

I think, looking back, that the adoption of the psychology or gospel of "plenty" in Bengal was a mistake.

Henry Braund, colonial administrator[91]

[87] Batabyal 2005; Bose 2011.
[88] *People's War*, 14 November 1943.
[89] Chatterji 1994: 106.
[90] *Statesman*, 22 May 1943; Chatterji 1994: 136.
[91] Braund 1944: 142.

In late 1942 the crisis in Midnapur and panic about the *aman* harvest caused both the price of rice and its spread across Bengali markets (as measured by the coefficient of variation of prices) to rise abruptly (fig. 2.2). This placed so much pressure on markets in neighboring Bihar that its governor felt "compelled to prohibit the export of any food-stuffs from Bihar except under permit."[92] Prices then settled briefly, but the removal of price controls and the Nawab of Dacca's declaration of a food shortage (see above) caused them to take off again in March. In Calcutta the price of rice rose from Rs. 10 (10 rupees) per maund in November 1942 to double that five months later. In late March the price reached Rs. 29 in Rangpur and Rs. 27 in Cox's Bazar (a fishing port south of Chittagong), and it hovered between Rs. 25 and Rs. 30 per maund in Patgram in the extreme north of the province. In early April rice cost Rs. 23 in Comilla and over Rs. 25 in Dacca.[93] At the end of April Fazlul Huq challenged his successor to bring down the price of rice, since "if it was the fault of his [i.e., Huq's] ministry that the price of rice had gone up, let Sir Nazimuddin [his successor] bring it down."[94] In a warning to hoarders Suhrawardy claimed that current supplies by no means justified the high prices, which he was determined to use all his powers to bring down.[95]

The imposition of price controls on 20 August 1943 led to rice shortages even in Calcutta. Many dealers found it virtually impossible to obtain rice; others disposed of their stocks before the order came into effect and did not replenish them because they could not even purchase rice at Rs. 30 per maund, the maximum sale price. The ordinance also forced many rice dealers to close shop. Meanwhile Suhrawardy continued to warn traders against withholding stocks from the market.[96]

Between August and December 1943 a significant gap separated official and black market prices.[97] The black market price of rice rose to Rs. 40 per maund in Calcutta, but by mid-October rice was being sold openly at Rs. 50 to 60 in the eastern division of My-

[92] Mansergh 1971: 414 (Sir T. Stewart (Bihar) to Linlithgow, 23 November 1943).
[93] "Rice Price in Districts," *Statesman*, 14 April 1943.
[94] "Ministry Reviews Food Situation," *Statesman*, 1 May 1943.
[95] "Warning to Hoarders," *Statesman*, 2 May 1943.
[96] "Rice Scarcity in City," *Statesman*, 30 August 1943.
[97] Greenough 1982: 164–65; Brennan 1988: 544.

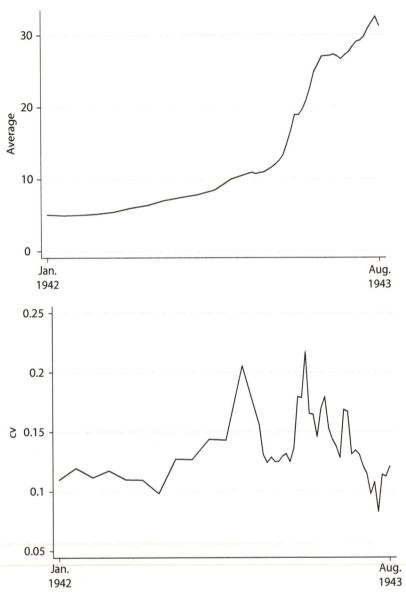

Figure 2.2 (a) Price of rice (in rupees per maund) and (b) coefficient of variation, Bengal 1942–43. Source: India Office Library, Famine Inquiry Commission Papers.

mensingh, and soon would reached Rs. 80 in parts of east Bengal.[98] Prices began to fall as soon as producers were reassured about the quality of the new *aman* crop. Traders began to dispose of existing stocks of old rice at Rs. 18 to 25 per maund for rice of medium quality. While considerable shortages persisted in some areas, the new crop began to appear in bazaars in the interior in late November and was being sold at about Rs. 16 per maund. The general opinion seemed to be that prices would continue to drop unless the government proceeded to buy up the crop, in which case cultivators and speculators would stockpile rice, driving the price back up again.[99]

A few weeks later, however, supplies had dried up again in the eastern division of Mymensingh, where dealers from Dacca and elsewhere were buying it up at prices above the controlled rates.[100] In mid-January 1944 the price of rice, which had fallen from Rs. 40 a maund to Rs. 11 or 12 as new grain began to come on the market a few weeks earlier, rose to Rs. 22, or Rs. 5 above the controlled price. Official sources, however, claimed that the price of rice was in fact falling; they reported prices of Rs. 15 at Howrah, Rs. 11–8 (i.e., eleven rupees and eight annas) at Contai, and Rs. 16–4 at Calcutta on January 17, against prices of Rs. 17, Rs. 12, and Rs. 17–8 a week earlier.[101] Government purchases of *aman* rice may have been partly to blame for any rebound; opposition spokesmen held that distress was persisting due to a "continued rise in the price of rice and paddy." In response to Suhrawardy's denial that prices were rising "throughout Bengal"—only in certain deficit areas—opposition spokesmen produced detailed evidence on price rises in the *mofussil* (rural districts).[102]

The relative buoyancy of prices in early 1944, given the general impression that the late 1943 *aman* harvest had been a good one, argues against the presence of excessive hoarding on a large scale at the height of the famine. It would be silly to claim that no merchants or traders tried their hand at speculation; the point is that had the

---

[98] Brennan 1988: 544; *People's War*, 21 November 1943; "Black Market Prices," *Statesman*, 22 October 1943. My citations from *People's War* are taken from photocopies kindly supplied by Lance Brennan.

[99] "Rice," *Statesman*, 1 December 1943.

[100] *Statesman*, 21 December 1943.

[101] "Rice Prices on the Decline," *Statesman*, 18 January 1944; 21 January 1944.

[102] "Rice Procurement in Bengal," *Statesman*, 2 February 1944.

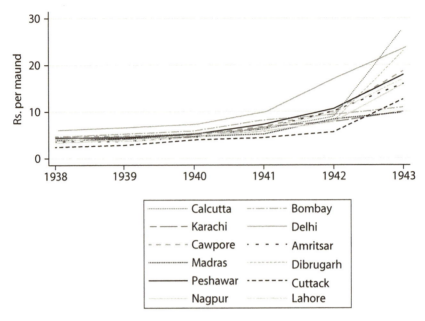

Figure 2.3 Rice prices in twelve markets in India, 1938/9 to 1943/4 (rupees per maund). Source: Knight 1954: 308.

famine-inducing prices of summer and autumn 1943 been mainly due to hoarding, then the release of hoarded rice thereafter would have forced prices down more than they actually fell. In early 1944 the *real* price of rice was roughly the same as two years earlier.

Three further points regarding prices bear noting. First, the literature has focused on price movements over time, paying less attention to price variation across the province. As noted earlier, the rise in the black market price of rice was much greater in east than in west Bengal at the height of the crisis, suggesting intra-provincial as well as inter-provincial balkanization. Second, the war forced up the price of rice and wheat across the subcontinent (figs. 2.3–2.5). Increases were relatively mild until 1942/3, but big in 1943/4. Figure 2.3 shows that the national market for rice became more segmented from 1940/1 on, while figure 2.4 shows that the market for wheat became so only in 1943/4. Note too how the gap between rice prices in Bengal and the rest of India (Delhi apart) widened in 1943/4 (as reflected in the increase in the coefficient of variation in fig. 2.5). The

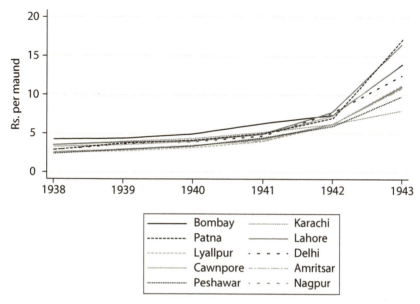

Figure 2.4 Wheat prices in ten Indian markets of the Indian subcontinent, 1938/9 to 1943/4 (rupees per maund). Source: Knight 1954: 308.

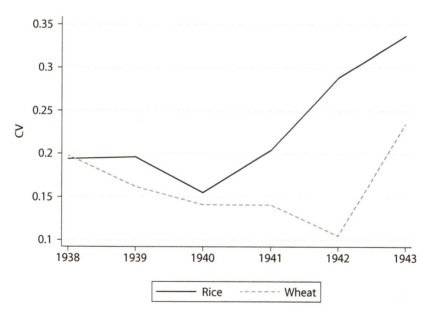

Figure 2.5 CV of rice and wheat prices, India 1938/9 to 1943/4. Source: Knight 1954: 308.

wide range of wholesale prices quoted for rice in early June 1943—
for example, Rs. 30–8 per maund in Chandpur-Puranberar (Bengal),
Rs. 18–2 in Purnea (Bihar), Rs. 12–10 in Bareilly (U.P.), Rs. 6–4 in
Larkana (Sind)[103]—suggests that the balkanization of Indian markets exacerbated Bengal's supply problems during the famine.

Such balkanization ruled out one of the remedies emphasized by
the classical economists: the cushion provided by free trade when
harvests fails, as the balance of trade in foodstuffs adjusts to relative
price movements.[104] Evidence from pre-industrial Europe (discussed
in detail in Essay 3) suggests that markets functioned more or less
normally during famines there. Certainly, there was no prospect of
this happening in Bengal in 1943. The "basic plan" devised in Delhi
in late 1942 envisaged Bengal obtaining 370,000 tons of rice—about
four percent of its annual requirements—from the rest of India in
the year beginning December 1942, whereas in the seven months
starting in December 1942 it actually received 44,000 tons.[105] During
the famine, the reluctance of neighboring provinces to supply Bengal was a frequent bone of contention, well captured by the remark
of the governor of neighboring Bihar, who had just imposed an embargo on food exports from that province. "By conviction," he confided to Linlithgow, "I hold with Adam Smith but in a crisis like this
I am prepared to accept 100% control."[106] Symptomatic, too, was the
response of representatives of the other provinces to Suhrawardy's
statement at an All-India Food Conference in July that Bengal was
"in the grip of a very great famine, probably of a size and nature that
may be equal to the Orissa famine of 1867": they greeted the suggestion by another delegate that "the only reason why people are starving in Bengal is that there is hoarding" with applause.[107]

The third notable point regarding prices is that in general, prices
rise during famine. A cost-of-living index for Bengal before and during the famine is lacking, but cost of living indices for the working
classes in three northern Indian cities report increases ranging from

[103] *ABP*, June 5, 1943.

[104] Ravallion 1987b. The evidence suggests that it rarely did so with sufficient speed,
however.

[105] Mansergh 1973: 43.

[106] Ibid., 414 (23 December 1942).

[107] Braund 1944: 30, 81.

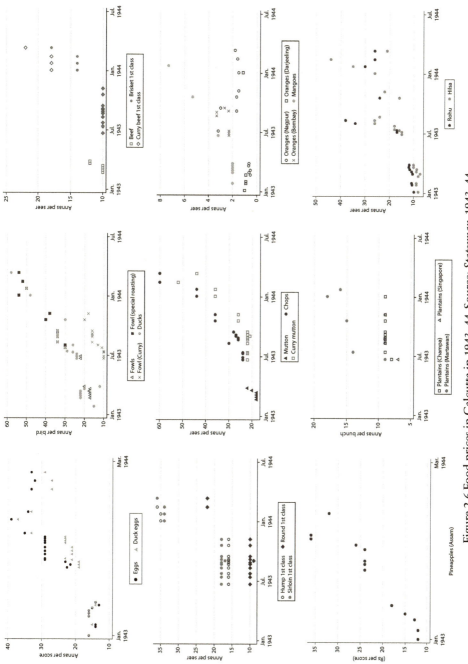

Figure 2.6 Food prices in Calcutta in 1943–44. Source: *Statesman*, 1943–44.

105 to 125 percent between January 1942 and January 1944.[108] Figure 2.6, which summarizes market price data for a range of food items (meat, vegetables, fruit, fish[109]) as reported in the *Statesman* between January 1943 and March 1944, confirms that price rises in Bengal were by no means confined to rice.

The "food drives" of June and August 1943 followed from the hoarding hypothesis. The first drive, which excluded the twin cities of Calcutta and Howrah, began on 7 June.[110] Local food committees, assisted by thirty thousand temporary workers, were charged with taking stock of resources available and "arranging for their equitable and amicable distribution amongst the village population as a whole." Suhrawardy, who described the food committees as an extension of the traditional *panchayat* (village assembly), promised not to intervene except "where persuasion has failed, or where a surplus in one area has to be transferred to a deficit area."[111] He promised that his officials would "enter every household and look under every *taktaposh* [a raised wooden bed with storage space underneath] and … drag out the hoards," and his officials held that the food drive was responsible for reported falls in the price of rice in a "number" of districts in early June.[112] Suhrawardy initially claimed that the province-wide drive had restored the poor's confidence and prompted the hoarders to let go of some of their stocks.[113] The campaign had a clear communal aspect to it, but the *Statesman* backed Suhrawardy's attempts at "getting out, from wherever it is, such hoarded food as exists … with what result is not yet clearly seen," and lauded his contribution to the assembly debate on the food situation.[114]

It took the authorities in Delhi longer to accept what was happening than Calcutta, and there was considerable tension between the

[108] Knight 1954: 307. The cities are Cawnpore (Kanpur in Uttar Pradesh), Ahmedabad (in Gujarat), and Lahore (now in Pakistan).

[109] Rohu is a variety of carp, hilsa a saltwater fish (fig. 2.5i).

[110] *ABP*, 6 June 1943, p. 5: In Rangpur, "The homes of a number of prominent citizens of the town were searched for illegal hoarded foodgrains. But no illegal hoarding has so far been discovered."

[111] "Food Committees for Bengal Villages," *Statesman*, 18 June 1943.

[112] *ABP*, 30 May 1943; "Food Committees for Bengal Villages," *Statesman*, 18 June 1943; *ABP*, 18 June 1943.

[113] *Statesman*, 6 June 1943.

[114] "More Food," *Statesman*, 2 July 1943; 9 July 1943.

two. While Herbert in Calcutta was arguing that disaster was inevitable "unless we can get foodgrains at once in sufficient quantities from outside," Linlithgow in Delhi still argued that the food drive was "show[ing] how much in fact was available."[115]

Suhrawardy, closer to the events on the ground, claimed that boats and carts had been used to conceal stocks; some, he said, had been shifted "into jungles."[116] Soon however, it was clear that the vast majority of the rural population was short of food, and that the drive had laid bare "an acute shortage." Unless large stocks were to be found in and around Calcutta, warned *Amrita Bazar Patrika*, the official "thesis" of Suhrawardy and the government of India would be "completely demolished."[117] Under pressure to provide disaggregated data on the outcome, Suhrawardy admitted that while he had no statistics, "the general picture was that in most places a deficit had been reported." Nor would Suhrawardy, whose mantra had by now switched to "To hope for the best and to prepare for the worst," reveal how any surpluses were disposed of.[118] Nalini Sarkar of the pro-Congress Swarajya Party conceded the drive's usefulness as an exercise in statistical intelligence, but wanted to know why the public had not yet been informed of its outcome, and whether enough hoarded food had been located to meet "the present situation." Given the government's heavy emphasis on hoarding, it was important that it published the results of the drive soon. Sarkar, a prominent business leader, did not believe that "very large hoarded stocks" existed.[119]

Criticism of the exclusion of Calcutta and Howrah led to a "food drive" directed against urban hoarders in early August 1943. August 7 and 8, 1943, were declared public holidays in order to facilitate house-to-house inspections in the two cities. The drive lasted from dawn to dusk on both days. The two-day drive employed police attached to the Department of Civil Supplies to deal with large merchants, local police to deal with small merchants, and authorized of-

---

[115] Linlithgow to Herbert, 11 July 1943; Herbert to Linlithgow, 2 July 1943.

[116] *ABP*, 24 June 1943.

[117] *ABP*, 7 July 1943 (editorial); 22 June 1943; 14 July 1943 ("in practically all places and districts deficits had been reported").

[118] *ABP*, 25 June 1943; "Food Situation Criticized," *Statesman*, 13 July 1943.

[119] "Food Conference in Calcutta," *Statesman*, 27 June 1943. Compare Tauger 2009: 35.

ficers drawn from the local civil service to deal with householders and smaller traders. It involved a total of 2,850 officers visiting 250,000 units, or an average of nearly 100 units each. Each policeman or official was accompanied by two volunteers (typically supporters of the Muslim League), in order to help and "generally to protect the interests of the people." In the case of merchants or shopkeepers, stocks of 20 maunds or more required a license. The official view was that 1.25 maunds per person (excluding children under 4) was sufficient for the rest of the year.

The "drive" was explained as a means of ascertaining stocks. According to the *Statesman*, "in several houses officers discovered stocks far in excess of the unit's requirements and these were duly 'frozen,' i.e. the groups were directed not to remove or in any way dispose of them until further notice." The search also unearthed "numerous instances of stocks above the amount permitted." In the following days the *Statesman* was silent on any unearthed hoards, although its European op-ed columnist continued to insist on the vital need to unearth "the millions of tons which would be required for consumption in the Provinces in which they were hidden."[120] Soon, however, Suhrawardy was conceding that in Calcutta stocks in the hands of consumers, traders, and employers were modest, and "we have all erred, and the main thing now for us is to get together and do all we can."[121] The "food-search" had revealed enough for a month's subsistence in the city, including stocks in the hands of government officials and employers.[122] An "I told you so" editorial in the nationalist *Amrita Bazar Patrika* noted that had the drive produced more than the proverbial "horse's egg," ministers would have crowed the news from the rooftops.[123]

In October a joint statement from the Bengal, Indian, and Marwari Chambers of Commerce expressed doubts "whether apart from the stocks which the government are fully aware and are virtually under their control, there are any appreciable undeclared stocks held by merchants in Calcutta or outside."[124] This assessment tallies with

---

[120] "Notes by Prodigal," *Statesman*, 29 August 1943.
[121] *Statesman*, 13 September 1943; 28 September 1943.
[122] Braund 1944: 88.
[123] "No Mere Civil Problem," *ABP*, 20 August 1943; Greenough 1982: 126.
[124] *People's War*, 31 October 1943.

a confidential memorandum prepared by the Government of India Food Department, and forwarded by Linlithgow to Amery on 7 September 1943, which found:

> The much-heralded "anti-hoarding" drive in the Bengal districts and in Calcutta has achieved very little that is positive. The Bengal Government themselves do not claim that it is more than a "food census," disclosing stocks in the districts amounting to rather more than 300,000 tons. The Bengal Government emphasises that this is "stock," and is in no sense "surplus," except to a negligible extent. In Calcutta itself practically no stocks were disclosed which would be classified as "hoards," or were held in contravention of the Foodgrains Control Order. [125]

The relatively small number of traders fined during the spring and summer of 1943 is further circumstantial evidence against large-scale speculative hoarding. Throughout the crisis the authorities campaigned against the twin offences of hoarding and profiteering. Traders who withheld stocks without declaring them, and traders who made a false declaration, were liable to fines, imprisonment, and the confiscation of their stocks. Retailers charging more than the controlled price were similarly liable and might be barred from carrying out business in the future or deprived of supplies of key items such as coal and kerosene. The non-trading hoarder, whose motive was fear, was not immune, but the main target of the campaign was the creature who, "for sheer greed, grabs and withholds from circulation the food of his fellowmen." [126]

In the circumstances, it is striking how relatively few traders were charged or convicted for hoarding and profiteering in rice during 1943. Thus, in the week ending 7 April 1943 thirty-nine cases of profiteering were detected; eighteen related to sugar, nine to kerosene, eight to coal, two to salt, and two to *atta*. In the following week 104 cases were dealt with, of which fifty-five related to sugar, twenty-five to kerosene, twenty to coal, one to mustard oil, and three to medicines. During the week ending 28 April, the Ministry of Civil Supplies proceeded against eighty-two people for profiteering and hoarding; twenty-nine cases related to sugar, and twenty-seven to

---

[125] Mansergh 1973, vol. 4, p. 197.
[126] "Bengal's Food Supply," *Statesman*, 9 April 1943, "Action against Hoarders," 10 April 1943.

coal. There were thirty-eight prosecutions for hoarding and profiteering in the week ending May 14, of which nineteen related to coal and ten to sugar. Of the nine people convicted for profiteering in Calcutta on May 27, one was fined for hoarding rice, five for profiteering in sugar, and three for profiteering in coal and coke. The total number of prosecutions in June came to 174, of which forty-eight related to sugar, thirty-two to coal, and thirty-four each to oil and kerosene. The total number of prosecutions for profiteering and hoarding reached 622 in July; 130 related to *atta* and flour, 115 to sugar, 92 to kerosene, 81 to coal, 52 to mustard, and only 43 to rice.[127] Again, of the 168 prosecutions for hoarding and profiteering in Calcutta in December 1943, twenty-eight related to kerosene, twenty-eight to medicines, twenty-one to coconut oil, eighteen to paper, and only fifteen to rice.[128] This would suggest that the authorities had no difficulty in discovering hoarders of other basic household commodities, who greatly outnumbered hoarders of rice.

The huge increase in forced land transfers during the famine is also consistent with a poor harvest. Hundreds of thousands of *ryots* (peasant cultivators)were forced to sell off some or all of their land; 1.7 million land transfers were made in 1943, and 22.9 percent of families were forced either to sell or mortgage all or part of their paddy land.[129] Chattopadhyay and Mukerjee noted that the price of paddy land varied from Rs. 150 to Rs. 200 "or a little more" in different areas in 1939; in 1943 their surveyors noted average prices of Rs. 258 in Contai, Rs. 184 in Diamond Harbour, Rs. 175 in Tangail, and Rs. 352 in Feni. Given that between 1939 and 1943 the cost of living more than doubled and the price of rice rose by considerably more,[130] this indicates a reduction in the real price of land. Sale values did not rise with sales; given the nominal (though not real) rise in the price of land, the average size of land transfers must have fallen during the famine.[131]

This implies that most of the sales were by smallholders normally reliant on agricultural labor to make ends meet, and who needed the

[127] "Hoarders and Profiteers," *Statesman*, 17 August 1943.
[128] "Calcutta Prosecutions," *Statesman*, 21 January 1944.
[129] "Sample Survey of Famine Districts," *Statesman*, 27 February 1944; Chattopadhyay and Mukherjee 1946: 10; Ó Gráda 2008; Das 2008.
[130] Knight 1954: 306, 307; Chattopadhyay and Mukherjee 1946: 31.
[131] Chakraborty 1997: 149.

cash to buy food. This is hardly surprising, but even P. C. Joshi, leader of the Communist Party, conceded that the middle peasantry also suffered in 1943. "How is it," he asked, "that even the middle peasant has to sell off; where did his rice go?" Joshi's answer—that "he got humbugged by the hoarder and tempted by the high price offered" and "began sinking to the status of a pauper"—lacked conviction. But that *nobody* had enough food in Joshi's view, except a small minority, "the zamindars, the rich jotedars, and the mahajans," surely implies a general supply shortage. The zamindars were big landlords and the jotedars major landholders and employers of labor, while the mahajans belonged to a business caste that specialized in moneylending.[132]

The Communists played a curious game during the famine. The party's support for the war effort following Hitler's invasion of the Soviet Union led to its legalization in 1942.[133] Its organizational and relief work won it plaudits during the famine, although its anti-Congress stance and uncritical support for the war alienated many. The party and its affiliates vigorously supported the food drives,[134] and even after the authorities conceded that there was a food availability problem, the party weekly *People's War* continued to target the hoarder. It reserved its greatest scorn for S. P. Mookerjee and the Hindu Mahasabha: "Dr. Shyamaprosad [Mookerjee] gives the lead, the Hindu hoarders pay the cash and call the tune, the Fifth Column gives the cadres." Although Mookerjee had courted the support of the masses by organizing relief on communal lines, his policies helped "not the Hindus of Bengal but only its Hindu hoarders," and he relied on "Fifth Column youngsters from the Forward Bloc [a nationalist movement that sided with the Japanese during the war], Anushilan [an anti-Stalinist Marxist movement], etc" to dole out the relief.[135] Economist Asok Mitra later castigated the Communists for their "tame emphasis on the need to prevent food riots and unearth hoarding," noting that "with the access they enjoyed at that time to information, they should have known that if anyone were hoarding

---

[132] *People's War*, 14 November 1943. Joshi's article was accompanied by graphic photographs of the famine taken by the young (and later famous) photojournalist Sunil Janah.

[133] Bhattacharya 1995.

[134] *APB*, 15 June 1943 (statement from Bengal Provincial Students' Federation).

[135] *People's War*, 14 November 1943.

to the point of forcing a famine on the country it was the central and provincial governments and their purchasing agents."[136] On the overall impact of the food drive one cannot fault the verdict of Kuruna Moy Mukerji, economist and author of a survey of the famine's impact in Faridpur in East Bengal:

> The negative results of the "Food Drive" in June 1943 further embarrassed the Government. These shook the people's confidence in the government on two counts. First, the precarious stock position revealed in the course of the "drive" was an evidence against the official view that withholding of stocks by the producers and consumers of rural areas played a part in causing the Famine. Secondly, the stock found to be in existence was so low that it not only directly torpedoed the Bengal and Central Governments" propaganda policy of "No shortage," but, at the same time, produced among people a paralysing sense of calamity, far surpassing even their own worst fears regarding food shortage. The actual shortage was found to be more serious and more acute than their own estimate of it so far. Thus reality outstripped popular imagination.[137]

Table 2.1 describes the impact of the famine on household debt by occupational group. The proportion of families in debt virtually doubled between 1943 and 1944. The "Other Agricultural" category refers to rent receivers and non-cultivating landowners (including widows). No group seems to have been immune; curiously, the table implies no striking difference between agriculturalists and non-agriculturalists.

To summarize: there *was* a food availability problem in Bengal, although its extent cannot be resolved with any accuracy. Some believed that the true situation was even worse than implied by the Nawab Bahadur of Dacca's declaration in February 1943, and that some of the *aman* crop (the main crop, harvested in November and December) in west Bengal rotted only after it had been harvested, but against this there is the assessment of the leading merchant and Muslim League politician, Mirza Isphahani, that the shortage in

---

[136] Mitra 1989: 258.
[137] Mukerji 1965: 49.

TABLE 2.1. Debt by Occupational Group, Bengal 1943–46

Occupational Group	Sample size		% Families in debt			Average loan per family [Rs.]		
	1943–44	1946	1943	1944	1946	1943	1944	1946
Cultivator	7,005	22,204	34.6	61.7	63.2	90.0	88.4	159
Agricultural labor (landless)	2,463	5,148	21.8	50.5	49.3	56.9	51.8	71
Other agricultural	907	2,604	33.9	56.8	56.0	115.1	115.9	306
All agricultural	10,375	29,956	31.4	58.6	60.0	87.6	83.3	158
Non-agricultural	4,394	16,658	25.6	52.6	42.1	79.5	79.2	120
Total	14,769	46,614	29.8	56.9	53.7	85.5	82.2	148

Source: Chakraborty 1997: 23.

1943, taking carry-over and the likely size of the *aus* harvest (harvested during the summer months) into account, was only one million tons.[138] In normal times, Bengal might have been resilient enough to cope with such a shortfall; in 1943, given military requirements and war-related disruption to trade and communications, this was a disastrous deficit. Informed commentary at the time, the failure of the food drive, and the high incidence of forced land sales by starving peasants all point to a deficit.

The Regional Dimensions of the Famine

As noted earlier, the impact of the Bengal famine was quite uneven by region (maps 2.1 and 2.2).[139] Calculations of its demographic toll are constrained by reliance on imperfect census and civil registration data. Yet estimates of vital rates before and during the famine imply that nearly two-thirds of the excess mortality between mid-1943 and mid-1944 and nearly three-quarters of the reduction of births in 1944 occurred in east Bengal, in divisions constituting present-day Bangladesh (maps 2.4 and 2.5, based on Maharatna 1996).[140]

[138] Linlithgow to Amery, 10 October 1943 (reporting a confidential conversation between Mirza Isphahani and the acting governor in October 1943), in Mansergh 1973: 390; Sen 1981: 82.
[139] Greenough 1982: 139–47; Maharatna 1996: 178–237.
[140] Maharatna's estimates imply 65 and 72 percent, respectively.

Map 2.4 Bengal: Percentage increases in deaths, July 1943–June 1944. From data in Maharatna 1996: 179–80, 200–201.

Map 2.5 Bengal: Percentage decline in births, 1944. From data in Maharatna 1996: 179–80, 200–201.

Two factors affecting the late 1942 *aman* crop—the Midnapur cyclone and an outbreak of brown rust disease (*Helminthosporium oryzae*)—were mainly confined to western Bengal. The role of brown rust disease is still unclear. In December 1943 Amery noted in his diary that the authorities were slow to recognize its effect:

> Had a talk at the office with Vigor, the food expert back from India.... As regards Bengal I gathered that the local administration did not begin to realise that the [rice] crop had been a failure until about April. It was quite a good looking crop and the fact that it suffered from blight was only gradually realised. One can only hope that the present promising crop may not be subject to the same disaster, or we shall be in a bad fix.[141]

Plant pathologist Paul Holliday and historian Mark Tauger support Indian plant pathologist S. Y. Padmanabhan in his claim that "nothing as devastating as the Bengal epiphytotic of 1942 has been recorded in plant pathological literature."[142] Official data, warts and all, confirm that the decline in agricultural output was proportionately greatest in the west (map 2.6). The extent of the damage caused by the fungus was not realized until the crop had been harvested; certainly the manner in which the cyclone dislodged flowering paddy plants in the coastal west (including most of Midnapore, Hooghly, and Howrah, and parts of 24-Parganas, Burdwan, and Birbhum) increased their vulnerability to fungus. Final crop forecasts by the director of agriculture[143] imply massive declines of over half relative to 1941 in the 1942 *aman* crop in the divisions of Burdwan, Bankura, Midnapur, Rajshahi, Rangpur, and Malda. Harvest deficits in divisions normally in deficit, located mainly in the east (map 2.7), were smaller. Map 2.8 describes the variation in adult literacy across the province in 1941; its south-north gradient hardly reflects relative famine intensity either.

---

[141] Amery 1988: 954.

[142] On the brown rust, see Amery 1988: 954 (entry for 7 December 1943); Padmanabhan 1973; Dasgupta 1984; Tauger 2004, 2009; Holliday 1998: 41. I am grateful to plant pathologist Paul Holliday for instruction on the likely role of the fungus. A memorandum by civil servant Stephen Hatch-Barnwell (IOL, Mss. Eur. D1022) further describes how "in 1942, the main rice crop was attacked by a fungal disease in epidemic form over a large part of Bengal, and, by the autumn it began to be apparent that there was going to be a major crop failure."

[143] IOL, Mss Eur., d911/8, Pinnell Papers, "Note on the acreage and yield of aus rice in Bengal in 1943."

Map 2.6 Bengal: Percentage change in rice output, 1942–43. Data from Pinnell Papers (IOL, Ms. Eur. 911/8).

Map 2.7 Bengal: Agricultural output per head, 1951. Data from Boyce 1981: 140–41.

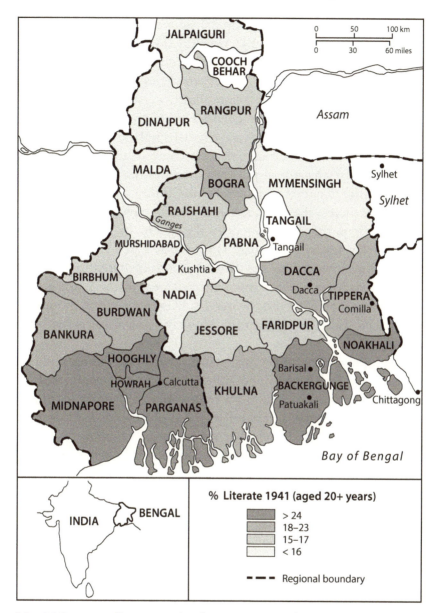

Map 2.8 Percentage literate 1941 (aged 20+ years). From data in the 1941 population census.

The pattern described in map 2.2 squares reasonably well with that of excess deaths (map 2.4), whereby the five worst affected divisions were Midnapur (in the west), Howrah (next to Calcutta), Murshidabad (in the north), Dacca (in the east), and Tripura (formerly Tippera, now a separate state abutting eastern Bangladesh).[144] Map 2.5 indicates that the declines in births were greatest in Dacca, Pabna, Faridpur, Tippera, Mymensingh, and Murshidabad (in that order). The demographic outcome in the largely urban and industrial division of Howrah muddies the water. Although births hardly declined in Howrah—indicating that the crisis was less severe there—the death rate rose considerably. This anomalous outcome is perhaps explained by the deaths in Howrah of migrants from nearby rural areas. However, as noted above, map 2.2 singles out Howrah, and the division is also included in an October 1943 assessment of the worst affected areas by the acting governor of Bengal.[145] Note too the overlap between some of the worst-affected areas (e.g., Midnapore, Howrah) and those with high literacy rates.

The following cross-sectional statistical analysis, loosely replicating that by Joel Mokyr and others for mid-nineteenth-century Ireland,[146] is based on data from twenty-four of Bengal's divisions, and excludes the more urbanized divisions of Howrah and Hooghly. The aim is to discover whether the range of variables described below help explain the regional variation in vital rates. The dependent variables are the changes in the birth and death rates.[147] *DDRA* is the increase in the death rate in July 1943–June 1944; *DDRB* also includes excess deaths in July–December 1944. *DBR* is the reduction in the birth rate in 1944. These are regressed on:

---

[144] Maharatna 1996: 190. Map 2.5 is derived from data in Maharatna 1996: 179–80, 200–201.

[145] Rutherford to Linlithgow, 2 October 1943, in Mansergh 1973: 363. Rutherford's list was Midnapur, Howrah, 24-Parganas, Bakarganj, Noakhali, Bankura, and Dacca.

[146] Mokyr 1985; see also McGregor 1989; Ó Gráda 1999. Table 4.2 in Essay 4 below is in the same tradition.

[147] The demographic data are taken from Maharatna 1996, the Muslim percentage of the population from the 1941 census, and the agricultural output estimates from Boyce (1987: 140–41).

MAGQ: agricultural output per head
DAGQ: proportionate change in agricultural output
PCMUSLIM: Muslim percentage of the population
DENSITY41: population per square mile
PCURBAN: urban percentage of the population
CDR: crude death rate before the famine
YNGLIT: child and young adult literacy rate
PRATIO: ratio of rice price during the famine to its pre-famine level

The variables and the correlations between them are described in tables 2.2 and 2.3. One would expect that lower mortality would be associated with, for example, more agricultural land per head, higher literacy, and fewer people per square mile. One would also expect areas where mortality was high before the famine to be more vulnerable during it. The outcome of the regression analysis is described in tables 2.4 and 2.5. The columns I–IX represent the outcomes of using different variables. Surprisingly, perhaps, in table 2.4 the results using *DDRB* are somewhat stronger than those using *DDRA*. The only variables to pack a significant statistical punch were *DENSITY41*, *CDR*, *DBR*, and *YNGLIT*. High population density and a high non-crisis death rate were, indeed, associated with bigger increases in the death rate. Higher literacy rates among the young—a proxy for living standards in the recent past—had the opposite effect. Table 2.5 describes the outcome of modeling reductions in the birth rate; the results are broadly analogous. Again, high population density imposed a penalty through fewer births during the famine, whereas youth literacy offered some insulation against its impact.

Variables with small coefficients and little or no explanatory power included *PCURBAN*, *DAGQ*, and *PCMUSLIM*. The failure of *PCMUSLIM* does not come as a surprise, given its high correlation with population density. The failure of *DAGQ* supports an entitlements approach to the crisis in the following sense: eastern divisions experienced lower proportionate declines in the *aman* crop in 1942, but they were deficit provinces. The huge gap, documented earlier, between black market prices in east and west Bengal after July 1943

Table 2.2. Correlation Matrix of Variables Used

	DDRA	DDRB	DBR	MAGQ	DAGQ	PCURB	PCMUS	YNGLIT	CDR	PRATIO	DENS41
DDRA	1.00										
DDRB	.784	1.00									
DBR	-.417	.075	1.00								
MAGQ	-.070	.159	.413	1.00							
DAGQ	.168	-.104	-.429	-.700	1.00						
PCURBAN	.108	.055	.090	-.214	-.055	1.00					
PCMUSLIM	.176	.081	-.328	-.214	.326	-.527	1.00				
YNGLIT	.077	-.271	-.094	-.404	.195	.261	.037	1.00			
CDR	-.513	-.628	-.250	.014	.030	-.026	-.144	-.251	1.00		
PRATIO	-.141	-.190	.129	.597	-.405	-.144	.031	.093	.041	1.00	
DENSITY41	.643	.328	-.593	-.441	.443	-.110	.605	.374	-.443	-.173	1.00

Note: For definitions of the variables, see text.

TABLE 2.3. Summary Statistics of Variables Used

	Mean	Std deviation	Min	Max
DDRA	93.90	47.70	13.83	178.02
DDRB	121.17	66.12	20.40	271.83
DBR	−39.23	15.98	−65.75	−0.52
MAGQ	93.60	25.03	41.5	152.10
DAGQ	−32.86	21.75	−65.23	19.55
PCURBAN	5.73	5.87	1.08	24.41
PCMUSLIM	52.98	26.26	2.42	83.93
YNGLIT	6.72	2.15	3.18	11.55
CDR	20.93	4.07	12.80	29.50
PRATIO	4.49	0.69	2.78	5.95

Note: For definitions of the variables, see text.

TABLE 2.4. Modeling the Variation in Excess Mortality

	DDRA			DDRB		
	I	II	III	IV	V	VI
MAGQ	.737			.803		
DAGQ	.320			−.072		
DENSITY41	.128**	.085**		.083*	.168**	
PCURBAN	1.97			2.91		
PCMUSLIM	−.417			−.078		
YNGLIT	−4.73*	−4.89**	−3.47**	−14.5*	−16.4**	−14.9**
DBR			−1.81**		2.16**	−.694
CDR	−2.43	−3.60	−8.24**	−9.05**		−12.9**
PRATIO	−6.88			−20.5		
N	24	24	24	24	24	24
Prob > F	.017	.002	.000	.005	.006	.000
Adjusted R²	.467	.447	.516	.504	.378	.556

*z > 1.65 **z > 2

TABLE 2.5. Modeling the Variation in Lost Births

	VII	VIII	IX
MAGQ	.088		
DAGQ	−.028		
DENSITY41	−.049**	−.044**	−.034**
PCURBAN	−.695		
PCMUSLIM	.070		
YOUNGLIT	1.98**	.645	
DDR			−.116**
CDR	−2.41**	−2.47**	−2.89**
PRATIO	−4.22		
N	24	24	25
Prob > F	.002	.000	.000
Adjusted R²	.634	.637	.702

*z > 1.65 **z > 2

implies that market forces failed to move rice from where it was in relative surplus to where it was in relative deficit at the height of the crisis. Our price data fail to capture the market segmentation that became much more of a problem after mid-1943; perhaps this explains why data on rice prices by division up to mid-1943 (*PRATIO*) fail to account for the variation in births or deaths.

Conclusion

The Bengal famine is sometimes described as India's last, although this description can only be considered accurate because of changing national borders: most of its victims lived in the mainly Muslim area that would become East Pakistan between 1947 and 1971 and thereafter Bangladesh, an area that notoriously suffered severe famine again in 1974. The 1943–44 famine has become paradigmatic as an "entitlements famine," whereby speculation born of greed and panic produced an "artificial" shortage of rice, the staple food. Here I have argued that the lack of political will to divert foodstuffs from the war effort rather than speculation in the sense outlined was mainly responsible for the famine. Those in authority at the time knew that there was a shortfall but kept quiet about it. The War Cabinet in London chose not to act on it. Winston Churchill's lack of empathy for India and "all to do with it" mattered; his immediate reaction—Amery described it as "a preliminary flourish"—to Amery's last-ditch plea for more shipping on 10 November 1943 was a remark about "Indians breeding like rabbits and being paid a million a day by us for doing nothing about the war."[148]

Neither price movements nor the outcome of the food drives of the summer of 1943 support the case that there were massive hoards of rice being kept from the market in the hopes of further price increases. Markets did "fail" in another sense, however: the disruption of transport facilities led to huge increases in the price of rice in the east of the province, which suffered most during the famine, during the second half of 1943. The problem in Bengal in 1943 was not in-

[148] Amery 1988: 950. Churchill's malign role is highlighted in Mukerjee 2010.

ternecine strife, but the failure of the imperial power to make good a harvest shortfall that would have been manageable in peacetime. The famine was made inevitable by the authorities' failure to recognize publicly that there was a shortfall and by the extra demands on food imposed by the war effort. The famine was the product of the wartime priorities of the ruling colonial elite.

3

Markets and Famines

PRE-INDUSTRIAL EUROPE AND BEYOND

> I cannot approve of the course you seem to have taken, which is to
> prevent by all manner of means the shipment of grain from your re-
> gion: is it natural that you should want to keep the price of grain in
> Touraine at 14, 15, or even 18 livres per septier, when it is going to
> cost 25 to 30 livres in Blois and Orleans and 35 to 40 livres in Paris?
>> Controleur-general Orry to the intendant of Tours, 1740[1]

> I believe that we both are agreed that Sleeman's theory of free move-
> ment is the only possible solution; but at present we have got the
> exact opposite.
>> Sir John Herbert (Calcutta) to Linlithgow (Delhi), 8 June 1943[2]

The impact of markets on famines remains a contentious issue. One
intellectual tradition, dating back beyond Adam Smith to François
Quesnay, Claude-Jacques Herbert, and the French Enlightenment,
holds that free markets minimize the damage done by harvest failure.[3] According to this tradition, merchants who respond to market signals ensure that foodstuffs are directed where they are needed
most; measures that interfere with their freedom are therefore to be
avoided. In his article on cereals in the French *Encyclopédie* the great

---

[1] Cited in Ó Gráda and Chevet 2002: 709.
[2] Cited in Mansergh 1971: 1050.
[3] For more on Herbert and on Enlightenment economics generally, see Persson 1999:
7–10.

French economist François Quesnay wrote that "the pretext of remedying famines in a kingdom, by intercepting the trade in grain between the provinces, gives rise to further abuses which increase suffering, destroy agriculture, and decimate the revenues of the kingdom."[4] This anticipates Adam Smith's classic case for free trade in foodstuffs during what he called "dearths" in *The Wealth of Nations* (1776).

In a context where the stakes were very high the stern Scotsman certainly did not hold back: all "dearths" or supply shortfalls in Europe for the previous two centuries or more, he asserted, had been due to poor harvests, and not to collusion between grain merchants, though sometimes such shortages were exacerbated by warfare. Smith also distinguished between "dearths" and "famines," asserting that all European "famines" in the same period had been due to "the violence of government attempting, by improper means, to remedy the inconveniences of a dearth." He held that grain merchants, "without intending the interest of the people," minimized such outcomes by ensuring both intertemporal and interregional arbitrage.[5] The merchants' optimal selling strategy would generate consumption smoothing over the harvest-year, thereby minimizing loss of life;[6] those who "from excess of avarice" hoarded supplies too long in the false hope of even higher prices would be forced in due course to sell at a loss.

Smith's claims were ably re-articulated in 1800 by Thomas Malthus in the *Essay on the High Cost of Provisions* and in the 1830s by Irish economist Mountifort Longfield.[7] Longfield's less familiar application of Smith's logic to pre-famine Ireland is worth citing:

> High prices . . . have the most beneficial effect in mitigating the evil consequences of a scarcity, and preventing an absolute famine from resulting towards the end of the season. They provide effectually that the reduction in the usual consumption shall be spread equally over the entire year. They do not much diminish the entire portion to be con-

---

[4] Quesnay 1958: 494n, my translation.

[5] Smith 1976: 526–34.

[6] Well, not quite, since the cost of storage implies a gradual reduction in consumption over the harvest-year.

[7] Malthus 1800: 12–14; Longfield 1834: 52–58.

sumed by any one person or family, they only cause that portion to be given in the manner and at the times most beneficial to the consumer. To take an instance, suppose the crop of the ordinary food used in any country, as potatoes in Ireland, was to fall short in some year one-sixth of the usual consumption. If this scarcity did not indicate and in some measure correct itself by an increase of price, the whole stock of provisions destined for the supply of the year would be exhausted in ten months, and for the remaining two months a scene of misery and famine beyond description would ensue. But this in fact does not take place, for prices do rise and cause an immediate diminution in the ordinary daily consumption, so that the existing stores hold out until the season for an arrival of a new supply. Undoubtedly some distress is endured during this interval, from the want felt by many of the poor of a proper quantity of food; but this distress is necessarily incident to a diminished supply, and would be incalculably increased instead of being diminished, if human legislation should attempt to regulate the prices.[8]

The focus in this passage is on consumption smoothing across the harvest-year, but the same Smithian tradition holds that the unimpeded functioning of markets during famines also minimizes the spread of prices across space:

In an extensive corn country, between all the different parts of which there is a free commerce and communication, the scarcity occasioned by the most unfavourable seasons can never be so great as to produce a famine; and the scantiest crop, if managed with frugality and œconomy, will maintain, through the year, the same number of people that are commonly fed in a more affluent manner by one of moderate plenty.... [A]s corn grows equally upon high and low lands, upon grounds that are disposed to be too wet, and upon those that are disposed to be too dry, either the drought or the rain which is hurtful to one part of the country is favourable to another; and though both in the wet and in the dry season the crop is a good deal less than in one more properly tempered, yet in both what is lost in one part of the country is in some measure compensated by what is gained in the other.[9]

[8] Longfield 1834: 53–54.
[9] Smith 1976 ("Digression concerning the Corn Trade and Corn Laws"). Note that "corn" here means wheat, not maize.

Thus by reallocating grain from areas in relative surplus to those in relative deficit, the market mechanism should produce a net reduction in the damage done—and deaths caused—by any harvest failure

Another more populist tradition counters that, on the contrary, well-functioning markets may exacerbate famines by removing food from where there is insufficient purchasing power for it to richer, less affected areas. It is in this sense that economists Jean Drèze and Amartya Sen have written of "English consumers attract[ing] food away, through the market mechanism, from famine-stricken Ireland to rich England, with ship after ship sailing down the river Shannon with various types of food" during the Great Irish Famine of the 1840s.[10] This tradition supports, by implication at least, those "moral economy" redressers who in the past attempted to block the outflow of grain in order to reduce famine's impact. Radical historian Edward P. Thompson's panacea for famine—send cadres of food-riot instructors to countries at risk—is very much in this tradition.[11] The rioters might succeed in preventing exports, seizing food, or forcing prices down, always with the aim of exacting concessions or transfers from the better off.

A third tradition holds that markets may simply not function well during famines, for a variety of reasons. Grain producers might tend to underestimate the harvest—or manipulate information about it—and hold back supplies, resulting in intertemporal misallocation. In that case false hopes of yet higher prices might generate "bubbles" in markets for staple foodstuffs, resulting in disastrous entitlement failures. Confusing signals and panic are particularly likely in wartime, and Amartya Sen's classic study of market failure in a famine context refers to India, or more specifically Bengal, during World War II. Or the problem could be spatial, as when local or regional markets might become segregated because bad weather disrupts communications. Famine conditions producing "noisy" or unreliable information about the true supply situation could have the same effect.

[10] Drèze and Sen 1989: 22.
[11] As cited in Bohstedt 2010: 89.

The ability of merchants and markets to gauge supply correctly in such circumstances is an empirical matter, and Smith's presumption has been questioned by others, then and since, including the well-known English agronomist Arthur Young. Unlike Adam Smith, Young did not fully trust grain merchants' ability to judge the size of the harvest accurately, and as secretary of the Board of Agriculture he urged the necessity of an annual national agricultural census, which would guide the decisions of consumer and producer alike. Yet Young's skepticism regarding all-knowing merchants did not affect his faith in market forces. In *Travels in France* Young stressed the role of markets in minimizing the danger of famine, and denounced the strong anti-speculator sentiment of the *cahiers de doléance* of 1789. In *The Question of Scarcity Plainly Stated*, prompted by the English near-famine of 1800—also the spark for Malthus's more famous *Essay on the High Cost of Provisions*—he argued that the harvest shortfall was "great and real [and] a very high price a necessary consequence," against critics who blamed artificial manipulation by hoarders and speculators.[12]

A fourth possibility is that the absence of competitive markets in normal times might lead to profiteering by powerful middlemen such as flour millers and moneylenders during famines.[13] Smith was alert to this possibility, but believed that, while it might have been possible to restrict competition in "the spiceries of the Molluc-cas," it would be impossible to create such an "extensive monopoly" in the case of staple foodstuffs. Those who traded in grain, be they farmers, bakers, or merchants, were simply too dispersed and too nu-merous to enter into a monopolistic conspiracy.[14] Again this is an empirical issue: the power of shopkeepers in backward, crisis-prone economies to exploit local monopoly power is a recurring theme in accounts of famine.

The issue of how markets work during famines is an important one for our understanding of famines, past and present, and for the policy measures undertaken to confront them. Table 3.1 summarizes the outcomes mentioned above. There are four possible outcomes:

---

[12] Young 1793: vol. 2, 401; Young 1801; Rashid 1980: 497, 499; Gazley 1973: 416–17.
[13] Drèze and Sen 1989: 22, 90–91, 143–44, 155; Persson 1999: 41–42.
[14] Smith 1976.

TABLE 3.1. How Markets Influence the Impact
of Famines

		Markets	
		Work	Don't Work
Famines	Worse	1,1	1,2
	Better	2,1	2,2

well or poorly functioning markets can make famines better or
worse. Adam Smith's perspective is represented by outcome (2,1):
markets that work prevent or at least alleviate famines. The populist
suspicion of markets is represented by outcomes (1,1) and (2,2); in
the first case, those market forces that draw food "down the river
Shannon" make matters worse, while in the second, anti-market actions that prevents the ships from traveling help alleviate the crisis.
The view that markets exacerbate famines because they fail to function as in non-crisis times—as reflected in Arthur Young's fears in
the 1790s—is represented by outcome (1,2).

Smith's preoccupation was with the influence of markets in the
event of a harvest shortfall. That influence hinges on the degree of
market integration in non-crisis times. But in backward, famine-
prone economies facing high transport costs and (perhaps) cumber-
some controls on interregional trade, the scope for trade in non-
famine years may be limited. This is a reminder of another way in
which markets can reduce the probability and gravity of famines:
market integration, by ensuring that different regions pursue their
comparative advantage, increases steady-state aggregate output and
incomes, thereby reducing the damage done by any given proportionate harvest shortfall. This mechanism is emphasized in the work
of French Enlightenment writers,[15] but Smith's concern—as in the
historiography of markets and famines generally—was with the impact of famines on the normal functioning of markets.

The verdict of empirical analyses on market response during famines is mixed. The official inquiry into the Great Bengal Famine of
1943–44 argued that the rise in food prices was "more than the natu-

[15] See Persson 1999; Rothschild 2001: chap. 3.

ral result of the shortage of supply that had occurred." Sen's classic inquiry into the same famine pointed the finger at farmers and grain merchants for converting a "moderate short-fall in *production* ... into an exceptional short-fall in *market release*" (emphases in original). The famine was due in large part to "speculative withdrawal and panic purchase of rice stocks ... encouraged by administrative chaos."[16] Martin Ravallion's classic study of the 1974 Bangladesh famine broadly corroborates Sen's findings. He also found market failure, concluding that excess mortality was, "in no small measure, the effect of a speculative crisis." Rice prices rose dramatically because, as Arthur Young envisaged might happen, merchants badly underestimated a harvest that turned out to be more or less normal. Prices then fell back just as fast. Ravallion also found evidence of "significant impediments" to trade between the capital city, Dhaka, and its main sources of supply during this famine.[17]

Joachim von Braun and Patrick Webb's study of famines in Sudan and Ethiopia in the mid-1980s also deems them to have been exacerbated by weak spatial integration of markets. Price explosions, price controls, and market disruptions were "commonplace." Roadblocks restricted interprovincial movements of grain and people, and food supplies for the armed forces were extracted from farmers and traders at fixed prices. The result was sharply rising marketing costs and severe market segmentation.[18] In a sophisticated study of local grain markets in Niger in the 2000s, Jenny Aker finds differently; her analysis of detailed market and transactions cost data shows that market failure did not cause the crisis that struck that impoverished economy in 2005. On the contrary, she found that markets were "partially integrated and efficient," and that prices were sensitive to supply shocks. Drought reduced the spread of prices across markets, which, as she notes, is hardly consistent with the case for market failure during crises.[19] Another study along similar lines on the Sahel argues that price data should supplement biophysics and weather-based

[16] Sen 1981: 76; Bhatia 1967: 323–24.

[17] Ravallion's *Market and Famines* (1987a) is the classic economic analysis of the Bangladesh famine. See also Ravallion 1997: 1219–21. Quddus and Becker (2000) analyze the functioning of food markets in Bangladesh further.

[18] Webb and von Braun 1994: 47–55; also von Braun, Teklu, and Webb 1999: chap. 6.

[19] Aker 2010a, 2010b.

models of agricultural production as a means of predicting harvest shortfalls and preventing food crises. It shows, using contemporary data from Sahelian markets in Mali, Burkina Faso, and Niger, that prices are excellent signals on about both present and future food availability.[20]

However, formal studies like these of how markets worked during pre-twentieth century famines are very few.

Famines in India

During the Great Bengal Famine of 1943–44 commentary sometimes harked back to another great Bengal famine, that of 1770 (known by the Bengali calendar as *Chhiattōrer monnōntór,* "the famine of 1176"), in which allegedly "nearly one-fifth" to one-third of the population perished, and when "the roads and the streets were filled with the dead and dying; the inhabitants fed on prohibited and abhorred animals; the child on its dead parent, the mother on her child."[21] Although the famine of 1770 lived on in collective memory, it is poorly documented. Death rates of one in three are almost unprecedented during famines, and such an exceptional mortality toll is not easily squared with the later claim that the receipts of the East Indian Company in Bengal in the wake of the famine were "very much better than had been anticipated, and in fact did not show the deficiency that might have been expected to follow such depopulation." And even though in reality the Company's net revenues from Bengal and Bihar fell from £1.76 million in 1768–69 to £1.42 million in 1769–70 and £1.27 million in 1770–71, the claim that one-third of all Bengalis perished during the famine carries little conviction. Rajat Datta, who has shown that the commonly cited toll of ten million deaths is "a largely inflated number," is careful to add that "two million dead in the space of six or seven months still remains a very high number."[22] Again, a dramatic fall in food output

[20] Araujo, Araujo Bonjean, and Brunelin 2012; Araujo Bonjean and Simonet 2014.
[21] Hamilton 1820: I, 44; Brewster 1830: 83; Fiske 1876; BPP 1832: General Appendix, 11 (for quotation).
[22] Campbell 1874: 420–21; Bowen 1991: 104; Prasad 1960: xxxii, 107, 181, 418–19; Datta 1990: 102–8.

and severe famine are implied by the threefold rise in the price of rice in 1770—and in places prices rose by much more for a time—although a trebling of prices during famines is not exceptional. The increase in the price of rice was accompanied by a doubling of the price of *gur* (an Indian sugar product). Prices returned to their pre-famine norm in the following year.[23]

Much later, a retired colonial official predictably blamed the 1770 famine on government interference with grain markets:

> The province had a certain amount of food in it and this food had to last nine months. Private enterprise if left to itself would have stored up the general supply at the harvest, with a view to realizing a larger profit at a later period in the scarcity. Prices would in consequence have immediately risen, compelling the population to reduce their consumption from the very beginning of the dearth. The general stock would thus have been husbanded and the pressure equally spread over the whole nine months, instead of being concentrated upon the last six. The price of grain, in place of promptly rising to three-halfpence a pound as in 1865–66, continued at three-farthings during the earlier months of the famine. During the latter ones it advanced to two pence and in certain localities reached four pence.[24]

The author of this passage, the learned William Wilson Hunter, knew how to invoke his Smith and Malthus. Yet elsewhere, describing famines and markets in Bengal in the early 1870s, Hunter sounded a less dogmatic note. The small price margin that defined the difference between scarcity and plenty, he observed, explained "the invariable and urgent demand" by the poor to prohibit food exports during famines. While declaring that he "would not be understood to advocate that demand," he also admitted that market forces were insufficient to keep food from leaving famine-afflicted Bengal in the early 1870s, and that the facts "explain, and to some extent justify" the cries for an embargo.[25] Shades of E. P. Thompson and of Jean Drèze and Amartya Sen!

[23] Bayley 1818; 568; Drèze and Sen 1989: 91.
[24] Hunter 1868: 43.
[25] Hunter 1874: 16–17.

That restrictions on the movement of grain out of Bengal made much difference in 1770 is highly dubious. The instinct of the Court of Governors of the East India Company, in faraway London, was to seek to restrict exports of foodstuffs, but it had no way of ensuring that this was being done. It worried about servants of the Company who "influenced by avarice [sought to] monopolize the chief articles of the support of the poor," and requested "a full and exact account of the quantity of rice which during the progress of this calamity has been exported into other parts from those provinces which suffered least by it together with the name of each proprietor of the rice so exported as well as the quantity thereof." Not surprisingly, the reply from its corrupt agents in Calcutta passed the buck on to indigenous traders who, "too often insensitive to the dictates of humanity, grasp at every opportunity of profiting by these practices."[26]

India seems to have experienced a respite from famine for some decades after 1770, but during the nineteenth century it also experienced several catastrophic famines. Worst were those in Orissa in the mid-1860s, in the Bombay and Madras presidencies in 1876–78, and those that straddled much of northern and western India in 1896–97 and 1899–1900. Indian demographer Arup Maharatna reckons that in aggregate these famines cost 17 million lives.[27] All were associated with massive rises in the prices of basic foodstuffs.[28] The economic context of these famines is contested. In the past the second half of the nineteenth century was usually described as one of impoverishment; more recent research indicates that real wages fluctuated wildly in the short run, but were more or less constant over the longer run.[29] There is uncertainty too about whether this period should be characterized as one of increasing frequency of famine, but even optimist Michelle McAlpine conceded that it was largely as a result of famines that India's rate of population growth in this era was so slow (less than 0.4 percent per annum) before 1900.[30]

[26] Prasad 1960: 107–8, 368–69.
[27] Maharatna 1996: 15.
[28] Maharatna 1996: 45, 53, 58, 64.
[29] Bhatia 1967: 7–8; Allen and Studer 2009.
[30] Bhatia 1967: 7–8; McAlpine 1983: 47–48, 71–83.

Debates about the link between markets and famines have a particular resonance for India. Famines in this period have been blamed both on market forces and on their absence. B. M. Bhatia, for example, argued that market integration increased mortality on the grounds that in crisis years such as 1876–79 it led to an increase in food exports.[31] Nor were unfettered markets likely to keep prices down during famines "in a country where grain trade in small towns and villages were monopolized in the hands of one or two dealers who often combined, withheld the supplies from the market, and raised prices."[32] Malabika Chakrabarti also refers to the manipulation of the food trade by local merchants in Bengal in 1896–97.[33] The authorities, on the other hand, believed in the efficacy of market forces as a form of famine relief. They saw free international trade in grain as a means of mitigating rather than exacerbating local scarcities; when famine threatened, the price mechanism would lead to a reversal of the balance of trade in grain as exports fell and imports rose. This argument was tested against Indian grain import data by Ravallion, who found that while market forces worked in the right direction, they did so too slowly to be of any use.[34]

In the later nineteenth century there were only very weak signs of the integration of wages and rents across regions that might have been anticipated from globalizing forces such as international trade and the railway. William Collins attributes this weak convergence to relatively low rates of internal migration and high climatic variability.[35] Still, Bhatia conceded that the spread of the subcontinent's railway network meant that "a failure of a crop over a limited areas comprising a few districts in a Province could not now cause distress amounting to famine."[36] Several authors since have linked the gradual diminution in the intensity of famines to the spread of the subcontinent's railway network.[37] But Bhatia, like Sen later, also added that the spread of the rail network could lead to the reduction of

[31] Bhatia 1967: 39.
[32] Bhatia 1967: 106.
[33] Chakrabarti 2004: 432.
[34] Ravallion 1987b.
[35] Collins 1999.
[36] Bhatia 1967: 160.
[37] McAlpine 1983; Burgess and Donaldson 2010.

food stocks "even in remote corners of the country" and that "the food situation everywhere was getting more difficult."[38]

The Law of One Price (LOP) stipulates that prices may deviate from their equilibrium values, but that properly functioning markets will arbitrage away significant deviations from equilibrium prices. In other words, in a well-integrated market persistent price differences between regions will stem largely from transport costs. Irish-born, Paris-based Richard Cantillon, writing in the 1720s, was probably the first to describe the LOP as both an equilibrium condition and an adjustment process:

> The price difference between the capital and the provinces must pay for the costs and risks of transport, or otherwise cash will be sent to pay the balance and this will go on until prices in the capital and in the provinces reflect the level of these costs and risks.[39]

LOP implies that integrated markets will prevent the widening of gaps in prices between regions during famines. This may be seen from the simple hypothetical example outlined in table 3.2. Let row P_N describe prices in the four fictitious regions (A, B, C, and D) in normal times (N): the mean represents the average of those prices, and σ and CV their standard deviation and coefficient of variation, respectively. The P_F rows reflect prices in times of famine (F). Let T represent the (constant) costs of shipping grain from a region to the most expensive region. Given T, the prices in row P_N reflect the Law of One Price because the price in D (4.5) equals the price in A (2.0) plus the cost of shipment T to D (2.5), and so on. Next, let $P_{F(1)}$ and $P_{F(2)}$ describe what prices would be in the absence of trade in two situations of harvest failure, $F(1)$ and $F(2)$. In $F(1)$ the failure is most serious in areas that are normally food-exporting. Unless T is affected, the higher prices obtaining in regions A and B will cause food to remain in them, and prices will remain at $P_{F(1)}$. In $F(2)$, the failure in the supplying areas is such that reverse flows of food from normally deficit regions are necessary to reflect the Law of One Price. Such flows would establish an equilibrium vector such as $P_{F(2)}$. In a

---

[38] Bhatia 1967: 160. Compare Sweeney 2008.
[39] Cantillon 1997: part II, chap. 5.

TABLE 3.2. LOP at Work: A Hypothetical Example

	A	B	C	D	Mean	σ	CV
P_N	2.0	3.0	4.0	4.5	3.38	1.11	0.33
T	2.5	1.5	0.5	0.0			
$P_{F(1)'}$	3.0	3.5	4.0	4.5	3.75	0.65	0.17
$P_{F(2)'}$	8.0	7.0	4.0	4.5			
$P_{F(2)}$	7.5	6.5	5.5	5.0	6.13	1.11	0.18
$P_{F(3)'}$	2.0	3.0	5.0	6.0			
$P_{F(3)}$	2.5	3.5	4.5	5.0	3.88	1.11	0.29

third scenario, $F(3)$, the failure is most serious in the consuming areas. In the absence of trade prices would be at $P_{F(3)'}$, but trade flows lead to the equilibrium vector of $P_{F(3)}$.

Note that σ, the standard deviation of prices across regions, is the same in $F(2)$ and $F(3)$ as in N, normal times, and less in $F(1)$ than in N. By the same token the Law of One Price implies a fall in the coefficient of variation (i.e., the standard deviation divided by the mean) of prices across different regions. Referring again to table 3.2, the 0.17 [$F(1)'$], 0.18 [$F(2)$], and 0.29 [$F(3)$] in the last column are all less than 0.33 [N]. A rise in σ would be consistent with the failure of the Law of One Price to operate, through markets becoming more segmented. In general, because famine prices, P_F, will exceed normal prices, P_N, unless T changes, with well-functioning markets arbitrage by traders will produce $CV(P_F) < CV(P_N)$. This implication of the Law of One Price is the product of smoothly functioning markets: whether it is borne out in practice offers one way of analyzing how markets function during famines.

We now apply this simple, partial test of how markets behave during crises to the important historical case of nineteenth-century India. In a study of the influence of the spread of the railway network on the expansion of market forces in India during the British Raj, John Hurd presented a rich data set on the average prices of wheat and rice in India and on their variation in districts (local administrative units) across the country over a six-decade period (1861–1921). Hurd inferred the spread of market forces throughout India from the decline in the coefficients of variation of the prices of rice and wheat across regions.[40] More recent work by Roman Studer confirms the presence of market integration in the second half of the nineteenth century, but argues that before then grain markets were "essentially local."[41] Be that as it may, Hurd's and similar data sets can tell us something about market behavior during crises. Whatever the reasons for the degree (or lack) of price variation across space in normal conditions—interlinkage of markets or independent processes—if markets become more segmented in times of crisis, price variation across regions can be expected to increase.

Hurd presents annual data on the prices per unit weight of rice and wheat, India's two largest crops in terms of acreage sown, and their coefficients of variation across 188 Indian administrative districts between 1861 and 1921.[42] After filtering the data to rid them of autocorrelation, the resultant series[43] produced the following correlations between the average price in a given year and the coefficient of variation in that same year:

Period	Wheat	Rice
1863–1921	−0.206	−0.305
1863–1890	−0.245	−0.298
1891–1921	−0.217	−0.399
1863–1914	−0.323	−0.344

The negative coefficients imply that relative price variation (CV) was low when prices were high. The outcome supports the hypothesis that in India between the 1860s and World War I food markets did not become more segmented during crises.

---

[40] Hurd 1975. Martin Ravallion (1987a: 114) rejected Hurd's analysis on the technical grounds that "if prices at different markets are generated by identical but independent stationary autoregressive processes then they will asymptotically converge to zero variance." As a result, claimed Ravallion, nothing about market integration should be inferred from trends in coefficients of variation. However, our interest here is not in trends but in responses to regionally uneven harvest shocks.

[41] Studer 2008.

[42] Hurd 1975: Apps. 6, 7.

[43] On the more technical details, see Ó Gráda 1997.

Four European Famines

The great American economic historian Robert Fogel once characterized famines in early modern Europe as due to anticipated rather than true harvest failures.[44] None of the four famines considered in this essay fits such a pattern. In one case—Finland in 1868—"the harvest of 1867 failed seriously: what was left amounted to about half the normal crop"—while the admittedly limited quantitative data available on France in 1693–94 and 1708–9 suggests that the harvests of those years were also severely affected.[45] The role of harvest failure in Ireland in the late 1840s hardly requires elaboration. All four famines exacted large death tolls and all feature prominently in the historiography of famine. All were regionally quite uneven, and the trigger in all cases was weather- or fungus-induced crop failure. In all four cases the resultant output loss was considerable, and was reflected in sharp increases in food prices.

The two earliest of these famines occurred in France towards the end of Louis XIV's reign. France was then a formidable military power, but its farming system struggled to feed its huge, mainly rural, population of 22 million. Bob Allen reckons that agricultural output per worker in late-seventeenth-century France was less than it had been two centuries earlier, and less than two-thirds of the levels attained in the Low Countries or in England around 1700.[46] Both famines were exacerbated by military campaigns on France's borders and further afield. In the first, excess mortality mounted in the fall of 1693 and would remain high for much of 1694. The estimated death toll of about 1.3 million people represented six percent of the population, prompting Marcel Lachiver's claim that for France this famine was a greater disaster in proportional terms than either the Revolution and Napoleonic Wars or the First World War.[47] The "big winter" of 1708–9 led to the second famine considered here. It struck at a time of grave economic crisis and enduring warfare be-

[44] Fogel 1992.
[45] Kaukiainen, 1984: 241; Lachiver, 1991: 118, 308–9.
[46] Allen 2000.
[47] Lachiver 1991: 200–205, 453; Cabourdin, Biraben, and Blum 1988: 206–9.

tween France and most of its neighbors. Excess mortality began to mount in mid-1709 and would reach 0.6 million before the end of 1710.[48] Both famines were regionally uneven in their impact. In 1693–94, west of an imaginary line from Bordeaux to Le Havre, southeast of a line from Carcassonne to Geneva, and northeast of a line from Geneva to Lille, the impact of the disaster on burials and births was relatively minor. But in the worst hit *départements* such as Lozère, Landes, Lot-et Garonne, Gers, and Cantal, deaths were four times that of a typical non-famine year. In 1709–10 central France was worst hit, and much of southwest France was less affected than in 1693–94. The west of France, less dependent on wheat, escaped relatively lightly, as it had done during earlier famines in 1649–52 and 1660–62.[49]

The Great Finnish Famine of 1868, Europe's second-to-last major peacetime subsistence crisis, received little attention at the time and is rarely discussed or analyzed outside Finland. Yet it was responsible for the deaths of over one hundred thousand people in a total population of 1.8 million. The historical context was severe harvest failure in the wake of several years of hardship in a poor and largely agrarian economy. Heavily forested and dotted with large lakes, and with only about one-twelfth of its landmass under cultivation, Finland in the 1860s was sparsely populated. Internal communications, though improving, were poor, particularly in bad weather. There was an increasing trade in grain between coastal Finland and Saint Petersburg, Tallinn, and Riga, but away from coastal areas the long-distance carriage of grain was on a small scale. On the eve of the famine rye, the staple food of the poor, accounted for well over one-half of grain production. The average yield ratio (i.e., output to seed planted) was only four or five to one. In 1868 mortality was highest in the central provinces of Vaasa and Kuopio and in the remote northern province of Oulu.[50]

---

[48] Lachiver 1991: 361, 381–82. On the broader European climatic context, see Lamb 1982: 43.

[49] Ó Gráda and Chevet 2002: 712–14.

[50] For background see Kaukiainen 1984; Kiiskinen 1961; Lefgren 1973; Häkkinen et al. 1991.

Finally, the Great Irish Famine (1846–52) was not just a watershed in Irish history but also a major event in world history, with far-reaching and enduring economic and political consequences.[51] It resulted in the deaths of about one million people—more, indeed, if deaths in the destinations of Irish famine emigrants are included.[52] Whereas poor grain crops were the proximate causes of the other famines, in Ireland the culprit was the potato. The potato, in which Ireland had a comparative advantage due to its damp climate, produced twice as much food per acre as grain, but its low yield ratio and its perishability were decided disadvantages.[53] In 1845, *Phytophthora infestans,* a plant disease new to Europe, destroyed about one-third of the potato crop, and in the following year it destroyed most of it. After a season's remission it also ruined the harvest of 1848. Excess mortality would persist for two or three years more in some regions. The Irish famine thus lasted longer than the other three and, relatively speaking, was the most devastating of all.

An Error Correction Approach

Did markets in France in the 1690s, in Ireland in the 1840s, or in Finland in the 1860s work as posited by LOP? Here I use an error correction model (ECM) approach to test whether the reaction to emerging disequilibria was slower during a crisis than in normal times. The discussion in this section is the most technical in the entire book, although the nonspecialist should still be able to gain an intuitive grasp of the main points. In the case at hand, the model estimates the speed at which the price in one area returns to its equilibrium value after a change in the price in another area.

I estimate the following simple and familiar representation of the error correction model:[54]

---

[51] For more see Ó Gráda 1999; Crowley, Smyth, and Murphy 2012.

[52] Mokyr 1985; Boyle and Ó Gráda 1986.

[53] Austin Bourke 1993; Rosen 1999).

[54] Alogoskoufis and Smith (1995) provide a good introduction to ECM. Before estimating an ECM the individual price series has to be tested for stationarity. In all cases the hypothesis that the individual series had a unit root could be firmly rejected. Estimation with differences

$$\Delta P_{i,t} = a + b\Delta P_{A,t} + c\text{FAM1} + d P_{i,t-1} + e P_{A,t-1}$$
$$+ f\text{FAM2} + g\text{FAM3} + u'_{it}$$

where $\text{FAM1} = \text{FAMDUM}.\Delta P_{A,t}$

$$\text{FAM2} = \text{FAMDUM}.P_{i,t-1}$$

$$\text{FAM3} = \text{FAMDUM}.P_{A,t-1}$$

Here P is the natural log of price, A is Region A, and i is any other region. Writing the model in this way offers the intuitive interpretation that agents adjust to $P_{i,t}$ from $P_{i,t-1}$ in response to changes in P_A (with b measuring the short-run effect). Moreover, the model posits the long-run relation $P_i = (e/d)P_A$. Changes in P_i are caused by shocks to P_A, and the extent to which the system is out of equilibrium is represented by the lagged error correction term. Since P_A is expected to adjust upwards·if P_i is higher in the previous period, we expect $d < 0$. The ratio (e/d) measures the equilibrium ratio between P_i and P_A; in the absence of transport and other transaction costs, $d = e$. The most important coefficients here are b and d.

The impact of the periods of severest harvest failure and famine—1693–94 and July 1708 to June 1710—on the adjustment process is captured by the coefficients on the interaction terms FAM1, FAM2, and FAM3. Note the italics for coefficients $c, f,$ and g in tables 3.3, 3.4, and 3.5, representing estimated values; in the markets in France and in Finland shown in these tables, $c > 0$ means that markets were better synchronized during the crisis, while $f > 0$ and $g < 0$ implies slower adjustment than in normal times.

The towns and cities included in the analysis of France are Paris, Toulouse, Angoulême, Grenade-sur-Garonne, Pontoise, Rozay-en-Brie, Albi, and Montbatzon. Four of these were significant in size at the time: Paris (with a population of about 0.5 million), Toulouse (40,000), Angoulême (10,000), and Albi (10,000). There would have been little or no trade in grain between Toulouse and Paris in this

---

in the logs of prices and the gaps between the logs of price pairs produced results very like those reported here. Other studies in this vein are Bassino (2007) and Studer (2008).

period in normal years, since Parisians relied on their supply of grain or flour from a well-defined hinterland stretching about 200 km in all directions around it.[55] Similarly, Toulouse and Angoulême did not normally trade in grain, though they were linked by navigable river and coastline via the major port city of Bordeaux. Three of the other pairs—Paris-Pontoise, Paris-Rozay, and Toulouse-Grenade—are markets within short distances of each other. Pontoise, a town of a few thousand people on the river Oise and epicenter of the Vexin region, was one of the main grain markets in the Paris basin, while Grenade was only a short distance downriver from Toulouse. Rozay-en-Brie, in the heart of one of France's main grain-producing regions, also supplied the Paris market. Montbatzon was a small market town near Tours. The choice of towns for this analysis was constrained by the need for monthly wheat price data.[56]

The model yields the results described in table 3.3. They confirm what a textbook account would predict about these markets in normal years. Note that N refers to the number of observations and F to the value of the F-test, a measure of the significance of the regression in question. First, the b coefficients are all positive, ranging from 0.121 for Montbatzon-Angoulême in 1680–99 to 0.886 for Grenade-Toulouse in 1680–1712, and the d coefficients are all negative, ranging from –0.055 for Angoulême-Toulouse in 1680–1699 to –0.646 for Grenade-Toulouse in 1680–99. Second, the spread of coefficient values is consistent with distance and communications. The closer the markets to each other, the bigger the coefficients; in other words, the stronger were the co-movements and the bigger the adjustments to disequilibria.[57] Thirdly, the c's are mostly positive and in some cases emphatically so, and none of the negative c's is statistically significant. Evidence of stronger co-movements during the famine months may reflect the power of the famine "signal" relative to the background noise. Twelve of the fourteen f's in table 3.3 are negative, in-

---

[55] Chevet and Guery 1985; and Kaplan 1984: 88–98.

[56] The data (for which I am grateful to David Weir and Jean-Michel Chevet) refer to market or *mercuriale* prices. Gaps were very few and these were plugged by simple interpolation.

[57] Moreover, the values of d/e, representing the equilibrium price ratios between P_A and P_I, are broadly plausible: prices were highest in the receiving areas.

TABLE 3.3. Pairwise Error Correction Model Estimates: Monthly Data

coefficient	Angoulême/ Toulouse	Grenade/ Toulouse	Batz/ Toulouse	Pontoise/ Paris	Montbatzon/ Paris
a	0.203	−0.483*	−0.334*	−0.480*	0.461
b	0.269*	0.886*	0.245*	0.512*	0.164*
c	0.132	−0.007	0.312*	0.111	0.122*
d	−0.062*	−0.543*	−0.116*	−0.218*	−0.254*
e	0.031	0.574	0.146*	0.251*	0.111*
f	−0.067	−0.236*	−0.194	−0.385*	−0.041
g	0.091	0.236*	0.207*	0.480*	0.016
N	395	395	395	227	227
F	18.6	209.8	27.0	64.3	17.8

coefficient	Angoulême/ Toulouse	Angoulême/ Toulouse	Grenade/ Toulouse	Grenade/ Toulouse	Albi/ Toulouse
a	−0.020	−0.177	−0.357*	−0.478*	−0.002
b	0.235*	0.349*	0.787*	0.721*	0.380*
c	−0.003	0.224*	−0.034	0.291*	−0.013
d	−0.055*	−0.195*	−0.6458	−0.492*	−0.393*
e	0.064	0.143*	0.648*	0.516*	0.388*
f	−0.013*	−0.028	−0.302*	−0.272	0.118
g	0.009	0.076	0.357*	−0.272	−0.087
N	239	156	239	156	197
F	4.8	16.9	124.5	45.1	7.8

coefficient	Montbatzon/ Toulouse	Montbatzon/ Toulouse	Montbatzon / Angoulême	Montbatzon / Angoulême
a	0.231	−0.510*	0.206*	−0.348
b	0.190*	0.241*	0.121	0.391*
c	0.421*	0.255	−0.227	0.306
d	−0.134*	−0.285*	−0.122*	−0.236*
e	0.088*	0.281*	0.087	0.252*
f	−0.365*	−0.023	0.019	−0.302*
g	0.401*	0.086	0.495*	0.348*
N	239	156	239	156
F	17.2	15.4	5.4	23.1

N = 239 (1680–1699); N = 227 (1680–1698); N = 395 (1680–1712); N = 156 (1700–1712); N = 197 (1696–1712).

Note: Coefficients c, f, and g are italicized.

* significant at 1%

TABLE 3.4. ECM Estimates for France (1680–98): SURE Estimation

coefficient	Angoulême	Grenade	Toulouse	Montbatzon	Pontoise	Rozay
a	−0.116	0.379*	0.624*	0.502*	−0.481*	−0.373*
b	0.143*	0.070	0.066	0.165*	0.526*	0.331*
c	−0.108	0.259*	0.214*	0.135*	0.096	0.066
d	−0.115*	−0.192*	−0.195*	−0.263*	−0.257*	−0.106
e	0.101*	0.082*	0.070*	0.133*	0.286*	0.122*
f	0.080	−0.160*	−0.106	−0.030	−0.352*	−0.388*
g	−0.075*	0.089*	0.060	0.025	0.353*	0.343*

Notes: The z-values give the confidence level of the outcome. For example, a value of 1.96 denotes a confidence level of 95%.

Coefficients $c, f,$ and g are italicized.

* $z > 2$.

dicating faster adjustment in crisis months. However, the absence of asterisks (*) indicates that the values are weakly determined for the most part, however (as are the g's). This suggests that responses varied little between normal and crisis years. Finally, dividing the 1680–1712 period into 1680–99 and 1700–12 suggests that the reaction of wheat prices in 1709–10 was somewhat stronger than in 1693–94.

Table 3.4 reports the results of estimating the adjustments in six grain markets to price movements in the great city of Paris between 1680 and 1698 as a system of seemingly unrelated regressions (SURE).[58] The outcome is basically as in table 3.3 except that the coefficients are nearly always better determined. In sum, these French data imply markets that were better integrated than indicated by the historiography, and fail to support the hypothesis that markets for grain performed "worse" during the two famines than in normal times.

Our Finnish data refer to rye, then by far the most important of Finland's grain crops, from October 1858 to December 1873. Table 3.5 describes the response in seven of Finland's eight provinces to price movements in the province of Viipuri, again using the SURE estimation method. For this analysis Viipuri was chosen as a likely market leader because it was on the coast and located next to Russian markets, and therefore most likely to be the channel for outside

[58] The standard BreuschPagan test emphatically rejects independence ($\chi^2(15) = 267.3$).

TABLE 3.5. ECM Estimates for Finnish Provinces (1858–73): SURE Estimation

coefficient	Oulu	Vaasa	Mikkeli	Uusimaa	Kuopio	Turku	Häme
a	0.280	0.225	−2.376*	−0.080	−0.041	1.260	−0.598
b	0.474*	0.331*	0.462*	0.441*	0.424*	0.349*	0.647*
c	0.980*	0.462*	0.716*	0.463*	1.253*	0.556*	0.964*
d	−0.153*	−0.117*	−0.250*	−0.263*	−0.224*	−0.217*	−0.370*
e	0.159*	0.111*	0.350*	0.266*	0.236*	0.165*	0.390*
f	−0.204	0.061	−0.236	−0.276*	0.046	0.107	−0.166
g	0.224	−0.071	0.231	0.337*	−0.062	−0.094	0.196

* $z > 2$

Note: Coefficients c, f, and g are italicized.

market influences. Again, separate estimation and SURE yield similar outcomes, and estimation with the latter is consequently more efficient.[59] As in France nearly two centuries earlier, prices were more synchronized during the famine than in other periods. The case for slower response during the famine is rejected by the generally small and weakly determined values of f and g.[60]

Finally, though the Irish famine was due to the failure of the potato, the behavior of grain markets is nevertheless of interest. Indian meal (or cornmeal) and oatmeal were the closest substitutes for the potato. Contemporary critics accused grain merchants of taking undue advantage of the situation and of making enormous profits through overcharging. Data on grain and oatmeal prices in Ireland are plentiful. Estimating a variant of the ECM described above with weekly oats prices between early June 1846 and the end of 1847 suggested strong co-movements and quick adjustment to disequilibria. Comparing the cities of Cork and Dublin, for example, implies that over half the response to a change in the Dublin price occurred within two weeks. Comparing movements in the price of oats in Dublin and Cork with those in London over a longer period also implies the rapid erosion of disequilibrium gaps.[61]

[59] The BreuschPagan test rejects independence even more emphatically ($\chi^2(21) = 613.3$) than in the French case.

[60] Elsewhere (Ó Gráda 2001) I examine the outcome of treating Vaasa as market leader and the reaction of prices in the remote northern province of Oulu to movements in the other seven provinces. The outcome corroborates the results reported in table 3.5 in this essay.

[61] Ó Gráda 1999: 141–43.

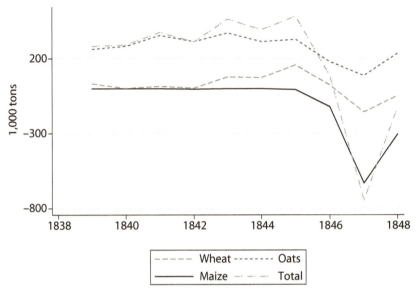

Figure 3.1 Net cereal exports, Ireland 1840–48. Derived from Bourke 1993: 168.

The more stereotypical view of market forces during the Great Irish Famine is reflected by the claim about "ship after ship sailing down the river Shannon with various types of food." But this claim ignores the reverse and much larger flow, also through the market mechanism, of maize or cornmeal from 1846 on. Exports of maize were never significant, and those of wheat fell sharply in 1846; only exports of oats continued to be sizeable (see fig. 3.1). Prohibiting the export of Irish oats or wheat at the start of the famine might have been worth consideration, but a smarter policy would have been to transfer entitlements by taxing the producers and consumers of those cereals more heavily and using the proceeds for the poor. But feeding the potato-eating Irish poor a luxury food like wheat during a famine would have been rather akin to following the solution of Jean-Jacques Rousseau's *grande princesse, "Qu'ils mangent de la brioche."*[62] The fundamental problem with relying on markets in Ireland in 1846–47 was that grain merchants were too risk-averse and the means of transport too slow to deliver the urgently needed imports in time.

[62] Rousseau 2000: 262.

Considering the evidence of this section as a whole, the outcome is broadly supportive of well-integrated markets both in normal and famine times. Co-movements between pairs of markets continued to be strong in crisis years, and in general the speed of adjustment is like that in normal times. The problem was that before the era of the steamship and the telegraph, adjustment to disequilibria was slow in both normal and crisis times.

A Spatial Perspective

As noted earlier, Richard Cantillon's Law of One Price (LOP) states that in a well-integrated market persistent price differences between regions stem largely from transport (T). It creates the presumption that, unless T changes, with well-functioning markets arbitrage will produce $\sigma(P_F) < \sigma(P_N)$. Alternatively, the coefficient of variation in prices (CV) should fall during famines. Note, however, that the bad weather often associated with famine conditions (as in France in 1708–9 and in Finland in 1868) might increase T, as would the disruption of trade by legislation or "moral economy" forces. Thus, and even more so given the possibility of a rise in T, to find no or little rise in the spatial spread of prices during famines would be consistent with markets not becoming segmented.

The contrasting outcomes in the maize markets of Botswana and Kenya in years of crisis in the early 1980s[63] are of interest here. In Botswana, where the average price of maize meal rose from 3.53 to 4.74 *pula* per bag between August 1980 and April 1983, the coefficient of variation across eighteen markets fell from 0.07 to 0.05, which is consistent with smoothly functioning markets. In Kenya, however, where the average retail price of maize rose from 2.42 to 4.61 Kenyan shillings per kilo between January and November 1984, the coefficient of variation across eighteen markets trebled from 0.15 to 0.45. The outcome is reported at the top of table 3.6. Such a rise is consistent with a serious segmentation of food markets, so that food was not directed to where it was most needed.

[63] See Drèze and Sen 1989: 144, 155.

Regional price data are available for all four European famines described here. Coefficients of variation for those famines, for those in Kenya and Botswana, and for two others are given in table 3.6. First I use annual data on a broad cross-section of forty French towns and cities[64] for insight into whether grain markets became more or less segmented during the famines of the mid-1690s, 1709–10, and the Great Frost of 1740. The first thing to note is that even in normal times the coefficients of variation across France at this point were very high, 0.2 to 0.4. Compare the eight statistical provinces that would constitute the Kingdom of Prussia where, thanks in large part to improved communications, in 1871 the coefficient of variation of wheat prices averaged 0.074 over the 1841–70 period, and that of rye prices, 0.117.[65] As may be seen from table 3.6, the coefficients of variation of wheat prices in France rose in 1693–95, 1709–10, and 1740. A disruption of normal patterns in times of crisis in France is also suggested by the impact of crisis on the correlation between wheat prices in the forty towns in year t and year $t+1$. Over the period 1671–1750 the average year-to-year correlation was +0.797, with a standard deviation of 0.152. However, the correlation plummeted from +0.770 in 1692–93 to +0.322 in the famine year of 1693–94 and +0.392 in 1694–95 before recovering to +0.722 in 1695–96. Again it dropped from +0.950 in 1706–7 to +0.271 and +0.233 in the following two years, rising to +0.599 again in 1709–10. In other words, the equalizing effect between markets could not keep up with famine conditions.

Let us turn next to potato prices in Ireland in the 1840s. Most potatoes grown in Ireland before the famine were for domestic or local consumption. One of the potato's disadvantages is that it was relatively costly to transport; Elizabeth Hoffman and Joel Mokyr reckon that one-fourth of the potato's value "evaporated" with every ten miles it traveled.[66] Nevertheless, there was an active local trade in

[64] The underlying database, kindly supplied by David Weir, refers to forty towns and cities.

[65] Estimated from *Zeitschrift des Königlich Preussischen Statistischen Bureaus*, vol. 11, Berlin: Royal Statistical Bureau, 1871.

[66] Hoffman and Mokyr 1984.

potatoes in Ireland before the famine, and most towns had their own potato markets.

Table 3.6 reports evidence from two sets of regional prices in Ireland, for 1840–46 and 1848–51, respectively. The first set summarizes data contained in a parliamentary report on potato prices in almost four hundred Irish towns between 1840 and 1846. The numbers are not ideal for our purpose, because they extend only as far as the harvest of 1845, the first to be affected by blight. Moreover, because they refer to the highest prices paid, they may well reflect a range of qualities and varieties across the country. In mitigation they refer to the prices paid in a single week in January, so they have the advantage of controlling for seasonal variation. In general, the observed interregional price gaps are smaller than what transport costs would indicate. This suggests that trade in potatoes and potato substitutes such as oats helped to arbitrage away disequilibrium differences. The second data set refers to a different, smaller sample of towns with potato markets. It includes 1848, when the ravages of blight were particularly severe. The standard deviations in the two panels are not strictly comparable. Note, however, that the coefficient of variation was lower in 1846 than in the preceding years, while in 1848 it was lower than in the years immediately following. This seems more consistent with orderly than segmented markets in the wake of the blight.

Two features of the Finnish data in table 3.6 are apparent. First, the coefficients of variation were very low throughout. Second, the coefficient of variation held its own in the famine years of 1867–68 relative to 1859–64 but was lower than in the immediate post-famine period (1870–73). In Finland both before and after the famine of 1867–68 grain prices were normally highest in the northern provinces of Oulu and Kuopio, with the mean price of rye in Oulu being on average 10–15 percent higher than that in Vaasa or Häme. However, during the famine years the proportionate price rises were greatest in the southwest, with the result that levels in Uusimaa, Turku, and Häme provinces were exceeded only by those in Oulu. The severe harvest shortfalls in the southwest in 1867–68[67] may ac-

<hr />

[67] Kaukiainen 1984.

TABLE 3.6. Spatial Variation in Prices

	Dates	CV
Botswana (grain)	Aug. 1980	0.07
	Apr. 1983	*0.05*
Kenya (grain)	Jan. 1984	0.15
	Nov. 1984	*0.45*
France (wheat)	1690–92	0.272
	1693–95	*0.401*
	1696–99	0.230
	1705–08	0.352
	1709–10	*0.438*
	1711–14	0.234
	1736–39	0.220
	1740	*0.391*
	1741–44	0.315
Ireland (potatoes)	1840–45	0.32
	1846	*0.29*
	1848	*0.12*
	1849–51	0.18
Finland (rye)	1859–64	0.049
	1867–68	*0.049*
	1870–73	0.059
Germany (potatoes)	*1816–17*	*0.356*
	1818–27	0.186
(rye)	*1816–17*	*0.311*
	1818–27	0.158
(wheat)	*1816–17*	*0.188*
	1818–27	0.099
India (rice)	1938/9–1942/3	0.210
	1943/4	*0.337*
(wheat)	1938/9–1942/3	0.152
	1943/4	*0.234*

Note: Famine years are italicized. In the case of Ireland, there are two datasets, one referring to 1840–46, the other to 1848–51 (see text).

count for the increases, and the poverty of Kuopio and Oulu for the failure of prices in those provinces to rise in tandem. Put another way, in Kuopio and Oulu an "entitlements" failure may have compounded the problem caused by poor harvests. However, the widening gap between prices in the southwest and in Viipuri (Viborg) in

1867–68 leaves unresolved the question why more grain did not flow west from Viipuri during the famine.

The 1870–73 data in table 3.6 show the earlier pattern reestablishing itself again in the wake of the famine. This suggests that in normal times small inter-provincial movements in grain seem to have been enough to maintain the pattern observed before and after 1867–68. At the height of the crisis, however, we can only speculate that inter-provincial trade or imports from outside Finland were insufficient to maintain the kind of equilibrium price vector assumed in our model. Indeed some inter-provincial flows may have been reversed. The lack of data on internal trade and the cost of transport preclude firm conclusions on this score.

In sum, there is some evidence from these European famines of rises in the regional variation in prices during crises relative to immediately preceding or succeeding years. The rises were modest, however: the fivefold rise in the standard deviation of prices across Kenya during 1984 offers some perspective. Further perspective is obtained from the situation in what would later become Germany-Prussia in 1816–17, during what John Post dubbed, with considerable historical license, "the last great subsistence crisis in the western world."[68] In these years poor harvests led to high prices and excess mortality in northern and western Germany, while harvests in East Prussia were bountiful. However, trade between different parts of Germany-Prussia was far from free: in German economist Friedrich List's oft-cited account from 1819, "numerous customs barriers cripple trade and produce the same effects as ligatures which prevent the free circulation of the blood."[69] In the circumstances, the spatial variation in prices was bound to increase. As table 3.6 makes plain, the coefficient of variation of both potato and rye prices across Prussia's eight statistical regions during the famine years of 1816–17 was double the average during 1818–27.[70]

Note too that in India in the harvest year of 1943/4, at the time of the Great Bengal Famine described in detail in Essay 2, the coefficient of variation of rice prices increased sharply above the average

[68] Post 1977.
[69] Cited in Henderson 1984: 22–23.
[70] Estimated from *Zeitschrift des Königlich Preussischen Statistischen Bureaus*, vol. 11, 1871.

of preceding years (from 0.210 to 0.337). Only part of this rise was due to the near-quadrupling in prices in Calcutta in 1943/4, however (without Calcutta the numbers are 0.219 and 0.299). The price of rice was also high in Delhi and in Dibrugarh (in North West Frontier Province, now part of Pakistan) in 1943/4. Note too that the variation in wheat prices across ten markets excluding Bengal also rose in 1943/4.[71]

Seasonality and Storage

As noted earlier, Adam Smith believed that grain merchants were best placed "to divide the inconveniencies of [a scarcity] as equally as possible through all the different months, and weeks, and days of the year."[72] If storing grain entailed merely raising prices in order to make a smaller harvest last the whole season, then it will have smoothened consumption and thereby reduced privation and deaths. If, on the other hand, it was based on an exaggerated view of scarcity, the release of a disproportionate amount of food later in the season will have led to losses and even bankruptcies. Sen and Ravallion have suggested that, on the contrary, speculative hoarding can exacerbate famine situations.[73] Their findings suggest an asymmetry in speculators' expectations about the state of the harvest: during famines, they tend to be too pessimistic. This may well sometimes be the case, but hard historical evidence on storage is scarce. The records of the Chartier farm, a large-scale family-run enterprise at Choisy near Paris,[74] offer one useful and exceptional illustration. In normal years such a farm would be expected to combine with grain merchants to produce something akin to consumption smoothing over the season. In the case at hand this meant small off-farm disposals between July and November. Figure 3.2 compares monthly off-farm grain sales in normal harvest-years and in 1693–94, and shows

[71] Knight 1954: 308. The rice prices refer to the twelve markets reported by Knight (1954). The wheat prices exclude Cuttack (Orissa Province), for which there is no quotation in 1943/4.

[72] Smith 1976: 533–34.

[73] Sen 1981; Ravallion 1987a.

[74] Moriceau and Postel-Vinay 1992: 225–26.

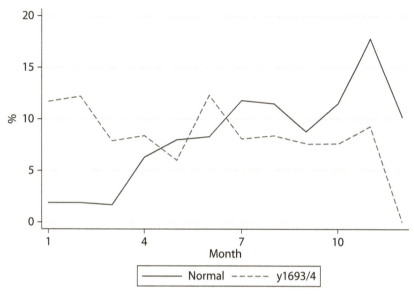

Figure 3.2 Sales of wheat at Choisy in the 1690s (monthly percentages). "Normal" is the average of the 1690, 1691, 1692, and 1694 harvest-years. Source: Moriceau and Postel-Vinay 1992: 226.

the Chartiers disposing of *more* of their grain in the early months of the famine harvest-year than in normal seasons. This is hardly consistent with hoarding. Alas, one Chartier swallow does not make a summer, and farm records as rich as theirs are the exception.

Here I build on an insight associated with D. N. McCloskey and John Nash (1984) but traceable back to Paul Samuelson (1957) in order to shed further light on the role of hoarding during the famines analyzed here.[75] In a classic paper McCloskey and Nash sought to infer storage costs and interest rates in medieval and early modern Europe from the seasonality patterns observed in grain prices. Their argument followed from the simple premise that those merchants and farmers who store grain must in equilibrium be rewarded for the opportunity cost of tied-up funds and losses from wastage during the storage period. A sawtooth price seasonality pattern is indicated, with low prices in the wake of the harvest giving way gradually to a maximum before the new harvest comes in. The more

[75] Samuelson 1957; McCloskey and Nash 1984.

TABLE 3.7. Seasonal Rise in Wheat Prices in France, 1680–1719: Monthly Data

	Paris*	Angoulême	Rozay	Toulouse	Mont-batzon**	Pontoise	Grenade
Mean Increase (%)	0.9	10.8	2.4	7.3	13.7	7.6	12.2
Standard deviation	28.1	35.9 49.0	28.8	49.2	47.4	31.1	
Increase in 1692–93 (%)	80.4	27.0 44.7	37.0	22.5	84.6	39.1	
Increase in 1693–94 (%)	21.5	29.8 40.4	53.1	50.0	40.0	61.8	
Increase 1708–9 (%)	——	171.8	256.5	108.9	248.1	242.7	112.5

* 1680–98. ** 1680–1715, 1698/99 missing.

important costs are fixed costs such as storage facilities and security, the less sensitive seasonal increases to the quality of the harvest. Abstracting from other complications, this means that in a well-functioning market seasonality would at most produce the same proportionate increases in prices in bad years as in good. Then lower-than-normal seasonal price rises during the crisis might indicate that producers were holding on to stocks in hopes of much higher prices at the end of the season. If, on the other hand, the seasonal price rise was faster than usual, this could reflect either the desperation of consumers or the fears of producers that their food stocks might deteriorate (as mentioned below regarding Irish potato crops) or be requisitioned. Hoarding during famines, in other words, implies smaller increases than usual from seasonal trough to peak.

In reality this presumption is complicated by the presence of carry-over stocks of grain from one harvest to the next, and in practice there is considerable variation or "noise" in the month-to-month and seasonal movements.[76] In table 3.7 I compare the average rises in wheat prices between September in year t (at the beginning of the harvest-year) and June in year $t+1$ (before prices are affected by the next harvest) in eight French towns between the 1680s and the 1710s. The outcome shows only weak traces of the seasonality pattern noted by McCloskey and Nash. On average, prices rose a little over the season, but they were subject to huge year-to-year variation. However, in the famine years of 1693–94 and 1708–9 the rises greatly exceeded the average, in 1708–9 soaring two or more standard devia-

[76] See, e.g., Persson 1999.

TABLE 3.8. The September–June Rise in Rye and Barley Prices in Finland, 1867–68: Comparison with "normal" years, 1859–66 and 1869–73

	Oulu	Uusimaa	Vaasa	Kuopio	Mikkeli
Rye					
Mean increase (%)*	9.6	8.1	11.3	12.2	13.8
Standard deviation*	13.0	9.2	8.3	11.9	13.1
Increase in 1867–68 (%)	22.9	31.5	29.0	38.1	43.7
Barley					
Mean increase (%)*	14.6	7.2	15.1	12.2	13.0
Standard deviation*	14.4	7.0	10.9	10.0	7.3
Increase in 1867–68 (%)	40.9	30.4	56.4	38.1	39.9

* Excluding 1867–68.

tions above it. In Toulouse, for example, whereas the average increase was 7.3 percent, that in 1693–94 was 53.1 percent, and that in 1708–9, 108.9 percent. The particularly sharp seasonal price rises during our two famines do not support the view that farmers or others hoarded early in the season in hopes that price would rise later.

Table 3.8 compares the average rises in rye and barley prices in Finland between September in year t and June in year $t+1$ in "normal" years (1859–66 and 1869–73) and in the famine year of 1867–68 in rural districts in the provinces of Oulu, Uusimaa, Vaasa, Kuopio, and Mikkeli. The outcome shows the seasonality pattern noted by McCloskey and Nash. In the average "normal" year both rye and barley prices were about ten percent higher in June than in the previous September, but the rise was subject to considerable year-to-year variation. Nevertheless, the rises during the famine year of 1867–68 were exceptional: double to treble the average, and double to four times the standard deviation of price rises in other, non-famine years. These sharp increases do not rule out the possibility that farmers or others hoarded early in the season in hopes that price would rise later, but surely they make it less likely.

Potatoes seem an ideal crop for this kind of simple framework, since there was no carry-over from one year to the next. Indeed, before the Irish Famine the prices of different potato varieties before the crisis were subject to marked seasonality. Moreover, the seasonal rise in prices was *greater* during the crisis than in normal times.

Cork city newspaper reports refer to the quantities of potatoes traded on six city markets between 1842 and 1848. On the eve of the famine, the outcome reveals a market that spread sales well over a harvest season beginning in early autumn. Comparing the pattern in 1845–46 with that in 1842–43, 1843–44, and 1844–45 indicates that the proportion of sales early in the season was higher than before. In 1846–47 again sales were proportionately higher early in the season. While this does not rule out speculation or hoarding on the part of potato suppliers, it certainly argues in that direction. In these data actions speak louder than intentions, but it seems clear that some traders sold quickly for fear that their supplies would not keep.[77]

Conclusion

We began our discussion with Adam Smith's assertion that in the two centuries prior to 1776 no famine had arisen in "any part of Europe ... but for the violence of government attempting, by improper means, to remedy the inconveniences of a dearth."[78] The French famines of 1693–94 and 1709–10 represented two more cases where, as in Ireland in the 1840s and Finland in the 1860s, the catastrophic nature of harvest failures overwhelmed functioning markets. If the state was to blame, it was for making inadequate entitlement transfers from rich to poor, not for undue meddling with food markets. It is curious how Smith, for all his allegedly wide reading, ignored these major French famines and indeed the notorious "seven ill years" of the 1690s on his own backdoor, though he noted[79] that he had "pretty exact accounts" of several dearths and famines. Whether a better understanding of the history of European famines would have caused him to modify his position must remain a moot point.

[77] Ó Gráda 1993: 116–21. This outcome is consistent with that indicated by the seasonal pattern in prices: see Ó Gráda 1999: 147–49.
[78] Smith 1976: 526. Several famines overlooked by Smith are mentioned in Essay 1 above. He also forgot the massive Italian famine of the 1590s (Alfani 2011).
[79] Smith 1976: 526.

During these famines, markets worked more smoothly than might have been expected on the basis of a reading of qualitative and fictional accounts. Though a spatial perspective on grain prices produced some evidence of slightly greater segmentation of markets during the famine, an error correction approach to regional price movements showed that in all cases the short-run effect captured by the co-movement of grain prices was more powerful during the famine than in other times. It also yielded evidence in most cases of a quicker-than-normal response to emerging disequilibria. Moreover, the data failed to support the claim that hoarding was more common during the famine than in normal years.

The contrasting trends in price movements in Kenya, Ethiopia, Niger, and Botswana during late-twentieth-century food crises were mentioned earlier. Let us end with a glance at the situations in Malawi and Niger in the 2000s and in Somalia in the 2010s. In Malawi movements in the spread of staple food prices are consistent with reasonably flexible markets. Figures 3.3a and 3.3b describe the monthly price of maize and the coefficient of variation for seventeen markets spread across the country, on which continuous data are available between 1997 and 2006. Note the broadly downward trend in the coefficient of variation, which is consistent with a gradual improvement in market integration. This trend, it is true, was disturbed for 3–4 months in early 2002, when the world's attention was focused on the threat of famine in Malawi. During those months markets did not function normally. Yet the significant point surely is that markets did arbitrage away the spread thereafter. The trend in average prices (fig. 3.3a) corroborates: prices *did* rocket in early 2002, but fell rapidly enough thereafter to prevent significant mortality.

Figures 3.4 and 3.5 contrast price movements in Niger and Somalia during their respective crises. In Niger the prices of sorghum (fig. 3.4a) and maize (fig. 3.4b), two staples, rose significantly in the early part of 2005 (although they had been rising steadily also during the previous year or so) and then fell very steeply in October and November of that year. Note, however, that the prices in all markets rose and fell together.[80]

---

[80] For more on Niger, see the interesting studies by Aker (2010a, 2010b).

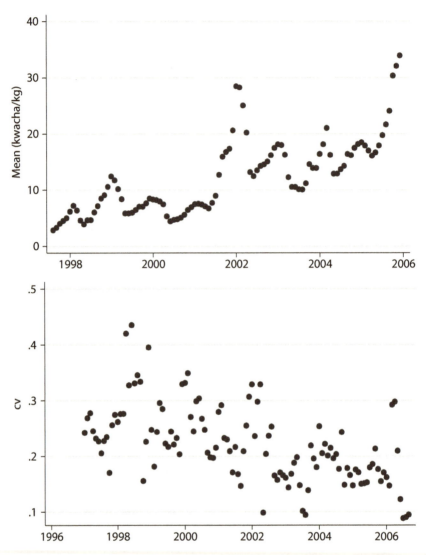

Figure 3.3 Maize prices in Malawi, 1998–2006. (a) Monthly prices at seventeen markets; (b) CV for monthly prices. Source: USAID Famine Early Warning System (www.fews.net).

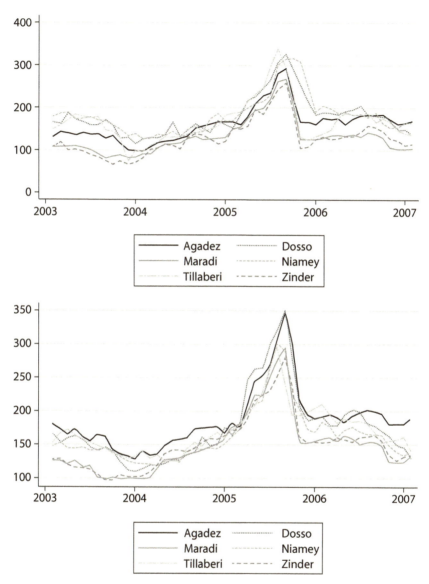

Figure 3.4 Prices on Niger markets for (a) sorghum and (b) maize (CFA francs per kg). Source: www.fews.net.

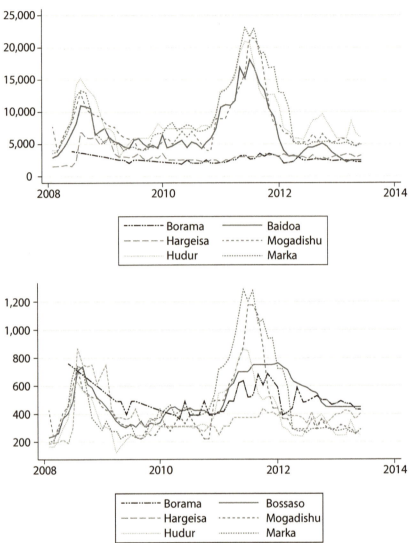

Figure 3.5 Prices on Somalia markets for (a) sorghum and (b) maize, before and during famine (100 Somali shillings per kg). Source: www.fews.net.

Figure 3.5 describes the prices of sorghum (fig. 3.5a) and maize (fig. 3.5b) before and during the famine in severely affected and less affected areas of Somalia. In towns such as Mogadishu, Baidoa, Hudur, and Marka the price of both products rocketed in mid-2011, and the peak easily exceed that reached during the global peak of 2009. In less affected towns such as Borama and Hargeisa in the northwest it was quite a different story. War certainly segmented grain markets within Somalia during the famine months.

None of the above outcomes rules out a further role for markets in exacerbating these crises. As noted at the outset, a fall in purchasing power in the worst affected regions could, as William Wilson Hunter suspected in Bengal in the 1870s (see above) and just as Drèze and Sen proposed over two decades ago, have aggravated one or more of them precisely because markets were so well integrated. Crisis-induced rises in foodstuff prices might not have been sufficient to deter food from leaving the worst-hit areas. While that is an issue worth exploring further, the evidence for the implied trade flows is lacking. It would seem that backward economies and low agricultural productivity, coupled with the lack of an adequate policy response from the authorities, rather than the failure of the markets for staple foodstuffs to work, were mainly responsible for the famines analyzed in this essay.

4

Great Leap into Great Famine

The situation in our country has not been very good for the past few years.... In 1959 and 1960 a number of things were done wrongly.... The most serious fault was that our requisitioning was excessive. When we did not have very much grain, we insisted on saying that we had. Blind commands were issued in both industry and agriculture.

Mao Zedong, 24 September 1962[1]

In 1959–61 China suffered the greatest famine in recorded history. The famine was mainly the product of the Great Leap Forward, a reckless and misconceived campaign aimed at greatly accelerating economic development after less than a decade of economic recovery and respectable growth in the wake of Liberation. The perceived need to catch up with the capitalist West—Mao hoped that China's industrial output would match Britain's within fifteen years—was a primary motivation. The policy shift had much in common with Stalin's Soviet first Five-Year Plan of 1928–32. Both Soviet planning and the Great Leap sought to place the burden of faster growth on a backward agricultural sector. Both relied on collectivization to generate the food required to sustain helter-skelter industrialization. And both resulted in massive excess mortality, almost all of it in the countryside. Of course, there were differences too: communal dining halls, backyard furnaces, and the campaign to eradicate sparrows were distinctively Chinese. In China the downside risk of failure was

[1] Schram 1974: 190.

even greater than in the Soviet Union, and the cost in lives accordingly much greater, both in relative and absolute terms. The combination of disastrous harvests and excessive requisitioning for urban consumption resulted in a massive, if regionally uneven, famine that lasted between 1959 and 1961. Estimates of excess mortality remain controversial; they range from the implausibly low 2 or 3 million recently proposed by some neo-Maoist scholars in China to the 50 or 60 million suggested by some of the Mao Zedong's most severe critics. The 20 to 30 million indicated by demographic analyses[2] would still make the Great Leap Forward Famine the costliest ever in terms of lives lost.

The authorities sought to prevent the news of famine from spreading, although word of conditions in China seeped out with refugees and through smuggled letters. When the International Red Cross offered help in early 1961, the Chinese Red Cross replied that the authorities were "fully capable of overcoming temporary difficulties caused by natural calamities."[3] A few commentators, such as Jesuit priest Laszlo Ladany, who ran *China News Analysis*, a digest published in Hong Kong, grasped the scale of what was happening. His reports described acute hunger, food shortages, symptoms of famine-related diseases, stillbirths, and even cannibalism and infanticide.[4] In hindsight, U.S. journalist Joseph Alsop's accounts of conditions on the ground in China were also quite accurate. Alsop's credibility was hopelessly compromised, however, by his insistence that Mao had engineered the famine as a means of reducing redundant population by one third in order to help fulfill his goal of making China "a military-industrial giant power." Most observers, expert China-watchers included, were not convinced by such reports, and several prominent Western visitors to China in those years—including Field Marshall Montgomery, Lord Boyd-Orr (head of the UN Food and Agricultural Organization), and François Mitterand (future president of France)—noticed nothing unusual.[5] Edgar Snow, blinded

[2] Several are discussed in Yang 2012: 394–430. See also Ashton et al. 1984; Ó Gráda 2009: 95–97.

[3] "China Denies Famine and Bars Aid Offer," *New York Times*, 17 February 1961.

[4] Leys 1990.

[5] "Le maréchal Montgomery n'a pas vu trade de famine en Chine populaire," *Le Monde*, 9 October 1961.

by ideological blinkers, declared that he had witnessed nothing worse than localized famine and widespread malnutrition during an extended visit in 1960. Western expert opinion found such assessments sounder than Alsop's high-octane columns. And so for two decades or more a massive three-year famine remained virtually hidden both inside and outside China.[6] Only in 1983, with the publication of official demographic data straddling the years of famine, did the Chinese authorities hint at the extent of the disaster. These data spawned a demographic literature that continues to grow. They also led to a broader analysis of the famine, its causes, its victims, and its perpetrators, both within and outside China. Finally, a famine that was both "hidden" and ignored for several decades is finally getting the scholarly attention that it requires.

Three works published in 2010–12 added enormously to the literature. Yang Jisheng's *Tombstone: The Great Chinese Famine, 1958–1962*—an abbreviated translation of *Mubei*, which created a sensation when it was published in Hong Kong in 2008[7]—was one of the publishing hits of 2012. Although *Mubei* was placed on a list of banned "obscene, pornographic, violent and unhealthy books for children" in Wuhan, capital city of Yang's own Hubei province, and studiously ignored by the official press, Yang reckoned that there were 0.5–0.6 million copies of *Mubei* circulating in China in 2012, counting original and bootleg versions.

Tombstone is also a very long book, even though ten of the Chinese fourteen provinces allocated chapters in the original were omitted in the translation. Readers could still be grateful for Yang's powerful accounts of the Great Leap Famine in the provinces of Henan, Sichuan, Anhui, and Gansu. The death of the author's stepfather as a famine victim in Hubei province lent his account an added intensity.

Yang's *Tombstone* arrived hot on the heels of Frank Dikötter's *Mao's Great Famine: The History of China's Most Devastating Catastrophe, 1958–1962* (Dikötter 2010; henceforth *MGF*). The main outlines

[6] Alsop 1962: 21–22; Bernstein 1983; Riskin 1996; Riskin 1998. Roderick MacFarquhar (1995: 694), founding editor of the *China Quarterly*, described Alsop as "more an avowed critic of the mainland regime than an objective analyst."

[7] http://www.bbc.co.uk/news/world-20410424). See also McGregor 2010; Johnson 2010.

of Dikötter's story would have been familiar already to Western readers from the works of Roderick MacFarquhar (1983), Jasper Becker (1996), Ralph Thaxton (2008), and others, but both Dikötter and Yang added much that was new and valuable. Dikötter, a prolific writer, was among Western scholars quickest off the mark in gaining access to public records, including party archives, formerly closed to historians, and *MGF* is informed by what its author describes as an "against the grain" reading of "well over a thousand" documents from cities and provinces spread across China (although excluding Anhui and Henan, two of the worst-hit provinces). In effect, Dikötter scooped many brave Chinese scholars such as Yu Xiguang, Cao Shuji, and Yang Jisheng who had been exploiting such records for a decade previously, but whose works remained untranslated into English and largely unknown outside China.[8]

Arriving just two years after *MGF* (which had some ungracious things to say about Yang and *Mubei*) and a few months after Zhou Xun's *The Great Famine in China* (2012),[9] *Tombstone* left readers spoilt for choice. Yang and Dikötter both relied on the kind of documentation reproduced in Zhou's volume—"sensitive" material surreptitiously accessed from official archival sources—which they supplemented with oral and written information gained from eyewitnesses. Indeed, Zhou's volume was a by-product of her time as Dikötter's research assistant; most of its 121 documents are a subset of the "well over a thousand" used by Dikötter.[10] Zhou's fine *Forgotten Voices of Mao's Great Famine* (2013), an oral history of the famine, is also a by-product of that collaboration. The similarities do not end there; Yang, like Dikötter and Zhou, provides plentiful horrific accounts of famine and state terror, as well as new estimates of excess mortality. Dikötter and Yang tally in their accounts of Mao's resentment of criticisms of policy pursued during the Great Leap by Liu

---

[8] Garnaut 2013a: fn8; see also Garnaut 2014b.

[9] A shortcoming of Zhou's useful volume is its relative brevity, particularly since some of its content is only loosely linked to the famine. This applies particularly to the twenty-two documents on religion—interesting in themselves, but mostly with little direct bearing on the famine. Zhou should have explained exactly how the material transcribed and published was selected.

[10] Dikötter 2010: x.

Shaoqi and others.[11] Moreover, all four accounts are highly politicized. Dikötter and Zhou blame the famine on Mao Zedong personally, but for Yang—no apologist for Mao—it proves that "a system without a corrective mechanism is the most dangerous of all systems."[12] Taken together, the works of Dikötter, Yang, and Zhou discredit the claims of latter-day neo-Maoists such as Yang Songlin, author of a new Chinese book on the famine, and cyberneticist Sun Jingxian, who insists that the famine caused very few deaths.[13]

While in *Tombstone* Yang pursues the Great Leap Forward and the ensuing famine from province to province, Dikötter opts for a broadly chronological narrative (chapters 1–16). This begins in 1953 with the death of Stalin, which Chairman Mao Zedong saw as an opportunity for asserting his independence of Moscow. It ends in 1962 with Mao being confronted by his own Nikita Khrushchev in the person of party vice-chairman Liu Shaoqi. The remainder of *MGF* describes the impact on the economy and the environment (chapters 17–21), and the cost in terms of lives ruined and lost (chapters 22–37). The tone throughout is one of abhorrence and outrage, and sometimes *MGF* reads more like a catalogue of anecdotes about atrocities than a sustained analytic argument. In style and approach it recalls Jung Chang and Jon Halliday's controversial *Mao: The Unknown Story* (2005); indeed, Chang led the praise for *MGF* on its back cover.

MGF has become the best-known account of the Great Leap Famine in our times. But should it be? It is, admittedly, more readable than Yang's account, but is not a comprehensive account of the famine. It is dismissive of academic work on the topic; it is weak on context and unreliable with data; and it fails to note that many of the horrors it describes were not unique to 1959–61, but recurrent features of Chinese history during the previous century or so. More attention to economic history and geography and to the comparative history of famines—as in Stephen Wheatcroft's famine research[14] and in Felix Wemheuer's *Famine Politics in Maoist China and the Soviet Union* (2014)—would have made *MGF* a much more useful

[11] Ibid., 335–37; Yang 2012: 505–12.
[12] Yang 2012: 496–97.
[13] Compare Lin 2013: 52–53; Riskin 1998.
[14] Wheatcroft 2008, 2011, 2012.

book. *Tombstone* shares some of the same weaknesses but it is far richer and much broader in its documentation and more measured in its critiques.

Poor China

Neither Dikötter nor Yang pays enough attention to the famine's historical context. Both Mao's popularity on the eve of the Great Leap and the extreme brutality of the Leap period followed more than two decades of murderous violence and misery for most Chinese. Estimates of the numbers of deaths caused by famines, droughts, and floods before the Communist take-over—80 million between 1810 and 1936 according to Deng Tuo, 18 million between 1910 and 1948 according to Xia Mingfang—may be exaggerated,[15] but they nevertheless add some context to the carnage of the Great Leap Famine. Walter Mallory famously dubbed China the "land of famine" in 1926 because it was extremely poor, and China in the 1950s was still extremely poor.

Famines are a hallmark of economic backwardness. How backward? Historical national accounting is an inexact art, particularly in the case of less developed economies such as China in the 1950s. Bearing this in mind, the best estimates of Chinese GDP per capita in the past imply that China on the eve of the Great Leap Forward was in economic terms one of the most backward places on earth. According to the reconstructions of Angus Maddison, Chinese real GDP per head in 1957 was only one-quarter of the global average in the 1950s and one-twelfth of today's global average. Despite having been (by Maddison's estimate) the twelfth-fastest-growing economy on the globe since 1950, China in 1957 was still ranked 120th out of the 140 economies included. Alternatively, only ten of the same 140 economies were poorer in 1970 (and only eight in 1980) than China had been on the eve of the Great Leap Forward.

The widely respected Penn World Tables[16] paint an even gloomier picture of the Chinese economy in this period. Their coverage is

---

[15] Compare Yang 2012: 13; Wemheuer 2014: 26–28.
[16] Feenstra, Inklaar, and Timmer 2013.

TABLE 4.1. Chinese GDP per Head in Comparative Perspective, 1952–58

Ranking	1952	1953	1954	1955	1956	1957	1958
Poorest	China 1 219	China 1 234	China 238	China 1 244	Zimbabwe 265	China 1 274	Zimbabwe 276
2nd	Ethiopia 327	Ethiopia 349	Zimbabwe 245	Zimbabwe 248	China 1 266	Zimbabwe 277	China 1 314
3rd	China 2 531	China 2 559	Malawi 285	Malawi 308	Malawi 309	Malawi 337	Malawi 336
4th	India 616	Sri Lanka 641	Ethiopia 349	Ethiopia 357	Ethiopia 362	Ethiopia 353	Ethiopia 368
5th	Pakistan 620	India 639	China 2 559	China 2 576	Sri Lanka 560	Sri Lanka 567	Sri Lanka 589
6th	Sri Lanka 660	Pakistan 652	Pakistan 632	Pakistan 617	China 2 611	Pakistan 625	Pakistan 622
7th	DRC 680	Uganda 697	Sri Lanka 639	Sri Lanka 652	Pakistan 638	China 2 639	Uganda 658
8th	Uganda 757	DRC 746	India 653	India 655	India 665	India 656	India 688
9th	Morocco 826	Thailand 779	Uganda 655	Uganda 666	Uganda 693	Morocco 662	DRC 734
10th	Egypt 831	Morocco 846	DRC 757	Morocco 733	Morocco 723	Uganda 708	Morocco 739
USA	14,634	15,015	14,420	15,135	15,138	15,113	14,731
N	62	64	67	71	71	71	71

Notes: China 1 and China 2 refer to the two variants proposed by Heston et al. N is the number of economies included in the database in any year. The numbers are 1996 purchasing power parity-adjusted U.S. dollars.

DRC = Democratic Republic of the Congo

Source: Heston, Summers, and Aten 2012.

much narrower for the 1950s than Maddison's, and their earliest data for China refer to 1952. Table 4.1 reports the Penn Tables' two alternative estimates for China and for the eight other economies with the lowest GDP per head in the world for each year between 1952 and 1958. They indicate that Chinese GDP per head in 1957 was between 1.8 percent and 4.2 percent that of the United States; by Maddison's reckoning the ratio was 5.8 percent. Low GDP per head was compounded by very unequal land and income distributions,[17] low life expectancy, and high infant mortality.

[17] Brandt and Sands 1992: Table 6.3.

Its backwardness made China very vulnerable to harvest failures and food shortages, both natural and man-made, and this is reflected in its recent famine history. For at least a century before 1949, major famines were probably frequent enough to warrant Walter Mallory's depiction of China as the "land of famine." The Taiping Rebellion is routinely reported as having cost 20 million lives, mostly from famine and disease. Neither R. H. Tawney's report in *Land and Labour in China* (1932) that the famine of 1849 "is said to have destroyed 13,750,000 persons" nor contemporary claims that the Great North China Famine of 1876–79 took a further 9.5 million to 13 million lives should be taken too literally, but such estimates nevertheless usefully underline the apocalyptic nature of those famines. Famine mortality probably declined thereafter. Yet Yang claims that China's most severe famine before the Great Leap Famine occurred in 1928–30, killing ten million people. Between 1920 and 1936, he added, "famine due to crop failures took the lives of 18.36 million people."[18] Again, these numbers seem on the high side. Still, Tawney witnessed the devastation that followed in the wake of the famines of the late 1920s, and famine in Anhui province in 1929 inspired Pearl Buck's *The Good Earth*. Nor did it end there. Famine in the Yellow River region in 1935 resulted in significant female infanticide in 1935–36, while the Henan war famine of 1942 produced its own catalogue of atrocities.[19] Again and again, what Dikötter dubs "traditional coping mechanisms"[20] had failed to prevent famine.

It bears noting too that the Great Leap Famine was most murderous in provinces that were infamously famine-prone in the past, such as Anhui, Sichuan, and Henan. In 1907, the *Guardian* placed Anhui at the epicenter of a major famine; four years later, an American account described Anhui's "fame of late years [as] only the bitter fame of her sorrow"; and in the 1920s, Anhui was the location of Pearl Buck's famine novel.[21] Between the 1920s and the 1940s, Sich-

---

[18] Yang 2012: 13.
[19] Garnaut 2013b.
[20] Dikötter 2010: 179.
[21] The *Guardian*'s account of "[t]he famine in China: four millions of starving people" singled out northern Anhui as the epicenter of a crisis in 1907, whereas before 1949, Huai-Pei (Huaibei) in western Anhui, an ecologically fragile region, was notorious for endemic unrest

uan was hit three times by major famines. The 1936 famine, the product of severe drought compounded by civil war, killed up to five million people in Sichuan and led to reports of widespread cannibalism, while it is estimated that another 2.5 million died in Sichuan in 1941.[22] Henan, another black spot in 1959–61, had been badly hit by the famine of 1876–78, and two million died there in a major famine in 1928–29. "Of all marks on my thinking," wrote U.S. journalist Theodore H. White in 1978, "the Honan famine [of 1943] remains most indelible."[23]

China's extreme backwardness on the eve of the Great Leap matters because it greatly increased its vulnerability to shocks and disequilibria, man-made or other. Had Chinese GDP per head in the 1950s been, say, twice as high as it was, the devastation wreaked by the Great Leap would presumably have been much less. The more economically backward a region or province was, the greater by far the downside risk of policy and harvest failure. In these circumstances, the Great Leap gambled monumentally with myriad human lives.

The Cold War context also mattered. Whereas Dikötter and Yang largely ignore Chinese fears of outside aggression both before and during the famine, Wemheuer has highlighted how the perceived threat of U.S. and, later, Soviet aggression was "absolutely central" to understanding Mao's behavior during the Great Leap Famine. Part of the rationale for rapid economic growth was that it would ease the burden of military expansion. In the meantime, Chinese vulnerability was obvious in 1955 and again in 1958 when the U.S. threatened it with military intervention if it persisted in its bombardment of the Nationalist-occupied offshore islands of Quemoy (Jinmen) and Matsu (Mazu).[24]

---

and high levels of female infanticide. See *The Guardian*, "The Famine in China," 1 January 1907; *Alliance Weekly: A Journal of Christian Life & Missions*, 9 November 1912, p. 88; Perry 1980: 51. Tawney and his wife stayed with the Buck family in Nanking in 1931 (Terrill 1973: 71).

[22] Wright 2000: 732–33.

[23] White 1978: 144. Even Becker (1996: 124, 130) concedes that pre-revolutionary Henan was known as the "land of the beggars" and that "since Emperor Zhu was born there" Fengyang county had been struck by famine "nine years out of every ten." Legend had it that no one would marry men from Fengyang villages because of their poverty (email communication from Stephen Morgan).

[24] Wemheuer 2014: 67–74; compare Chang 1988; Sheng 2008.

At the same time, Dikötter's *MGF* probably does not take sufficient account of how conditions improved between 1949 and 1958. National accounting aggregates for 1950s China are probably not very reliable, but the Maddison Project and the Penn World Tables propose similar growth rates in the pre–Great Leap era. The former reckons that Chinese GDP per capita grew by 42 percent between 1950 and 1957, while the latter indicate a growth rate about two-fifths between 1952 and 1958.[25] These estimates indicate significant growth, but China still remained among the very poorest countries on the eve of the Great Leap Forward (table 4.1). If the standard estimate of grain output of 200 million metric tons in 1958 is taken at face value, then there was enough food to provide an average daily intake of only about 2,170 kcal.[26] And if the output data are contaminated by Leap-style "winds of exaggeration" and refer to un-husked grain, then the picture is much less rosy and the margin for error by central planners much narrower. But the achievements of the pre-Leap years prompted a false optimism that much faster growth was feasible—catching up or overtaking Britain "in fifteen years."[27]

Again, regional economic disparities were wide: in the mid-1950s incomes per head in Heilongjiang and Liaoning in the northeast were three times as high as in Sichuan or Guizhou in the southwest, and daily calorie consumption per head is reckoned to have ranged from 1,700–1,800 kcal in Shanxi and Guizhou to over 3,000 kcal in Jilin and Heilongjiang.[28] Walker's national pre-famine average of about 2,000 kcal would translate into about 2,600–2,700 kcal per adult male equivalent, far lower than what was available to English workers on the eve of the Industrial Revolution, and far short of the 3,400–4,000 kcal needed for the physically demanding farm work that was standard in China.[29] A casual glance at the data suggests that mortality was highest where incomes were lowest and where

---

[25] Feenstra, Inklaar, and Timmer 2013; Maddison Project 2014 (http://www.ggdc.net/maddison/maddison-project/home.htm).

[26] Dikötter 2010: 132; Ashton et al. 1984: 622; compare Meng, Qian, and Yared 2010.

[27] Dikötter 2010: 14, 15, 73; compare Wemheuer 2014: 113.

[28] Walker 1984.

[29] Ibid., 345; Kelly and Ó Gráda 2013: 1147.

TABLE 4.2. Accounting for Excess Deaths: Cross-sectional Evidence Using Robust Regressions

	Using Cao death rate				Using Yang death rate			
Y	−1.648	−2.864	−1.238	−1.112	−0.952	−0.454	−0.806	−0.458
DPROD2	0.820		0.836		0.568		0.497	
PCPROCUR	0.905	2.191			0.636	0.026		
N	21	20	21	21	27	28	27	28
Prob > F	.0002	.006	.0001	.039	.0057	.166	.0039	.053

Note: Robust regression estimates to control for outliers; all coefficients except those italicized are statistically significant at 1%.

Source: Data from Yang (2012: 395–96 [Cao's estimates], 399–402, 411–15) and estimates of provincial incomes per capita 1955–57.

famines had been most common in the past.[30] Yang is more prepared than Dikötter to concede the Hobbesian character of life in pre-1949 China, but still perhaps not sufficiently.

Given doubts about the reliability of both production and demographic data, estimates of the link between such data at the provincial level must be treated with due skepticism. Nonetheless, in analyses that rely on cross-section variation rather than on trends over time, these data have their uses.[31] In the following simple exercise Y is pre-famine gross provincial product per capita, DPROD2 is the square of DPROD, the percentage change in grain production between 1958 and 1960,[32] and PCPROCUR is the percentage of provincial grain output requisitioned in 1959 and 1960. The first four regressions in table 4.2 rely on Cao Shuji's estimates of excess mortality, the second four on the "unnatural deaths" reported by Yang, divided by population in 1957.[33] The reported coefficients are elasticities. The outcome suggests that in all cases excess mortality was likely to be higher in provinces that were poor on the eve of the Great Leap, and in provinces suffering greater production shortfalls

---

[30] Despite Yang's claims (2012: 396).

[31] Compare Kung and Lin 2003; Meng et al. 2010; Kung and Chen 2011.

[32] This produces stronger results than DPROD. In an earlier exercise (Ó Gráda 2008) it was found that proxies for the harvest and regional income alone explain about half the variation in excess mortality during the Great Leap Forward.

[33] Yang 2012: 395–96, 411–14.

(since *DPROD* was uniformly negative). Using Cao Shuji's estimates of excess mortality by province (on which more below in "Numbers Matter"), adding the procurement rate improves the explanatory power of the model, although it does not change the size of the other coefficients much. The regressions employing Yang's own mortality estimates pack a weaker explanatory punch. The impact of low incomes on death rates underlines the vulnerability of poor regions to misguided policy.

Three Parts Nature?

Thomas Robert Malthus and his followers underestimated the role of human factors in exacerbating and mitigating famine in the past, even in very backward economies. As John Post pointed out in his classic account of famine in northwestern Europe in the 1740s, even very poor economies could escape "famine conditions and crisis mortality [by] import[ing] grain supplies, adequate welfare programs, and … effective … public administration." This message is also an important implication of Amartya Sen's entitlements approach to famine analysis.[34]

Malthusian interpretations of famine in China begin with Malthus himself, and most analyses of pre-1949 Chinese famines continue to be strictly Malthusian. Consider the following from Ralph Thaxton:

> In the spring of 1920, a severe drought gripped the lower part of the North China Plain, settling over northern Henan, western Shandong, and southern Hebei provinces. This long drought extended into the spring of 1921. As a result, several million farmers perished in what came to be called the North China Famine of 1921.[35]

No room for human agency there! Dikötter's stance is the polar opposite. He repeatedly cites variants of Liu Shaoqi's quip (picked up

---

[34] Post 1984: 17; Sen 1981.
[35] Thaxton 2008: 26.

by Liu from peasants in his native Hunan) that the Great Leap Famine was three parts natural and seven parts man-made,[36] but only to reject Liu's "three-tenths Malthusian" interpretation in favor of one that rests entirely on human agency.

Contemporary Chinese sources highlighted *ad nauseam* the difficulties caused by drought and flooding in 1959–61, and this is still a key feature of Chinese apologetics on the Great Leap Famine.[37] For a time, Western journalists and historians echoed this view. *Time* magazine, for example, described the havoc allegedly wreaked by the "God of Water" in mid-1959 as follows:

> [N]ature this spring took a cruel hand in China, as it so often has before. While flooding rains fell over huge chunks of Central China, the provinces of Kirin and Hopei were parched by drought. In Szechwan, a force of 40 million Chinese was working desperately to keep a wheat crop, badly weakened by unseasonably warm weather in the spring, from toppling over. In Honan, 5,000,000 farmers were battling swarms of insects, and six other provinces were plagued by plant fungus. Finally, last week, came official reports that "the worst flood of the century" had been raging through the provinces of Kiangsu and Anhwei, Fukien and Kwangtung, then over Honan, swirling down the North and West rivers toward heavily populated Canton (pop. 1,500,000) itself. Hundreds of thousands of townspeople were pressed into working on the embankments, and the dikes of Canton held.

Several times between 1959 and 1961, *Time* linked China's apparent retreat from utopianism during the summer of 1959 to the rains, and interpreted Chinese weather reports as a means of preparing the population for food shortages during the following winter; but it did not question the veracity of the weather reports. Moreover, *Time* also described the impact of adverse weather in the neighboring countries of Formosa (as it referred to Taiwan) and Japan. In August 1960 *Time* noted the mention of famine in official Chinese sources, but in the following April it again took at face value the comment of a Chinese diplomat that during the previous summer for forty days

---

[36] Dikötter 2010: 121, 178, 335.
[37] Chris Buckley, "New (Approved) Assessments," *The Economist*, 9 September 2013.

one could drive a car along the bed of the Yellow River.[38] That remained the standard view for over two decades: an eminent Harvard Sinologist declared in 1969 that conditions such as those experienced in 1959–61 "would have meant many millions of deaths in the areas most severely affected" but for the effectiveness of public policy and the transport network. Roderick MacFarquhar's pioneering account of the famine, which appeared in 1983, also highlighted adverse weather as a factor.[39] Reliable information was at a premium; even the "fabled sinologists" in the British Embassy in Beijing had no inkling of what was happening.[40]

Dikötter does not deny the challenges posed by adverse weather, but instead blames the environmental destruction caused by the Great Leap Forward for greatly magnifying the damage attributable to weather shocks alone. There is surely something to this: overambitious and badly executed dam construction projects during the Great Leap increased the impact of floods and led to the alkalinization of water tables in the North China plain and elsewhere.[41] But anecdotes are an inadequate substitute for more rigorous meteorological analysis.

Tombstone denies the role of extreme weather events entirely, but its account is hardly conclusive either, since its verdict is based on national weather averages across a landmass the size of Europe. That makes little sense, because even within provinces the weather was subject to considerable variation.[42] Sinologist Chris Bramall notes that during the famine rainfall at the median weather station in the vast province of Sichuan was only four percent higher than normal,

---

[38] *Time*: "The God of Water," 6 July 1959; "The Far East: The Rains Came," 24 August 1959; "Red China: Forward in Reverse," 22 August 1960; "Subversion on the Farm," 17 October 1960; "Red China: Pactmanship," 21 April 1961. See also Dwyer 1962. According to Ci and Yang (2010: 72) the 1960 drought in the "middle reaches" of the Yellow River lasted 110 days (24 March to 17 July), during which period rainfall was less than 13 mm. The result was a layer of dry soil one meter in thickness. The affected area contained a population of 11.5 million. See too "Peking Disaster Cry Sincere?," *Christian Science Monitor*, 31 December 1960.

[39] Perkins 1969: 303; MacFarquhar 1983: 322; on memories of flooding in Shandong province, see Zhou 2013: 130–31.

[40] Dikötter 2010: 345.

[41] Ibid., 179–84; Murphey 1967; Shapiro 2001; compare Zhou 2013: 107–8.

[42] Yang 2012: 453–56; Dikötter 2010: 174–88. Yang refers in passing to adverse conditions in Xinyang (pp. 25, 27), Henan (pp. 72, 76), and Anhui (p. 305).

but that this conceals very high precipitation in some districts and serious drought in others. Still, Bramall reckons that in Sichuan as a whole the weather played only a subsidiary role; in 1959—the driest year—only one-eighth of Sichuan's food availability decline could be attributed to bad weather.[43] This is small compared with Y. Y. Kueh's estimate, based on rainfall-yield simulations using 1930s data, of an average annual shortfall of 36 percent in Sichuan's rice yields in 1959–61. Still, Kueh insisted that "even without natural disasters, the agricultural depression was inevitable."[44]

While Dikötter and Yang are doubtless correct in their judgment that the authorities greatly exaggerated the role of the weather, its true impact remains to be determined. Researchers have only begun to use abundantly available direct meteorological measures that are not subject to misreporting.[45] In the absence of systematic analysis of these data, all one can say is that data from several Chinese weather stations show signs of exceptionally adverse weather shocks in 1959–61, though certainly not enough to account for the dramatic crop deficits claimed in official statistics.[46]

Neither Dikötter nor Yang has much to say about the role of geography, but Anthony Garnaut has plausibly attributed the spatial variation in mortality in part to transportation networks. He argues that remote areas, where requisitioning grain was more costly, tended to escape relatively lightly, because the political leadership could risk putting local needs first.[47] The implication that cadres weighed the marginal costs of requisitioning against marginal benefits is as tantalizing as it ironic. Measuring the impact of such interaction between politics and geography would be a useful exercise.

---

[43] Bramall 2011: 1000.

[44] Kueh 1984: 80–81; Kueh 1995: 195, 224.

[45] For example, Garnaut 2009; Meng, Qian, and Yared 2010. A very useful source on weather station data is: "Chinese Famines: Famine Period 1958–62: Weather" (http://www.famine.unimelb.edu.au/weather_stations.php).

[46] Weather stations reporting exceptionally adverse weather conditions in this period include Chengdu, Sichuan (four wet summers in succession in 1958–61); Baoding, Hebei (drought in August 1960); Yiehang, Hubei (drought in July–August 1959); Beijing (heavy rainfall in July–August 1959); Nanning, Guanxi (heavy rainfall in June 1959, drought in June 1960); Lanzhou, Gansu (heavy rainfall in August 1959); Jinan, Shandong (a very dry 1960); Zhengzhou, Henan (very dry in July 1959).

[47] Garnaut 2014a.

What Did the Victims Die Of?

Throughout history most famine victims have succumbed to disease, not to literal starvation.[48] Weakened immune systems and social disruption have allowed diseases present in normal times to play havoc during famines. The character of famine mortality has been radically changed by the epochal breakthroughs in medicine associated with the germ theory of disease as well as the advent of penicillin. In this respect one can speak of "modern" famines, as distinct from "traditional" famines. The Soviet famines of the 1930s and World War II mark a historical break; they killed millions of people, but most of these perished from literal starvation, not from infectious diseases. Violetta Hionidou's classic study of famine in wartime Greece notes that "starvation played by far the dominant role in raising mortality in the almost total absence of epidemics,"[49] and the same holds true for other World War II famines in the western Netherlands and in the Warsaw ghetto before its destruction by the Nazis. The editor of an academic study of the Leningrad blockade notes that

> In contrast to many other famines there were no major epidemics during the siege, even though hygiene in winter 1941–42 was at a much lower level than normal due to the breakdown of sewerage and running water. The explanation would appear to lie in a combination of unfavourable climatic conditions for the spread of epidemic diseases ... and the preventive measures taken by the Leningrad authorities, notably their mobilization of an exhausted population in spring 1942 to cleanse the city of the filth accumulated over the winter.[50]

In pre-1949 China economic backwardness made infectious diseases such as cholera, typhus, and malaria endemic, and most famine deaths were from such diseases and from dysentery. So what did the victims of the Great Leap Famine die of? Most accounts imply death by starvation rather than by disease. Ladany mentioned swollen bel-

[48] Mokyr and Ó Gráda 2002.
[49] Hionidou 2006: 192.
[50] Barber and Dzeniskevich 2005: 8.

lies and people collapsing in the fields and dying (the likely product of famine edema). Bernstein notes the repeated use of the term *"e si"* (death by starvation) in an account from Fenyang in Anhui Province, while Chang's account of famine in Sichuan contains several references to "edema" but does not mention infectious diseases. Chu's evocative account relies mainly on second- or third-hand accounts from refugees; it implies that edema (formerly known as dropsy) took a heavy toll, but most of the epidemics mentioned are not classic famine-related epidemics.[51] Thaxton links most deaths in the village of Da Fo in 1960 to "edema," and this is corroborated by the most detailed study of the causes of death to date, Yixin Chen's analysis of public health gazetteers from Anhui province.[52] Although Chen convincingly argues that the faulty data in the gazetteers underestimate the death toll from diseases such as dysentery and malaria, he nevertheless concedes the primary role of edema and literal starvation. Becker attributes this small proportion of deaths from infectious disease to the stringent enforcement of public health regulations, even at the height of the crisis; Dikötter concurs and wonders why disease did not carry off more "before terminal starvation set in."[53] References to deaths from typhus, typhoid, malaria, measles, or cholera are also lacking in *Tombstone*. This could be an oversight, but more likely it reflects the same perversely "modern" feature of the Great Leap Famine, the primacy of starvation as the cause of famine deaths. Whereas in earlier Chinese famines such diseases did most of the killing, in 1959–61 "disease" was a euphemism for edema, dysentery, and starvation.[54]

The primacy of starvation as the cause of famine deaths during the Great Leap Famine is rather striking and poses somewhat of a conundrum for demographers studying the famine. Before the 1950s only war-induced famines in economies with effective public health regimes, such as the western Netherlands in 1944–45 or Leningrad in 1941–43, and, to some extent, the Soviet Union in the early 1930s, followed such a pattern. Does this imply that the Maoist public

[51] Leys 1990; Bernstein 1983: 36; Chang 1991: 306, 308, 313; Chu 1964: 73–76. For more references to dropsy and hepatitis, see Asian People's Anti-Communist League 1962: 60, 63, 66, 93.

[52] Thaxton 2008: 209, 253; Chen 2010.

[53] Becker 1996: 198; Dikötter 2010: 286.

[54] Yang 2012: 217–19.

health campaigns of the early and mid-1950s influenced the causes of deaths during the Great Leap Famine, if not the death toll itself? Could it be that the authorities' attempts to control migration limited, even if unintentionally, the spread of infectious diseases? Chen gives due credit to achievements registered before the Leap; by then three traditional killers—smallpox, plague, and cholera—had been virtually eliminated and large-scale immunization campaigns carried out.[55] Reluctant to allow public health improvements a role, Dikötter surmises, albeit without supporting evidence, that the Chinese peasantry succumbed to starvation quickly, "reducing the window of opportunity during which germs could prey on a lowered immunity."[56]

The Horrors of Famine

We return in this section to the topic of famine cannibalism, already familiar from Essay 1. Dikötter reports several cases like the following in *MGF*:

> Date: 25 February 1960. Location: Hongtai Commune, Yaoheija Village. Name of Culprit: Yang Zhongsheng. Status: Poor Farmer. Number of People Involved: 1. Name of Victim: Yang Ershun. Relationship with Culprit: Younger Brother. Number of People Involved: 1. Manner of Crime: Killed and Eaten. Reason: Livelihood Issues.
>
> Date: March 1960. Location: Hongtai Commune, Xiaogou Gate. Name of Culprit: Zhu Shuangxi. Status: Poor Farmer. Number of People Involved: 2. Name of Victim: [void]. Relationship with Culprit: Husband and Elder Son. Number of People Involved: 2. Manner of Crime: Corpses Exhumed and Eaten. Reason: Livelihood Issues.[57]

And Yang's account of cannibalism in Henan province is no less graphic:

> At least twenty cases of eating human flesh were recorded in Xinyang's Luyi, Xiayi, Yucheng, and Yongcheng counties. In Pangwang Village, an

---

[55] Chen 2010.
[56] Dikötter 2010: 286.
[57] Ibid., 322.

eighteen-year-old girl, Wang Yu'e, drowned her five-year-old cousin, Wang Huailang, and ate him. Huailang's elder sister Wang Xiaopeng was also driven by hunger to eat her brother's flesh.[58]

Famine cannibalism is also a recurring theme in Yang's long chapter on Anhui, the worst affected province of all in 1959–61, and there are detailed reports from elsewhere too of both survivor cannibalism and murder for human meat. The evidence traumatized Yang: "I did not foresee this level of cruelty. There was cannibalism in the ancient time in famines. People used to talk about 'exchanging children to eat', because they could not bear to eat their own children. But this was much worse."[59] Zhou Xun's collection of official documents[60] reproduces documents from Gansu and Sichuan which also list and name several perpetrators and victims.[61] Such horrific evidence will shock nonspecialists in famine and Chinese history, as it is surely intended to do. Naming names adds to the horror, although one wonders whether it was really necessary or advisable; in *Forgotten Voices* Zhou chose to conceal the identities of her interviewees "in order to protect their privacy and for political considerations."[62]

But horrific as these lists are, accounts of cannibalism were hardly new in the "land of famine." Three stock phrases regarding cannibalism recur in gazetteers' accounts of the "incredible" North China famine of 1876–78, in which millions perished: "people ate each other," "exchanging children and eating them" (as Yang notes in the quotation above), and variants of "people ate each other to the point that close kin destroyed each other."[63] A mere three decades before the Great Leap in Sichuan's Wanyuan county, "people got used to the idea of eating human flesh in order to survive":

This flesh was bought in quarters, at prices that varied by a factor of one or two depending on whether it had been taken from a corpse or from a person killed for the purpose. In the east of Sichuan at the beginning of May 1936, the going rate was 500 copper pieces for a

[58] Yang 2012: 41–42.
[59] As cited in McGregor 2010.
[60] Yang 2012: 278–79, 289–90, 302–04 (Anhui); 141–44 (Gansu); 41–46 (Henan); Zhou 2012: 59–71.
[61] Dikötter 2010: 320–23; Wemheuer 2010: 191.
[62] Zhou 2013: 11.
[63] Edgerton-Tarpley 2008: 223.

pound of flesh from a corpse and 1,220 copper pieces a pound if it was freshly killed.[64]

Seven years later an American journalist working for the London *Times* in Henan reported in his diary a mother's arrest for having eaten the flesh of her deceased six-year-old daughter. This prompted a Chinese friend to remark that "if they start eating dead, they'll soon be eating live people," which perhaps explains why the unfortunate mother was reportedly buried alive "for punishment and example."[65] *Time* magazine journalist Theodore White also referred to accounts of cannibalism in Henan in 1942–43; he wrote about parents tying children to a tree "so they would not follow them as they went in search for food"; "larger" children being sold for less than ten dollars; and a mother who was charged with eating her little girl merely denying that she had killed her.[66]

Kathryn Edgerton-Tarpley, author of a fine study of the Great North China Famine of the 1870s, surmises that such accounts were "primarily metaphorical expressions of the catastrophic destruction of the family unit wrought by the famine";[67] alas, the evidence from more recent famines argues otherwise. Historians of famine are familiar with such stories;[68] Yang and Dikötter are not. Still, widespread[69] cannibalism in a society allegedly on the verge of "the ultimate paradise of human history"[70] was in a league of its own.

Leaders and Followers

The profound economic naiveté that defined the Great Leap and the gullibility—initially, at least—of Mao Zedong and a majority of the Communist Party has often been described before. So has defense

[64] Bianco 2001: 153.

[65] Harrison Forman diary, December 1942–March 1943, University of Wisconsin-Milwaukee, collections.lib.uwm.edu/cdm/ref/collection/forman/id/50.

[66] Citations are taken from reports by White from *Time Magazine*, 26 October 1942 and 22 March 1943; see also White and Jacoby 1946: 163.

[67] Edgerton-Tarpley 2008: 225.

[68] Arnold 1988: 16, 19; Ó Gráda 2009: 63–68; Ó Gráda 2013.

[69] Zhou Xun was told by survivors in the Xinyang area of Henan, an epicenter of the famine, and in Anhui that "almost every village had cannibal incidents and some people even ate their own children" (http://www.youtube.com/watch?v=61fQ2zHXxuE).

[70] Yang 2012: 250.

minister Peng Dehuai's brave attempt at halting the "rash advance" of the Great Leap at the Lushan Party Conference of July–August 1959, but Yang's lengthy account of that episode[71] is the best we have. Alas for the Chinese people, Peng failed to convince Mao that there were "different rules for politics and economics, and that's why ideological education cannot replace economic work."[72] Instead, a majority accepted Mao's stance that "in a big country like ours, always taking the slow and steady route will lead to disaster."[73] What did the masses think? Yang concedes—and this should not be forgotten—that "in all fairness, the people's genuine aspirations lay behind much of the folly of the Great Leap Forward."[74]

For a year or two, millions of "true believers" and "hot-headed youths" wanted to believe—and Chairman Mao certainly believed at the outset[75]—the spectacular stories of achievements in agriculture and industry (dubbed "sputniks" to reflect their spectacular character) that would have been the envy of Joseph Stalin's norm-breaking Stakhanovites. The "sputnik" yields culled by Yang from the *People's Daily* reached 64 metric tons per hectare of wheat on a farm 2,800 meters above sea level in Qinghai and 450 t/ha of rice in a hilly part of Guangdong by September 1958. Even Mao's credulity was stretched by a claim of 50,000 kilos per *mu* (750 t/ha) in Tianjin.[76] Yields in China today average only about 7 t/ha for rice and 5 t/ha for wheat. Dikötter's depiction of this aspect of the Great Leap Forward is excellent and corroborates the more theoretical case previously advanced by economists and economic historians.[77] The prospect of bountiful harvests led to the mass diversion of labor out of agriculture, with calamitous consequences for food availability.

After Lushan nobody dared point to the state of the emperor's clothes. When Mao inspected Henan, provincial leader Wu Zhipu covered up the starvation;[78] there were myriad cover-ups at the local

---

[71] E.g., Schram 1974; Li 1994: 313–23; Yang 2012: 350–93; Wemheuer 2014: 119.

[72] Yang 2012: 357.

[73] Ibid., 103, 263.

[74] Ibid., 125; but see also Wemheuer 2010: 190.

[75] Yang 2012: 497; Li 1994: 278.

[76] Ibid. 200, 327–28, 497.

[77] Such as Yao 1999; Li and Yang 2005; Bernstein 2006; and Wheatcroft 2008, 2011.

[78] Yang 2012: 81; Wemheuer 2010: 186–87.

level,[79] and even senior officials could not communicate freely about what was really happening. One of Mao's cousins told him, "You live in Beijing, as remote as the emperors of old, and you don't know what is happening."[80] According to his personal physician—invoked as a reliable source by Dikötter—Mao was both depressed by bad news and annoyed at how people hid the truth from him. But "the vexation of falsehood" was part and parcel of the system, and "negative feedback" was lacking.[81]

How much did Big Brother know? Although many stories of edema and even starvation deaths at the local level reached him during 1959 and 1960, Mao failed or refused to link these to systemic failure and nationwide famine.[82] We are told that Mao was "visibly shaken" when presented with graphic reports of famine from Xinyang in Henan province in late October 1960. The news from Xinyang set in train moves that would mark "the beginning of the end of mass starvation."[83] Blaming the tragedy on the usual counterrevolutionary suspects, Mao nonetheless had "abusive cadres" removed. In that same month Mao, under pressure from critics of the Leap, ordered the redeployment of a million workers from industry to agriculture in Gansu province, citing the truism that "no one can do without grain."[84] Various concessions to the peasantry followed, and in January 1961 a chastened Mao told the Ninth Central Committee Plenum that "socialist construction ... should take half a century."[85] For the millions who died in 1959 and 1960, it was already too late. China lacked an all-seeing, all-knowing Soviet-style secret police during the Leap. Too much reliance was placed on poorly monitored regional agents and thuggish local cadres. Why else would it take a visit to his home village in Hunan in April 1961, much too late, for party vice-chairman Liu Shaoqi to discover the

[79] Yang 2012: 39, 49.

[80] Ibid., 51, 52, 279, 192; compare Gao 2011: 179; Thaxton 2008: 231–32; Li 1994: 279, 283–84.

[81] Yang 2012: 497, 103; Dikötter 2010: 346; Li 1994.

[82] Yang 2012: 447–48; Li 1994: 339; Riskin 1998: 119.

[83] Wemheuer 2010: 187–90; Wemheuer 2014: 120; Dikötter 2010: 116, 118 (source of quote).

[84] MacFarquhar 1983: 323.

[85] Barnouin and Changgen 2007: 188.

dimensions of the disaster? That visit and what followed are well documented.[86]

What Liu saw converted him overnight from supporter to harsh critic of the Great Leap Forward. Central-planner-in-chief Li Fuchun's reaction to the reports from Xinyang was that misguided policies (which he had championed) had cost lives. In a speech in Hunan to party strategists in mid-1961, he pithily summarized what have become textbook criticisms of central planning: "too high, too big, too equal, too dispersed, too chaotic, too fast, too inclined to transfer resources." However, there was really no central planning during the Great Leap. Those with the requisite expertise were condemned to manual labor, and adequate statistics—a key requisite—were not collected. Li Fuchun's remarks are therefore best interpreted as a critique of ideological dogma combined with economic anarchy. Thanks to a form of "closed" governance of their own creation, Mao and the party leadership seem to have discovered "destruction on a scale few could have imagined" rather late in the day.[87]

None of this absolves Mao from responsibility for the policies that caused the greatest famine ever. But reckless miscalculation and culpable ignorance are not quite the same as deliberately or knowingly starving millions.[88] Few of the countless deaths in 1959–61 were sanctioned or ordained from the center in the sense that deaths in the Soviet Gulag or the Nazi gas chambers were.[89] While Dikötter's stance on the famine is evident from his book's title, Yang flatly denies that Mao ever said (or meant literally) that "it is better to let half of the people die so that the other half can eat their fill."[90] Yet if intent was lacking, both the scale of the disaster and the failure to confront it stemmed from the edifice that Mao, his comrades, and their "upwards of 60 million cadres of various ranks"[91] built.

---

[86] Yang 2012: 436; Zhou 2012: 158, 162–64; Dikötter 2010: 119, 329.

[87] Yang 2012: 116–23 (quotation on p. 122).

[88] Jin 2009: 152.

[89] On the comparison with Soviet planning in the 1930s, see Wheatcroft 2001, 2008; Wemheuer 2014.

[90] Yang 2011; compare Garnaut 2013a; Zhou 2012: 25.

[91] Yang 2012: 168.

Politics help explain why the intensity of the famine varied from region to region.[92] In Sichuan, for example,[93] the extremism of party secretary Li Jingquan was a key factor in determining the scale and duration of famine. This tallies with the findings of a recent study by Chen Yixin contrasting the role of province-level politics in Anhui and Jiangxi "under the same Maoist sky." In Anhui another radical, Zeng Xisheng, a native of Hunan, veteran of the Long March and friend of Mao, diverted five million peasants from the land to over-ambitious irrigation projects, with disastrous consequences, while in neighboring Jiangxi a home-grown collective leadership did what they could to cancel the Leap's excesses.[94] So provincial boundaries mattered: Anthony Garnaut's map of county-level diminution of 1958–62 cohorts with provincial boundaries superimposed high-lights the role of borders. The contrast in famine severity across the Sichuan-Shaanxi and Sichuan-Yunnan borders is striking. The same holds for the Jiangxi-Anhui border, while some of Qinghai's borders can be predicted with confidence from its county cohort depletion rates.[95]

Yang accepts that the intensity of the famine also varied consider-ably within provinces. Yet his long chapter on Sichuan, which dwells on the malign influence of Li Jingquan, takes insufficient account of the marked contrasts in mortality inside that vast province, where differences in cadre responses to central government policy were de-cisive in determining the scale of famine.[96] Again, in Fenyang in Anhui province, the focus of an extended account in *Tombstone*,[97] the suffering was even greater than in Anhui as a whole. Estimates by Cao Shuji[98] suggest that mortality in that province was subject to a marked south-north gradient, with the death rates in the northern counties of Su and Taihe being nearly ten times those of Wangjiang and Dongxi in the south.[99] Such contrasts suggest that interpreta-

[92] Ibid., 155.
[93] Ibid., 197–247; see also Goodman 1980.
[94] Chen 2011; see also Chen 2009.
[95] Garnaut 2013b.
[96] Bramall 2011: 998.
[97] Yang 2012: 270–86.
[98] Cao 2005.
[99] My thanks to Anthony Garnaut for supplying me with Cao's county-level data; these also highlight Fengyang as one of the worst affected counties.

tions that lean heavily on the zeal of the provincial party leaders like Li Jingquan and Zeng Xisheng leave a lot unexplained; more disaggregated analyses are needed.

The Great Leap placed local cadres under pressure to deliver. One former cadre in Sichuan declared that "the job of a good official is to guard the people while listening to the upper leaders. Bad leaders just listen to upper leaders." Easier said than done; this cadre had sailed pretty close to the wind himself more than once.[100] It was easier to be a bad cadre than a good one, particularly in the "grey zone" that famines entail. Zhou's oral history of the famine records very few positive stories about cadres in Gansu province, but dozens of negative ones. Yang, like Dikötter, implies that most cadres buckled under the pressure. He also claims that they were less likely to die than either ordinary commune members or landlords and rich peasants.[101] Jeremy Brown and Gao Hua are more positive: Gao claims that "the great majority of cadres shared in the hardship of the masses," while Brown has documented how in the northeastern city of Tianjin municipal and central leaders went to "extraordinary lengths to prevent urban starvation."[102] Brown may be right, but it must be said that Tianjin's party secretary faced fewer food distribution challenges than his counterpart in, say, Sichuan. Brown's case study is a reminder that although the Great Leap privileged the cities, urbanites were also at risk; indeed, Felix Wemheuer devotes a long chapter in his recent comparative study of famine politics in China and the Soviet Union to the issue of "preventing urban famine by starving the countryside."[103]

Famines bring out the worst in people, but why were some cadres more brutal and more cowardly than others?[104] Lacking micro-level studies of groups of cadres,[105] we can only speculate that factors such

[100] http://xiakou.uncc.edu/chapters/history/famine.htm.

[101] Yang 2012: 49, 42; Zhou 2013: 53–54, 58–59, 96–97; compare Kung and Chen 2011.

[102] Gao 2011: 194; Brown 2011: 247. In a detailed account of Wuwei county in Anhui based on local party records, Cao Shuji (2010) accused the prefectural and provincial party committees of murder, on the grounds that they had full knowledge of the state of grain supplies and knew that excessive requisitioning was causing mass mortality. But he concluded that headquarters in Beijing might not have been informed.

[103] Wemheuer 2004: 115–53. Compare Yang 2012: 339; Zhou 2012; Wheatcroft 1997.

[104] Yang 2012: 155, 398–99, 405–6.

[105] Compare that by Dora Costa and Matthew Kahn (2009) on the very different context of the U.S. Civil War.

as birthplace (local or not), ideological stance, hunger, fear of retaliation, and previous participation in violence all counted. The responses from center and periphery depended on, but could also exacerbate, the informational gap between the center and the regions.

A Unique Famine

The famine's setting, the rash and disastrous attempt at rapid economic modernization known as the Great Leap Forward—and not just its size—made it unique. One striking feature of *Tombstone* is the paucity of references to shops, moneylenders, pawnbrokers, or prices. And because there were no landlords or private farmers, there were no evictions and no distress sales. Did markets function at all? They did, if only to the extent that commune members in some provinces continued to cultivate minute parcels of land and to raise pigs and ducks. We know too that some people sold their children,[106] and that pre-cooked human flesh was sold as pork in Anhui;[107] and Zhou reproduces documents on hunger-induced prostitution and black markets in Sichuan.[108] In *Tombstone* there is also a hint of a market in kind for sex; and there are fleeting references to fines and to profiteering and to black markets.[109] But that China lacked a functioning, integrated market economy during the Great Leap surely made the famine worse.

Tellingly, neither public action nor private charity—dominant themes in the historiography of pre-1949 Chinese famines[110]—plays much part in *Tombstone* either. Accounts such as that from Gansu's Tongwei county in December 1960, where the authorities were shamed into a relief effort that "reclaimed eighty thousand souls from the brink of death," or from Linhuai in Anhui, where an influential cadre sent five thousand kilos of soy pulp—and was reported

---

[106] I am grateful to Felix Wemheuer for alerting me to the "selling and giving away of [660,000] sons and daughters" in the spring of 1961 mentioned in *Zhongguo zaiqing baogao 1949–1995* 1996: 276. The number given is suspect, however: the same source is silent on 1959 and has 10,688 for 1960.

[107] Yang 2012: 439–40, 302.

[108] Zhou 2012: 132, 134, 135–37, 129–31.

[109] Yang 2012: 196 223, 224, 226, 478; Wemheuer 2010: 191.

[110] E.g., Will 1990; Li 2007; Fuller 2011.

for "right-deviating thinking" for doing so—are exceptional. True, late in the day, policies aimed at saving lives, such as importing grain, and abolishing features of the Great Leap such as communal dining, were implemented.[111] But at the height of the famine, public works, soup kitchens, workhouses, private philanthropy, and foreign aid: these are the dogs that didn't bark in 1959–61. Why relieve a nonexistent famine?[112]

Another unusual feature of the period was the many violent deaths, mainly from beatings and other forms of physical abuse associated with the Great Leap Forward. The perpetrators were cadres, the victims often recalcitrant and bewildered peasants, mainly men, suspected of hoarding or stealing food.[113] But who was most likely to die in the "classless" society being created during the Great Leap? Yang[114] notes only that peasants were much more likely to succumb than cadres, but a loose hierarchy of suffering by socioeconomic class may be inferred from the impact on the number and timing of births during the famine. A mother's low occupational status or lack of education were strong predictors of the likelihood of a miscarriage or infant death, whereas higher status was linked to the greater likelihood of induced abortion.[115] Some of these patterns may be seen in figure 4.1, derived from the 1982 China fertility survey. The mean age at marriage rose more in badly affected provinces (Sichuan, Anhui) than in less affected provinces (Jilin, Heilongjiang; see fig. 4.1a); the percentage of women giving birth within two years of marriage fell more in rural than in urban areas (fig. 4.1b); the number of marriages rebounded powerfully in the wake of the famine, and more so in rural than in urban areas (fig. 4.1c). The survey also

[111] Yang 2012: 151–52, 279; Wemheuer 2010: 179.
[112] Compare Wemheuer 2014: 222.
[113] Zhou 2012: 31–35, 139.
[114] Yang 2012: 42.
[115] Cai and Wang 2010.

Figure 4.1 Marriage and birth in China, before, during, and after the Great Leap Famine. (a) Comparison of mean age at marriage in four provinces (1958–62). (b) Percentage of women giving birth within two years of marriage. (c) Urban and rural marriages 1950–65 (index, 1955 = 100). Source: China Population Information Centre 1988: vol. 2.

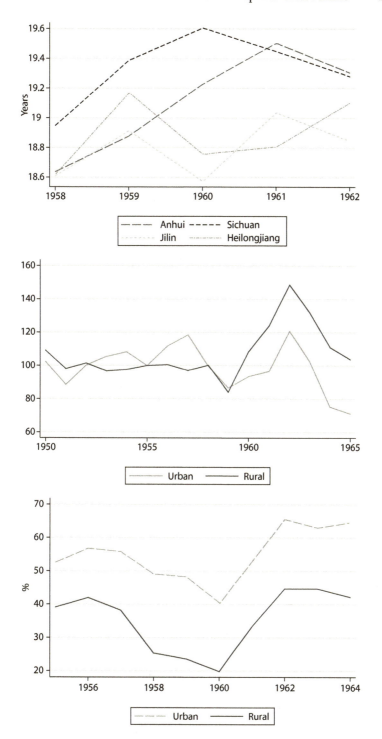

indicates that the fertility of the better off, represented by mothers who had attended senior middle school, was less affected.[116]

The role of migration during the Great Leap Famine requires further study. Migration as a coping strategy is a classic feature of famine, and homeless vagrants are often the first casualties of famine. Therefore, it may come as no great surprise to read that the first recorded case of cannibalism in Anhui involved a "vagrant."[117] References to migration in the oral historical accounts collected by Zhou (see below) are common. Official population statistics also imply that migration played a role: outmigration was greatest from the worst-affected provinces, such as Anhui, Guizho, Henan, and Gansu, while provinces that escaped relatively lightly, such as Tianjin, Guangdong, Heilongjiang, and Jilin, absorbed large numbers of immigrants during the crisis.[118] Were these migrations an artifact of fallible data? To what extent were they state-assisted, to what extent did they evade official attempts to prevent them? The ambiguous history of migration during the Great Leap is well captured in *Tombstone*, which rather equivocates between arguing that migration was impossible (due to the system of household registration introduced in 1958) and that it was common.[119] It seems likely that without the safety valve of migration, the famine might have been deadlier still.

Numbers Matter

Excess mortality is a measure both of a famine's severity and—to a greater or lesser extent depending on the historical context—of the culpability of those deemed responsible for it. This explains the focus on quantifying mortality in many accounts of famine; other measures of famine severity, such as the extent of price increases and the number of evictions, also attract special attention. Quantifica-

---

[116] Cai and Wang (2010: 147) infer from the 1988 fertility survey that 1959 was when infant and child mortality increased most, when the marriage rate dropped most, and when miscarriages and abortions increased. The "observed maximum impacts of the famine are mostly delayed effects of the adversity in 1959."

[117] Yang 2012: 302; Zhou 2012: 139–40; compare Li 2007: 233–34; Will 1990.

[118] Ó Gráda 2008: 17–18.

[119] Yang 2012: 20–21, 27, 29, 57, 127, 270, 473.

tion is not *MGF*'s strong point: it contains lots of numbers but few tables and no graphs. So we read that "between 1 and 3 million people took their lives" by suicide during the Great Leap Forward; that in Xinyang in Henan province "67,000" people were clubbed to death by militias; that in some unspecified location "forty-five women were sold to a mere six villages in less than half a year"; that "at least 2.5 million … were beaten or tortured to death" during the Leap; and that delays to shipping in the main ports during some unspecified period cost "£300,000."[120] An estimate of 0.7 million deaths from starvation and disease in labor-correction camps between 1958 and 1962 is obtained by applying an arbitrary "rough death rate" of two-fifths to a guess at the camp population at its peak.[121]

The main basis for Dikötter's claim that "up to two-fifths of the housing stock turned into rubble" seems to be a report describing conditions in Hunan province from Liu Shaoqi to Mao on 11 May 1959, after Liu had spent a month in the region of his birth.[122] On page after page of *MGF*, numbers on topics ranging from rats killed in Shanghai to illegal immigration to Hong Kong are produced with no discussion of their reliability or provenance: all that seems to matter is that they are "big."

The cost of famines in lives lost is often controversial, because famines are nearly always blamed on somebody, and excess mortality is reckoned to be a measure of guilt. It is hardly surprising, then, that Dikötter's brief account of the famine's death toll arrives at a figure far beyond the range between 18 million and 32.5 million proposed hitherto by specialist demographers.[123]

Rather than engage with the competing assumptions behind these numbers, Dikötter selects Cao Shuji's estimate of 32.5 million and then adds 50 percent to it on the basis of discrepancies between archival reports and gazetteer data, thereby generating a minimum total of 45 million excess deaths. Much hinges on what "normal"

---

[120] Dikötter 2010: 304, 117, 294, 261, 298,156.

[121] Ibid., 289.

[122] Ibid, xii, 169. Elsewhere, however (p. 119), Dikötter describes Liu's visit to his home region in April 1961 as his first trip there in four decades.

[123] Ibid., 324–34; compare Yao 1999; Peng 1987; Ashton et al. 1984; Cao 2005.

mortality rates are assumed, since the archives do not distinguish between normal and crisis mortality. The mortality rate in China in the wake of the revolution was probably about 25 per thousand. It is highly unlikely that the Communists could have reduced it within less than a decade to the implausibly low 10 deaths per thousand adopted in *MGF*.[124] Had they done so, they would have "saved" over 30 million lives in the interim! One can hardly have it both ways.

Famines invariably also result in fewer births.[125] Sometimes the births are lost, sometimes (as to some extent in China in 1959–61) they are postponed. Surprisingly, perhaps, Dikötter has little to say on this aspect, but his attempts at quantification again are hardly convincing. Elementary human biology suggests that the drop in the number of births in one region of Yunnan province from 106,000 in 1957 to 59,000 in 1958, which Dikötter mentions twice,[126] refers mainly to conditions before the Leap. And his implied claim[127] that marriage rates rose during the famine would, if verified, represent a first in the global history of famine.[128]

Another feature of the famine's demography touched on only in passing in *MGF* is its disproportionately rural dimension. Data collected from Anhui gazetteers by Cao Shuji,[129] although probably subject to under-recording, are highly revealing on this aspect. Anhui's proportionate population loss was the highest in China, but whereas the death rate in its urban areas rose by 260 percent, in rural areas it rose almost eightfold. The rates of population change in rural and urban Anhui also differed, but there was a dramatic rebound in births in both rural and urban areas in the wake of the famine.[130]

Finally, as Dikötter highlights, not all Leap deaths were famine deaths. His anecdotal evidence on the terror campaigns waged by local cadres is compelling, although his figures for deaths in the

---

[124] Dikötter 2010: 331.
[125] See Banister 1984: figs. 2–6.
[126] Dikötter 2010: 68, 254.
[127] Ibid., 260–61.
[128] The number of marriages in Yunnan in the 1982 Chinese one-per-thousand fertility survey fell from 3,998 in 1958 to 3,393 in 1959, and then rose to 4,219 in 1960 (China Population Information Centre 1988: vol. 1, pp. 78–79).
[129] Cao 2005: Appendix 3.
[130] Ó Gráda 2011: 196.

"gulag" ("at least 3 million"), by suicide ("between 1 and 3 million"), and from torture and beatings ("at least 2.5 million") are just weakly supported guesses.[131]

Yang devotes a whole chapter[132] to the demographic scale of the 1959–61 famine. He begins with calculations derived from the well-known official population data published in 1984, which yield an estimate of "unnatural deaths" of 16.2 million.[133] Next he uses provincial data available since 1986, which he deems more reliable, to calculate excess deaths by province; these add up to an aggregate 21 million.[134] After a survey of three well-known estimates by foreign scholars,[135] Yang turns to research by Chinese scholars. Dismissive of the estimates of both mainstream demographer Jiang Zhenghua (17 million) and economist Chen Yizi, who fled China in 1989 (43 million), he opts for 36 million, which he judges "still too low."[136] Yang's dismissal of the wilder "sputniks" of 50 to 60 million lent credence by Becker[137] and Dikötter is salutary, but his own chosen figure may still be too high.

Why? Dikötter's reaction to a critique of his "minimum of 45 million" was to ask if "a one per cent rate of death is too low to be considered normal ... would it really change that much if we doubled it to two per cent?"[138] The answer, most emphatically, is that it would. Given that China's population on the eve of the famine was about 650 million, a crude death rate of 20 per 1,000 rather than 10 per 1,000 would have entailed 20 million fewer deaths during the "three difficult years." But instead of attempting to answer his own ques-

---

[131] Dikötter 2010: 291, 298, 304.

[132] Yang 2012: 394–430.

[133] Ibid., 409.

[134] Ibid., 411–16.

[135] But overlooking Ashton et al. (1984), Peng (1987), Luo (1988), and the useful review by Riskin (1998). Zhao and Reimondos (2012) came too late for Yang's possible consideration.

[136] Yang (2012: 427) and Riskin (1998: 113) note that Chen Yizi's estimate is unverifiable. Bramall (2011: 992fn9) rejects it on the grounds that it was part of a 'remit of discrediting the Maoist regime.' Bramall also raises the possibility, plausible yet unverifiable, that some "officials exaggerated deaths to evade or diminish state-imposed grain procurements."

[137] Becker's "sputnik" of 3 million excess deaths in North Korea in the 1990s—"more victims that in Pol Pot's Cambodia"—might be compared with Spoorenberg and Schwekendiek's estimate of between 240,000 and 420,000 (Becker 2005: 211–12; Spoorenberg and Schwekendiek 2012: 133–58).

[138] See Dikötter's response in Wemheuer 2011: 163.

tion, Dikötter pits historians who have spent time in the archives against those who have attempted to make sense of the patchy and fallible demographic data available.[139] Yang is emphatically one of the latter, although the 3,600 or so folders that Yang collected in thirteen different archives filled his apartment; more were kept "in the countryside at a friend's house for safekeeping."[140] Still, a key weakness of the three estimates of excess mortality underpinning Yang's proposed 36 million is that they too rely on an implausibly low pre-famine death rate. Thus Ding Shu treated the 1957 mortality rate (10.8 per 1,000) as the non-crisis norm, while Jin Hui used the averages of 1956–57 and 1962–63 (10.6 per 1,000), and Cao Shuji used the averages of 1957 and 1962 (10.4 per 1,000). Such rates are too low, and Western demographers such as Banister and Ashton et al.[141] have suggested corrections.

Under-recording of births and deaths was pervasive not just before the Great Leap Famine, but also during it. Again, Ashton et al., Banister, and others have proposed adjustments. However, estimates of infant and child mortality based on retrospective fertility surveys[142] imply that their corrections may have been on the high side. Banister's numbers—underpinned by what she candidly described as an "arbitrary estimation process"—suggest that life expectancy at birth reached a minimum of 24.6 years in 1960,[143] whereas Zhao and Reimondos, using much higher quality data, produce a figure of 32.5 years for 1959–60.[144] Since the latter's simulations refer only to six of the worst affected provinces (Anhui, Gansu, Guizhou, Henan, Qinghai, and Sichuan), the aggregate death toll implied by their results is lower than the 30 million proposed by Banister. The price in lives lost exacted by the Great Leap Famine will never be known precisely. Zhao and Reimondos's results make the case for a total much lower—perhaps ten million lower—than that proposed by Yang; the cost in lives lost remains staggering, nonetheless.

---

[139] Ibid., 164.
[140] Johnson 2010. Yang began work on *Mubei* in 1996.
[141] Banister 1987; Ashton et al. 1984: 637–42.
[142] Zhao and Reimondos 2012.
[143] Banister 1987: 116.
[144] Zhao and Reimondos 2012: 342–43.

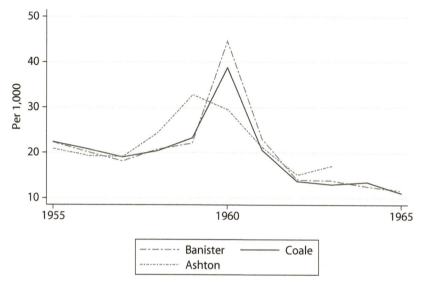

Figure 4.2 Western estimates of the crude death rate in China, 1955–65. Sources: Ashton et al. 1984; Banister 1987; Coale 1984.

An added consideration is that famines usually kill off many vulnerable and sickly people who would have died soon in any case. As a result, typically mortality in the wake of famines is lower than what it would have been in their absence.[145] Both official data and the revisions of Coale, Banister, and Ashton et al.[146] suggest that this was a factor in China after 1959–61 (see fig. 4.2). The ensuing deficit in deaths, though hardly dramatic, should also be included in assessments of the famine's demographic toll.

Meanwhile, famine amenorrhea, reduced libido, and spousal separation reduced the birth rate.[147] The finding that women with no surviving sons on the eve of the famine experienced the lowest fertility decline during it[148] may also point to a Malthusian preventive check at work: those with sons already were presumably under less pressure to bear a child. Retrospective fertility surveys reveal that

[145] This effect is evident in, for example, France after 1694 (Lachiver 1991: 480) and in Finland after 1868 (Mitchell 1975: 109).

[146] Coale 1984; Banister 1987; Yang 2012: 408, 418; Ashton et al. 1984.

[147] Cai and Wang 2010.

[148] Zhao and Reimondos 2012: 340.

there was a reduction too in the number of marriages and an increase in mean marriage age. Moreover, the big rise in marital fertility and the birth rate in the immediate wake of the famine—more than at any other point during the 1950s or 1960s—also implies that some births were postponed rather than lost during the famine. This means that Yang's estimate of forty million births lost is excessive.

A Perspective from Oral History

Zhou Xun's documentary history of the Great Leap Famine has already been mentioned. Her *Forgotten Voices of Mao's Great Famine* (2013) is a very different work from the others, being the first book-length oral history of the Great Leap Famine.[149] It is based on interviews with "nearly a hundred" famine survivors, organized around eight themes such as "the tragedy of collectivization," "starvation and death," and "surviving the famine." Informants were selected in a rather haphazard fashion: a woman selling herbs on a village street in western Sichuan; a chef encountered by accident at a street market near Chengdu, the capital of Sichuan; a woman "sitting against a wall and petting rabbits in a basket" just west of Chengdu; another whom Zhou "ran into by accident in a small market town not far from Pengshan"; a shy man encountered at a roadside café in Anhui who became talkative after "a few cups of alcohol and a hot meal"; "an old neighbour of my family"; Zhou's father; and so on.[150] An anthropologist friend recommended some of the others.[151] Most are what Zhou describes as "illiterate peasants"[152]—and keep in mind that in China as recently as 1980 nearly half of adult women were illiterate—but they also include several who were students at the time, as well as a few former teachers and medical practitioners. Some still lived in poverty in the 2000s; a few had made it out of poverty, as emigrants in Hong Kong and London.

---

[149] Gail Hershatter (2011), based on a series of interviews with elderly women in Shaanxi province, is not about the famine, but contains many references to it.

[150] Zhou 2013: 243, 24, 59, 276, 86, 101, 224 (in the sequence cited).

[151] Zhou 2013: ix–x.

[152] Zhou 2013: 9.

A disproportionate number of Zhou's narrators—about one-half—live (or were living at the time) in her native province of Sichuan. Very often her informants lived in remote, almost inaccessible places: "farther up in the mountains" of northern Sichuan; "a mountainous village in eastern Shandong province"; "deep in the mountains of Liangshan."[153] Whether people living in such remote areas were more or less likely to suffer during the famine remains a moot point, not broached by Zhou: although they did not escape collectivization, their very remoteness may have shielded them more than other places against the worst of the grain procurement campaigns.[154] Or, alternatively, those campaigns may have come as a particular shock in hitherto isolated communities.

Some of Zhou's narrators were mere toddlers or young children in 1959–61, some were then already in their forties. Zhou does not dwell on the traps laid by autobiographical memory, nor on the evasions and silences and chronological confusions associated with oral history as a source.[155] Dropping her original plan to have all her informants answer the same set of questions, she simply invited them to talk. This turned out to have been a wise decision, and Zhou's sorting of their reflections by theme is effectively done.

It all sounds rather random and unscientific. And still, serendipitously, it works. On nearly every page, the obscenity of the famine is brought home in the depictions of its deaths, its cruelties, its insanities, and its horrors. True, many of these stories, especially those describing survival strategies, could apply to *any* major famine. Stories of how famines turned children against parents and the strong against the weak, and made liars and thieves and (in extremis) even cannibals of decent people have been told about other famines, in China and elsewhere. But there is much that resonates of China in the 1950s too. And the anecdotal, autobiographical character of the narratives lends these accounts a compelling potency and immediacy.

After brief introductions, Zhou lets her informants speak for themselves. She has the knack of getting complete strangers to reveal

[153] Zhou 2013: 56, 63, 87.
[154] See Garnaut 2014a.
[155] On some of the pitfalls, see Ó Ciosáin 2004; Ó Gráda 2006: 223–33.

very personal stories of hardship and loss. Her sources trusted her—often, according to her, breaking down in her presence—and her decision in turn to conceal their identities is a measure of her respect for them. The overall impact is of convincing and sincere accounts.

Nearly one-third of the book is taken up with collectivization and the propaganda and pressures associated with the Great Leap. This focus on context matters, since the consequent diversion of labor and grain from the countryside was a key factor behind the famine. The tragic accounts of communal dining halls without adequate food, of slaving long hours, of the expropriation of cooking utensils and domestic furniture, and of incessant pressure from Party cadres are compelling. Sections on unnatural disasters and on death follow. The rest of the book is concerned with the impact of the famine on the cities, survival strategies, and memories of the famine.

The quest for survival was reflected in substitute foods (insects, earth, chaff, tree bark, poisonous plants, etc.), in antisocial behavior, and in migration. The oral record, significantly, is silent on organized resistance and food riots, though she records several individual actions of defiance. The role of migration as a path to survival is a recurring theme in *Forgotten Voices*. Some were fortunate enough to be able to escape to Macau and Hong Kong, but Zhou also mentions migration from Gansu to Henan, from Shandong and Henan to the northeast, and from Hunan in central China to Yunnan in the far southwest. One narrator fled with his brother from Fushun county in southern Sichuan to Liangshan Yi Autonomous Region in 1959, exaggeratedly claiming to have covered "more than one thousand kilometers" on foot in a week.[156] Cities were also magnets for those seeking food and work. Those who managed to leave survived; "they were all very capable people"; "if I had not run away, I'd have starved to death too." Some deserted dependents in fleeing. That so many found it possible to escape despite the efforts of the authorities to stop them is in itself telling.[157]

Most of the evidence on party cadres is very negative. They were "real tyrants"; they were "fearsome" and "brutal"; they stole food;

---

[156] Zhou 2013: 260–61.
[157] Zhou 2013: 160, 142, 262, 183–84.

they were "like slave owners"; "they only cared about themselves."[158] Some narratives spin a more positive tale: "cadres were under a lot of pressure in those days"; they "had to be fierce, or else no one would follow their orders"; they risked being purged for underperforming; "my father (a cadre) was an honest man"; cadres saved a camp laborer's life by having his stomach pumped out; a cadre in Anhui gave a teenager a bowl of rice to feed her dying father.[159] As local agents, cadres were caught between a rock and a hard place; either to bow to the "Wind of Exaggeration" fanned by the Great Leap or to risk getting beaten up for telling the truth.[160]

It would be tempting to infer a narrator's experience from mention of the loss of family members in the famine. Thus in mountainous Langzhong county in northern Sichuan, Wei Dexu watched people die, but they did not include members of his own family.[161] Another distanced reference to deaths comes from an informant in Sichuan's Renshou county, who says that "you could see people drop dead while walking."[162] However, moving and vivid reports of deaths of siblings and parents and near relatives are all too frequent.

Zhou provides plenty of evidence straight out of the "grey zone" inhabited by those living through famines.[163] Discord over food within families is a recurrent theme.[164] An in-law of one of Zhou's informants in Sichuan refused to feed a weak grandson. When remonstrated with about this refusal, her reply was "Why don't you feed him yourself?" The little boy died shortly afterwards. Stealing communal food was also endemic. In Sichuan's Pengshan county "thieves constantly came across other thieves." When there was nothing left to steal, some engaged in cannibalism: with no dogs or cows left, "people had to fill their stomachs with something."[165]

The oral evidence is not always consistent. So at the construction site of the Xichong reservoir in Yunnan's Luliang county "many peo-

---

[158] Zhou 2013: 23, 45, 76, 46, 53, 59.
[159] Zhou 2013: 33, 96, 89, 97, 230, 236.
[160] Zhou 2013: 74–76, 87–88.
[161] Zhou 2013: 49.
[162] Zhou 2013: 52.
[163] Compare Mac Suibhne 2013.
[164] Zhou 2013: 220, 222, 250, 257.
[165] Zhou 2013: 252, 249, 260.

ple died," whereas at the site of the Banqiao dam in Henan's Suiping county "no one died," that is, the dying were moved elsewhere lest a government inspection team discover the truth about conditions on the ground.[166] On the whole the role of the weather is discounted, but in Huang county, Shandong, "it rained savagely" in 1960 and 1961 while in Gansu "there were sandstorms all the time" (pp. 130, 132). According to another informant in Renshou county, food was scarce, not because of the weather, but because "all the young and strong labourers were sent to make iron and steel" and "the crops were left to rot in the fields" (p. 137).

Zhou makes much of the environmental damage caused by the Great Leap Forward (pp. 78–79, 105–8). Certainly, some of it was immediately obvious; what is less clear is whether the losses resulting from dust storms and alkalinization of water were already a problem before 1960–61, or whether future problems were widely predicted at the time. Today, the warnings of hydrologist Huang Wanli against the construction of gigantic dams during the Great Leap are universally acknowledged as brave and prescient, but Huang's warnings were more about silt and sedimentation than salinization and alkalinization.[167] On this, Zhou's narrators may have the advantage of hindsight over the madcap enthusiasts for big dams and small backyard furnaces during the Great Leap.

While Mao's personal, genocidal culpability is central to the accounts of Dikötter and Becker, he is quite a remote—though hardly sinister—figure in Zhou's narratives. One informant notes that "militarization was Mao's idea" (p. 39), another that he stressed the need for "self-reliance" (p. 42); one remembered Mao's visit in 1958 to Xushui, a village famous for its communistic feats, but he "couldn't see him" (p. 70); another, barber Feng of northern Sichuan, referred to the head of his brigade as a crook, "the type of person that Mao once warned us about" (p. 58). But that is about it. Moreover, to Zhou's evident surprise, Mao's memory was revered almost everywhere she went. In Henan's Suiping county, devastated by the fam-

---

[166] Zhou 2013: 78, 80.
[167] Shapiro 2001: 48–64.

ine, "in almost every home there was a portrait of Chairman Mao" (p. 284), while an old neighbor of Zhou's in Chengdu claimed that "if it wasn't for Chairman Mao, who liberated us, we would not be able to enjoy today's good life" (p. 283). An old villager, wondering why Zhou was dwelling on the past, explained that while under Mao people learned to appreciate life by eating bitter food, "these days life is not too bad for many people" (p. 277). Zhou does not attempt to resolve the "disconnect" between the follies of the Great Leap Forward, the violence, and the deaths, on the one hand, and Mao's role, on the other.

Had Zhou interviewed her subjects a generation ago, would their verdict on the part played by Mao in the famine have been the same? Oral history, like all history, often tells us as much about the present as the past. Its strength lies in the searing anecdote and the local detail, not in sophisticated analysis of political decision-making at the top. The Chinese poor were as remote from Mao and Beijing in the 1950s as the Irish poor were from Lord John Russell and London in the 1840s. The willingness of Zhou's witnesses to let Mao off the hook in the 2000s, though important, hardly resolves the extent of Mao's culpability in the 1950s. That issue remains controversial. As we have seen, for some (like, say, Dikötter or Becker) it is enough to declare the famine "Mao's Famine"—and Zhou's subtitle also echoes this sentiment. Others (like, say, Bernstein or Wheatcroft or Wemheuer) hold Mao culpable for engaging in an ill-conceived and reckless attempt at forcing a desperately backward economy to catch up, which ended in catastrophe.[168]

It may be useful to dwell briefly on how the material in *Forgotten Voices* compares with oral evidence on the Great Irish Famine of the 1840s (which has already been featured in Essay 3). Like the material collected by the Irish Folklore Commission between the 1930s and the 1950s, the Chinese evidence focuses almost entirely on the local and the anecdotal. Just as the Irish material is silent on the likes of Treasury undersecretary Charles Trevelyan, the Chinese material is silent on provincial party secretaries such as Wu Zhipu of Henan or

---

[168] Dikötter 2010; Becker 1996; Bernstein 2006; Wheatcroft 2011, 2012; Wemheuer 2014.

Li Jingquan of Sichuan, who feature prominently in *written* histories of the famine. However, the Chinese oral record is more explicit and more immediate than the Irish in its accounts of violence and death. The Irish evidence is doubly vicarious in that the narrators related second-hand information from people who very often described the sufferings of third parties who fared worse during the famine than themselves. Indeed, hardly anywhere in the IFC archive do we encounter an informant who admits that somebody in the immediate family of his own forebears suffered a famine-related death, or that one of her own people entered the workhouse as an inmate. Compare the following examples from Ireland in the 1840s and China in 1959–61:

> Patrick Reilly, Culleagh, tells of people found along the roads weak with hunger, grass on their mouths and who were brought to the poorhouse. [County Cavan]

> Auld Mrs Corcoran, the wife of Peter Corcoran, went into Granard workhouse and took three children out of it. [County Longford]

> More than once I heard my grandfather, who lived down here in Magh Adhair and who was a married man during the famine, say that there were so many making for the poorhouses that there wasn't accommodation for half of them. [County Clare]

> Anthony Dwyer's father told him that he saw people dead, dying and staggering about at a rest house in Knockroe, a short distance on the Cashel side of Golden. [County Tipperary]

> Bat had an old horse and when the opportunity arose, it was Foxy Bat's horse that would convey people to the Beathach workhouse. [County Kerry]

> "You have the brand of the Union [workhouse] on you," is what people were told. [County Kerry]

> To be buried in a workhouse coffin was regarded as a slur on the friend and on the deceased. [County Galway][169]

---

[169] Ó Gráda 2006: 227.

My father starved to death in 1961. It's really hard for me to talk about that time. [Crying] In those days there weren't even any coffins for those who died. The bodies were just covered up with some earth, and their feet were often exposed outside.... [Shandong province]

I had nine children, and two starved to death during the time of the famine. In those days even adults couldn't get enough to eat, and it was even worse for children ... Cry? I am a man, I could bear it. But it's different for women. My wife wept. How did I feel? What could I do? They were my own children ... Their little bodies were thrown away. The best we could do was to ask some people to cover up their bodies with earth.... [northern Sichuan province]

In those days there were no roosters crowing any more. In the end, the head of the militia went to the canteen and got a handful of rice from the staff there. He put it in my hand. I ran home ... My father died while I was feeding him. It was in 1959. He was only in his forties. [She wept at this point]. [Anhui province][170]

Literally none of the Irish accounts convey a real sense of "having been there." And whereas in Ireland there is much on workhouses and soup kitchens and evictions and shopkeepers, in China the emphasis is on cadres and state violence and propaganda and communal dining. This is not the place for a systematic comparison between themes in Zhou's narratives and Póirtéir's[171] excellent compendia, but such a comparison would be a worthwhile exercise.

What Yang Did Not See

Yang Jisheng's *Mubei/Tombstone* and Frank Dikötter's *MGF* are landmark volumes in the historiography of Chinese famines. Indeed, they have been heaped with so much praise that any criticism of either work risks being misinterpreted as famine denial or pro-regime apologetics. That is far from being the motivation here. While neither *MGF* nor *Tombstone* may add much reliable economic and de-

---

[170] Zhou 2013: 162, 169, 236.
[171] Póirtéir 1995, 1996.

mographic data, what they reveal about what really happened in 1959–61—and the same may be said of Zhou's *Forgotten Voices*—will influence future analyses of the Great Leap Famine. Their perspective on two of the abiding mysteries of the famine—how much people knew, and how come so many people, inside and outside China, seemed not to know—will not please everybody. Both Dikötter's and Yang's damning accounts offer their own insights on these puzzles, as does Yang's brief autobiographical intrusion at the beginning of *Tombstone*.

Had Dikötter focused more on the implications of northern China's "dry and dusty countryside [and] an alkaline soil that hardly yielded enough grain for villagers to survive on,"[172] or on the economic historian R. H. Tawney's famous depiction of the Chinese peasant just a generation before the Great Leap Forward as "standing permanently up to his neck in water, so that even a ripple is enough to drown him,"[173] he might have produced a more rounded account of the tragedy. *MGF*'s reliance on fresh archival sources and interviews and its extensive bibliography of Chinese-language items are impressive, but its bite-size chapters (thirty-seven in all) and breathless prose style—replete with expressions like "plummeted," "rocketed," "beaten to a pulp," "beaten black and blue," "frenzy," "ceaseless," "deafening noise," "frenzied witch hunt"—are often more reminiscent of the tabloid press than the standard academic monograph. If Yang Jisheng is destined to be China's Alexander Solzhenitzyn, Frank Dikötter has replaced Jasper Becker as its Anne Appelbaum.[174]

The ignorance of the outside world about events in China in 1959–61 has already been remarked on. The only article in the *Irish Times* in 1960 to contain both the words "China" and "famine" dwelt on how droughts and floods had brought about "China's Year of Disasters." Innocently citing the *People's Daily*, the *Irish Times* recorded how "many old peasants who still remember the pains of pre-liberation natural calamities say nobody could guess how many people would have died from this if we had not formed people's com-

---

[172] Dikötter 2010: 47.

[173] Tawney 1966: 77.

[174] Author of *Gulag: A History* (New York: Doubleday, 2003) and *Iron Curtain: The Crushing of Eastern Europe, 1944–1956* (London: Allen Lane, 2012).

munes." In its ignorance of the reality, the *Irish Times* was echoing a broader silence on the Chinese famine. It was likewise in the French daily *Le Monde*. That newspaper carried a report of Field-Marshal Bernard Montgomery's claim that he had seen no signs of a famine on a recent visit to China, and one of "massive purchases" of Canadian and Australian grain in 1961; but that was all.[175] Yang Jisheng should have been in a better position to know. He grew up in Hubei, a province that features little in either *Tombstone* or Zhou's *Documentary History*,[176] and which (unlike neighboring Anhui and Henan) escaped the Great Leap Famine with relatively little harm. His admission that, as an adolescent in the late 1950s, he was oblivious to the famine, even though his seventy-year-old stepfather died of starvation, sustains *Tombstone*'s broader narrative. Only during the Cultural Revolution, when Hubei's then governor referred openly to the famine, did Yang realize that his "family's tragedy was not unique."[177] By suggesting that such ignorance was widespread within China, Yang's confession puts a new gloss on the failure of so many, like engagé American journalist Edgar Snow, the "fabled sinologists" of Beijing's British embassy lampooned by Dikötter, and renowned Harvard scholar Dwight Perkins—who declared in 1969 that "few if any had starved outright" and that "the regime had averted a major disaster"—to realize what was happening.[178] But it doesn't explain their ignorance. Just how the biggest famine in human history (in absolute, not in relative terms) remained "hidden" within and outside China for so long is a question still awaiting a full answer.

---

[175] "Pour combattre la famine 40 navires sont affrétés à Londres pour la Chine," *Le Monde*, 6 February 1961; "Le maréchal Montgomery n'a pas vu trace de famine en Chine populaire," *Le Monde*, 9 October 1961.

[176] Zhou 2012: 116–17.

[177] Yang 2012: 11.

[178] Mirsky 2010; Dikötter 2010: 345; Perkins 1969: 166, 303–19; Riskin 1996. Snow, according to Mirsky, "didn't bother to see" the famine. Contrarian voices such as *China News Analysis* (1961, as cited in Leys 1990), the Asian People's Anti-Communist League (1962) and Chu (1964) were ignored or not heard.

5

Famine Is Not the Problem
—For Now

> In all ages of the world except the present, want of food has caused
> wholesale destruction of the people.... But gradually the effects of
> increased wealth and improved means of communication are mak-
> ing themselves felt nearly all over the world; the severity of famines
> is mitigated even in such a country as India; and they are unknown
> in Europe and in the New World.
>
> Alfred Marshall[1]

The Changing Nature of Famine

Controversies about the nature and existence of famines are not
new, and they are ongoing. Some are about issues of guilt; some
about famine denial; some about the very definition of famine. Famines are catastrophic, out-of-the ordinary events, but what passes for
extraordinary in a rich society with a normal mortality rate of, say,
ten per thousand is very different from what passes for extraordinary
when the normal mortality rate is thirty per thousand. By the same
token, a crisis that would have been deemed a "dearth" or a "*disette*" a
few centuries ago might be dubbed a famine today. A concise definition of famine that straddles such a range of events is impossible.

The difficulty is highlighted by the current United Nations definition of famine. The UN deems a famine to exist nowadays when

---

[1] Marshall 1920: 163.

three conditions are met. First, at least one-fifth of the population must be subsisting on fewer than 2,100 kcal of food per diem; second, more than thirty percent of children must be acutely malnourished; and third, daily death rates due to lack of food must reach two per 10,000 population or four per 10,000 children.[2] But in France two centuries or so ago *average* calorie consumption was probably no more than 2,000 kcal, and in Europe generally daily child mortality rates of over four per 10,000 would have been commonplace. So by the UN's definition, in Europe before the Industrial Revolution famine would probably have been the norm rather than the exception.[3]

In what follows, famine is defined differently. It is taken to mean "a shortage of food or purchasing power that leads directly to excess mortality from starvation or hunger-induced diseases."[4] This narrower definition reflects the facts that historically most famine deaths have been from infectious diseases and, taking a leaf out of Amartya Sen's entitlements approach to famine, that harvest failures are not always a necessary precondition for famine. The definition excludes situations of averted famine and of severe privation. But averted famines and situations of severe privation deserve to be documented and studied in their own right.

By any definition, famines have long been the stuff of controversy. For as long as the market mechanism has been employed to distribute food, in times of scarcity the poor have suspected the rich of plotting against them. And wherever, as discussed in Essay 3, the "moral economy" conviction that the haves were duty-bound to assist the have-nots in time of need has held sway, the poor and not so poor have attempted to extract concessions from the better off. Sometimes the ensuing resource transfers saved lives; sometimes, arguably, the opposite was true.

By the same token, excess mortality during famines is a particularly contentious topic, since it has been—and continues to be—invoked as a measure of guilt or policy failure. In the British House of Commons in 1847 opposition leader Lord George Bentinck fa-

[2] Purcell 2011; Howe and Devereux 2004.
[3] Kelly and Ó Gráda 2013; Breschi and Pozzi 2004.
[4] Ó Gráda 2009: 4.

mously berated the government for "holding the truth down" about
the famine that was devastating Ireland, and predicted a time "when
we shall know what the amount of mortality has been," and people
could judge "at its proper value [the government's] management of
affairs in Ireland."[5] Since 1847 commentators and historians have
talked up or talked down the death toll of the Great Irish Famine,
and their findings have often been good predictors of their stance on
culpability.[6]

The question of excess mortality during famines in India in the
late nineteenth century and in Bengal in 1943–44 is equally fraught.[7]
The same holds for Ukraine in 1932–33, Vietnam in 1945, and China
in 1959–61. In an address before the joint houses of the U.S. Congress in 2005 former Ukrainian president Viktor Yushchenko described himself as "a son of a nation that survived the most terrible
tragedies of the 20th century: the Holodomor famine that took away
20 million lives of Ukrainians *and the Holocaust*" (emphasis added),
but demographers who have studied the numbers carefully reckon
that the true demographic toll from famine in Ukraine in 1932–33
lay between 2.5 and 3.5 million.[8] Although Ho Chi Minh's declaration of Vietnamese independence on 2 September 1945 stated that
"from the end of last year to the beginning of this year, from Quang
Tri province to the north of Vietnam, more than two million of our
fellow citizens died from starvation," the likely toll was probably
closer to one million.[9] And, as seen in Essay 4, while *engagé* scholars
like Jasper Becker and Frank Dikötter insist that the Great Leap Forward Famine of 1959–61 exacted a toll of 45 to 60 million, demographers argue for an excess mortality of 20 to 30 million.[10]

---

[5] H.C. Debates, 29 March 1847; see http://hansard.millbanksystems.com/commons/1847
/mar/29/poor-relief-ireland-bill#S3V0091P0_18470329_HOC_105.

[6] Estimates range from 0.5 million to 1.0–1.5 million. Compare Green 1956: 126; Daly
1981: 20–21; Mokyr 1980.

[7] Sen 2009: 338–39; Dyson 1991; Maharatna 1996.

[8] "Ukrainian President Yushchenko's Address before Joint Session of U.S. Congress, 6 April
2005" (see http://web.archive.org/web/20061006021607/http://www.president.gov.ua/en
/news/data/print/173.html). Compare Wheatcroft 2001.

[9] "Declaration of Independence of the Democratic Republic of Vietnam" (see http://
historymatters.gmu.edu/d/5139/); Marr 1997: 104.

[10] On controversies about excess mortality in China, see Essay 4.

The demographic tolls of the world's most recent famines are also debated, but—apart, probably, from Somalia in 2011–12—they have been minuscule by historical standards. Malawi was the epicenter of a broader food crisis threatening southern Africa in 2001–2. In March 2002 Malawi's president, Bakili Muluzi, pleaded with the international community for aid to deal with a crisis that had put three-quarters of the population at risk, and almost immediately UN agencies and relief-oriented nongovernmental organizations (NGOs) set about addressing Malawi's "worst food crisis in half a century." In May 2002 the BBC was warning that "at least 10 million people face starvation in four southern African countries." Two months later aid agencies had upped the number, stating that "14 million people in southern Africa face starvation," and by February 2003 *Africa Recovery* was warning that "with 38 million facing starvation . . . business as usual will not do."[11]

Yet we now know that the eventual death toll in Malawi in 2002 was very low. In March 2002 an official source reported that about one hundred Malawians had died from hunger-related illnesses from the beginning of the year, while NGO sources informed the BBC that "more than 300 people ha[d] died of hunger" in the previous two months.[12] In May the BBC reported that "officially more than 100 people starved to death by March in Kasungu," the worst-affected district, in Malawi's "worst-ever famine."[13] The higher estimates of aggregate losses of "at least 500–1000" and "1,000–3,000" proposed by famine specialist Stephen Devereux of the University of Sussex imply an increase of about one percent above the normal death rate.[14]

In late 2005 Malawi was in trouble again, with aid agencies claiming that "at least five million people face starvation this winter," the World Food Programme declaring a funding shortfall of "at least $70

[11] BBC, "Millions at Risk in Southern Africa," 29 May 2002; "How to Donate to Famine Appeal," *The Guardian*, 25 July 2002; "Famine Spreads across Africa; with 38 Million Facing Starvation, 'Business As Usual Will Not Do,'" *Africa Recovery*, February 2003.

[12] "IRI Climate Digest April 2002: Climate Impacts—March" (http://www.iri.columbia.edu/climate/cid/Apr2002/impacts.html); "South Africa Threatened by Famine," 7 March 2002 (http://news.bbc.co.uk/2/hi/africa/1858880.stm).

[13] "Malawi's 'Worst-ever' Famine," http://news.bbc.co.uk/2/hi/africa/1985765.stm.

[14] Devereux 2002.

million," and Malawi's government warning that without outside help "hundreds of thousands of Malawians will die."[15] Happily, no major crisis materialized. Since 2005 a series of favorable seasons and generous subsidies through cheap fertilizers have increased the output of maize, the staple crop, substantially. By 2008/9 Malawi was a net exporter of maize, and it was almost as if its food supply problems were in the past. But if Malawi's recent famines or near-famines have been exaggerated, predicting the future on the basis of a few good years in succession is equally foolhardy. Whether seed and fertilizer subsidies offer an enduring and sustainable cure for economic backwardness remains moot. A related problem is that subsidies are of least assistance to poor farmers dependent on marginal soils and that the long-term viability of a program that subsidizes two million cultivators out of the public purse is questionable.[16]

In 2005–6 Niger was one of the poorest countries in the world. At the time only Guinea Bissau, Sierra Leone, and Burkina Faso ranked lower on the United Nations Development Program's Human Development Index.[17] Robert Malthus, a technological pessimist, would have been dumbfounded by the ability of Niger's farm sector to sustain a population increasing at a rate of 3–4 percent per year. Its ability to do so implies significant productivity gains in order to stand still—and considerable resilience in a context of threatened soil erosion and, indeed, desertification. Keeping food supplies per head constant when population is growing at such a pace requires greater efficiency and productivity gains than those achieved by European agriculture before World War II.[18] However, that growth occurred against a backdrop of increasing reliance on imports in bad

[15] Bill Corcoran, "Five Million Face Starvation in Malawi," *Observer*, 2 October 2005; Patrick Barkham, "Silently, Malawi Begins to Starve," *Guardian*, 19 October 2005. Both reports were filed in Nsanje district in southern Malawi.

[16] On the rise of cereal production, see "Food and Agricultural Organization: Malawi Country Profile 2014" (http://www.fao.org/countryprofiles/index/en/?iso3=mwi). On fertilizer subsidies, "Malawi Minister Admits Fertliser [*sic*] Programme Had Mistakes," *Nyasa Times*, 13 February 2013 (http://www.nyasatimes.com/2013/02/13/malawi-minister-admits-fertliser-subsidy-programme-had-mistakes-minister/); Ricker-Gilbert, Jayne, and Chirwa 2010.

[17] United Nations Development Programme, *Human Development Report 2007/2008*: 232 (*hdr.undp.org/sites/default/files/reports/268/hdr_20072008_en_complete.pdf*).

[18] Federico 2005: 240–41.

years and increasing output variability.[19] In 2005 estimates of 3.5 million people in a population of around twelve million at imminent risk of starvation—almost invariably including 0.8 million children—were much recycled. Fortunately, as it turned out, crisis-induced excess mortality in Niger in 2005–6 was also almost certainly minimal.[20]

Comparing Niger's 2005 crisis with that the major Niger famine of 1931, when drought and locusts destroyed most of the staple millet crop, offers evidence of progress made in the interim. First, the 1931 famine's toll in terms of deaths and emigration exceeded 150,000, with excess mortality in the tens of thousands.[21] Second, colonial tax exactions were a factor, as was the paucity of aid from France, of which Niger was a colony. During 1931 food aid totaled 140 tons for the 0.5 million living in the three worst hit districts of Niamey, Dosso, and Tillabéry, and much of that aid was in the form of loans. In the following year the authorities took their responsibilities more seriously, but food ordered for Niamey and Tillabéry in late 1931 had yet to arrive in July 1932. Relief was thus both inadequate and slow.[22] Third, the price of millet more than quintupled at its peak during the third quarter of 1931, whereas in 2005 the price at most doubled. Most vulnerable in 1931 were those nomadic pastoralists who relied on the market for their food, and who saw their resources and purchasing power (i.e., their entitlements in the sense of Amartya Sen) dwindle to almost nothing as livestock prices plummeted and food prices soared. Only the need to fund their tax burdens drove farmers to the market. In sum, the contrast between 1931 and 2005 could not be starker. That is not to deny Niger's extreme poverty in the 2000s and 2010s. In 2013 GDP per head in Niger ($800-$900) was the among the lowest in the world, while its total

---

[19] Cornia and Deotti 2008.

[20] A scholarly study published in 2008 attempted to estimate mortality on the basis of a sample survey carried out in the wake of the crisis. The highest daily mortality rate found was 0.7 per 10,000 in Zinder; for Niger as a whole the estimate was 0.4 per 10,000. Had that daily rate lasted for a year—which was far from being the case—it would convert to an annual rate of less than 15 per thousand, or considerably less than the annual death rate reported by international agencies for Niger in the early 2000s.

[21] Egg, Lenin, and Venin 1975: 18.

[22] Ibid., 45–47; see also Fuglestad 1974.

fertility rate was the world's highest and its mean female age at marriage among the world's lowest.[23] Like other mainly Muslim countries in north and western Africa, it has been largely spared the catastrophe of HIV/AIDS, but global warming poses a grave and deadly threat to Niger in the medium term.

Somalia in 2011–12

Somalia, where a famine was declared in July 2011, and where two months later the UN was claiming that "as many as 750,000 people could die"[24] within four months, is a different story than Malawi or Niger. In early February 2012 the UN declared the Somali famine over,[25] but also held that "tens of thousands of people have died after what is said to be East Africa's worst drought for 60 years." According to Oxfam, "Although it is impossible to calculate exactly how many people died as a result of drought, the UK government estimates that between 50,000 and 100,000 lives were lost between April and August 2011, more than half of them children under the age of five."[26]

Separating excess mortality from normal mortality in Somalia is not trivial, given that Somalia has not held an official census since 1975.[27] Moreover, the appropriateness of a UN famine benchmark of four deaths per 10,000 per diem for children under five years,[28] which translates to an annual death rate of 146 per 1,000, in a country where in normal, non-crisis conditions the mortality rate of under-five-year-olds was higher than that in the 2000s, seems ques-

[23] CIA, "GDP per capita" (2013 estimates), *World Factbook* (https://www.cia.gov/library/publications/the-world-factbook/rankorder/2004rank.html); CIA, "Country Comparison: Total Fertility Rate" (2014 estimates), *World Factbook* (https://www.cia.gov/library/publications/the-world-factbook/rankorder/2127rank.html); *The Economist*, "Birth Control in Niger Population Explosion: Runaway Birth Rates Are a Disaster," 14 August 2014.

[24] "Somalia Famine: UN Warns of 750,000 Deaths," http://www.bbc.co.uk/news/world-africa-14785304 (5 September 2011).

[25] "UN Declares Somalia's Famine Over," http://www.cbc.ca/news/world/story/2012/02/03/somalia-un-famine.html (3 February 2012).

[26] http://www.oxfam.org/en/pressroom/pressrelease/2012-01-18/thousands-lives-millions-dollars-lost-late-response-food-crisis-east-africa (18 January 2012).

[27] UNDP Somalia 1997: 3.

[28] Purcell 2011.

tionable. By the same token, per capita food consumption in Somalia was estimated at 1,734 kcal in 2001, whereas one of the UN's criteria for declaring a famine is 20 percent or more of the population receiving fewer than 2,100 kcal daily.[29]

Still, two studies of excess mortality in Somalia exist. The first, the 2013 study of excess mortality in Somalia by epidemiologist Francesco Checchi and demographer Courtland Robinson, funded by the UN Food and Agriculture Organization (FAO),[30] confirms that this crisis was of a different order than that of Malawi or Niger. The estimates in Checchi and Robinson's study, which received enormous coverage in the media, was widely reported as being "off the charts," with the famine killing "260,000 people," including "133k Somalia famine child deaths."[31] However, their study was more nuanced than the headlines implied. True, their "preferred" estimate was 258,000, but they also described in some detail alternative scenarios yielding excess mortality figures of 164,000 and 196,000, respectively.

One worrying limitation of the Checchi-Robinson study is the thinness of the survey data that underpin it. Its interpolations are based on 82 surveys carried out between March 2007 and July 2012, which contain information in total on only 3,249 deaths and 1,772 births. The coverage is very spotty; seventeen surveys were conducted before the famine, in 2007–10, and eleven after it, in 2012, but no single region is represented continuously. Moreover, 23 of the 82 surveys were conducted in camps for internally displaced persons (IDPs).

A second worrying feature of the study is the high proportion of children aged less than five years per household captured in the surveys. In 16 of the 70 surveys providing such data, over 28 percent of household members were aged less than five; in another 21 the percentages ranged between 25 and 27 percent, while the average for all 70 surveys was 24.7 percent. This is far in excess of that found else-

---

[29] E.g., http://www.bbc.co.uk/news/world-africa-14785304 (5 September 2011).

[30] Checchi and Robinson 2013.

[31] http://www.bbc.co.uk/news/world-africa-22380352; http://www.usatoday.com/story/news/world/2013/05/02/somalia-famine-child-deaths/2130511/.

where in eastern Africa (17 per cent in 2010).[32] Perhaps the extraordinarily high birth rates inferred from some of the surveys are a reflection of this. In seven of the 47 surveys providing data on the birth rate, the birth rate exceeded 60 per thousand; in Addun in northeastern Somalia in July 2011 it was 102.6 per thousand; in a pastoral region in Gedo in July 2011 it was 89.1 per thousand. As the authors concede:

> An implausibly high birth rate in mortality surveys may suggest over-reporting of household demographic events and lack of understanding of the recall period, *which would also lead to upward bias of the death rate.* An outstanding finding was the relatively high proportion of children under 5y old.[33]

A third feature of Checchi and Robinson's survey data is the implication that the birth rate was unaffected by the famine. Again as the authors admit:

> While there is considerable evidence that famines contribute to a decline in fertility, the FSNAU surveys done in 2011 and 2012 suggested that birth rates had not decreased significantly. . . . *If birth rates, in fact, had declined, then our model would overestimate births and thus overestimate the number of children under-five who were exposed to higher death rates during the emergency, i.e. result in artificially high death toll estimates.*[34]

One of the safest generalizations in famine demography is that famines reduce the birth rate.[35] The finding that, exceptionally, in Somalia in 2011–12 this was not so is possibly an artifact of dubious underlying data.

Checchi and Robinson's study is careful and transparent but, given the thinness of the underlying data and some perplexing features of the results they yield, their estimates of excess mortality must be regarded as provisional. Note that their total exceeds the es-

---

[32] 2010 data given in http://esa.un.org/unpd/wpp/Excel-Data/population.htm.
[33] Checchi and Robinson 2013: 73, emphasis added.
[34] Checchi and Robinson 2013: 57, emphasis added.
[35] Ó Gráda 2009: 102–8.

TABLE 5.1. Crude and Under-Five Death Rates in
Somalia, 2007–2012

Year	Under-5 Death Rate*	Crude Death Rate*
2007	1.8	1.0
2008	1.8	0.8
2009	1.2	0.6
2010	1.1	0.5
2011	3.6	1.3
2012	1.5	0.9

* 10,000 per diem.
Source: World Food Programme Somalia 2012: 44.

timate of 220,000 widely associated with the 1992–93 Somalia famine—an estimate that is also, however, subject to a margin of error.[36]

An alternative estimate may be inferred from World Food Programme Somalia's *Trend Analysis of Food and Nutrition Security in Somalia 2007–2012*. Its figure 11 reports overall and under-five daily death rates between 2007 and 2012, which are the basis for table 5.1 below. The under-five daily death rate easily exceeded the UN benchmark of 4 per 10,000 during the *hagaa* season (July–September) of 2011. A very rough guess at aggregate excess mortality may be inferred from comparing the estimated crude death rate in 2011 and 2012 to the 2007–10 average. That would imply an excess rate of 0.6 per 10,000 in 2011 and 0.2 per 10,000 in 2012, which translates into a cumulative rate of about three percent of the population or, given an estimated population of 10 million, an aggregate toll of 0.3 million. Thus the WFP data square with Checchi and Robinson's findings.

Somalia in 2011–12 differed from Malawi and Niger too, of course, in that its famine was linked to war and terror. Not only was it difficult to transfer aid to where it was needed most; for the employees of NGOs and others, it was a highly dangerous task. Médecins Sans Frontières (MSF) halted some of its operations at the height of the crisis, and in 2013 withdrew from Somalia altogether,

[36] Hansch et al. 1994: 20–24. This figure would imply a higher toll than for 2011–12 in proportionate terms, however.

citing the "untenable imbalance between the risks and compromises our staff must make, and our ability to provide assistance to the Somali people."[37] In 2010–12, over twenty aid workers, mostly locals, were killed in the course of their duties. Although most of these were Somali nationals, they included UN aid workers from places as far-ranging as Turkey, Belgium, and Indonesia.[38] The contrast with, say, Ireland in the 1840s, where travelers such as the American evangelist Asenath Nicholson, grandees like Lord Dufferin and the son of the Earl of Glasgow, or the Scottish journalist Alexander Somerville witnessed and documented the famine unthreatened and unimpeded, is stark.[39] The difficulties and dangers in Somalia prompted the head of MSF to accuse some agencies of "glossing over" the difficulties of getting aid to the worst affected areas "in order to convince people that simply giving money for food was the answer." He added that the use of phrases such as "worst drought in sixty years" obscured the man-made character of the famine.[40] In Somalia, where life is precarious even in non-famine situations, war led to famine. Yet the broader message as reflected in Malawi, Niger, and elsewhere seems to indicate that peacetime famines are become smaller and fewer. Is it time to declare famines history—for now?

Famine, Where Is Thy Sting?

Forecasting future prospects for the eradication of famine is perhaps foolhardy. In the 1960s and 1970s doomsday predictions were the order of the day. The predictions of Paul Ehrlich and William Dando are well known; in 1967 a lesser-known volume by William and Paul Paddock with the disturbing title *Famine 1975! America's Decision: Who Will Survive* defined India, Egypt, and Haiti as beyond help and

[37] "MSF Forced to Close All Medical Programmes in Somalia," http://somalia.msf .org/2013/08/msf-forced-to-close-all-medical-programmes-in-somalia/.

[38] Aid Worker Security database, https://aidworkersecurity.org/; UNICEF, "UN Condemns Killing of Aid Worker in Somalia," http://www.unicef.org/somalia/media_11649.html.

[39] Nicholson 1851; Blackwood and Boyle 1847; Somerville 1994.

[40] Tracy McVeigh, "Charity President Says Aid Groups Are Misleading the Public on Somalia," *Guardian*, 3 September 2011.

therefore not worth assisting.[41] A few years later, the more sober prognosis of the Club of Rome envisaged "negative feedback loops [involving] such processes as pollution of the environment, depletion of nonrenewable resources, and famine."[42] It was in this gloomy context that ecologist Garrett Hardin proposed his "lifeboat ethics: the case against helping the poor," whereby the weakest should be allowed to drown in order to save the rest.[43]

Less famously, perhaps, in 1963 the state of Maharashtra in the west of India passed a law called "The Maharashtra Deletion of the Term 'Famine' Act," which removed all references to "famine" in statutes referring to public relief. The relevant sections read:

> Whereas the agricultural situation in the State is constantly watched by the State Government, and relief measures as warranted by the situation are provided as soon as signs of scarcity conditions are apparent, so that there is no scope for famine conditions to develop:
>
> And whereas the term "famine" in the Bombay State Famine Relief Fund Act, 1958 and other laws on the subject in their application to the State has now become obsolete, and requires therefore to be deleted therefrom; It is hereby enacted in the Fourteenth Year of the Republic of India as follows.
>
> From the commencement of this Act, in all enactments relating to any of the matters enumerated in Lists II and III in the Seventh Schedule to the Constitution of India, in their application to the State of Maharashtra . . . , and in all instruments and other documents, the word "famine" shall be deemed to have been deleted.[44]

Less than a decade later, Maharashtra was struck by India's last famine (so far), in which "at very least" 70,000 people perished.[45] Bearing such caveats in mind, is there any point in peering ahead? Yes, insofar as studying the past helps us identify what makes famine more likely. And the recent history of famine suggests that we may

---

[41] Ehrlich 1968; Dando 1980; Paddock and Paddock 1967.

[42] Meadows, Randers, and Meadows 1972: 157. Compare Sauvy 1958; Pearce 2010.

[43] Hardin 1974; Ó Gráda 2009: 260–61.

[44] "The Maharashtra Deletion of the Term 'Famine' (Form Laws Applicable to the State) Act, 1963," http://bombayhighcourt.nic.in/libweb/acts/1963.40.html.

[45] Dyson and Maharatna 1992.

have reached the stage where famines—in peacetime—are history. If so, this is a noteworthy achievement for humankind. The reasons for this are not complex. The first is that increasing global incomes and food output make the problem more tractable. The second is the evolution of an informal, de facto global anti-famine contract, as reflected in the globalization of relief and the rapid responses to emerging crises.

But the caveat about peacetime conditions is crucial. Throughout history wars have caused or exacerbated famine, and the experience of World War II highlights the vulnerability of even relatively wealthy economies to total war. The claim that today famine is a serious threat only in places seriously threatened by war or self-imposed autarky claim finds corroboration in an annual list of countries requiring external food assistance compiled by the FAO. The list also provides the main reasons why aid is required. The FAO divides countries at risk into three categories: those facing exceptional shortfalls in aggregate production and supplies; those suffering "widespread lack of access"; and those faced by "severe localized food insecurity." In tables 5.2 and 5.3, which refer to predictions for 2009 and 2014 respectively, bold italics have been added to indicate reasons associated with human institutions rather than adverse weather or poor crops per se. The data imply that, more often than not, the main reasons given for food insecurity were civil conflict, poor governance, or the burden placed by HIV/AIDS. For added context, recent levels of the UN Human Development Index (HDI) and the total fertility rate (TFR) in the affected countries are also reported when available. A drawback of the data provided by the FAO is the lack of time frame for "the main reasons" given, but the broader point still surely holds.

New Variant Famine: A Receding Threat?

In 2003 famine specialist and human rights activist Alex de Waal and HIV/AIDS specialist Alan Whiteside published an influential and widely cited paper on what they termed "new variant famine" in which they proposed that the character of food crises in southern

TABLE 5.2. Countries in Crisis Likely to Require External Assistance, 2009

Nature of Food Insecurity	Main Reasons	HDI Ranking 2009	TFR 2009
Exceptional Shortfall in Aggregate Food Production or Supplies			
Kenya	Adverse weather, *lingering effects of civil strife*	144	4.56
Lesotho	Low productivity, HIV/AIDS pandemic	155	3.06
Somalia	*Conflict*, economic crisis, adverse weather	—	6.04
Swaziland	Low productivity, HIV/AIDS pandemic	141	3.45
Zimbabwe	*Problems of economic transition*	—	3.19
Iraq	*Conflict* and inadequate rainfall	—	4.26
Widespread Lack of Access			
Eritrea	Adverse weather, *IDPs, economic constraints*	164	4.72
Liberia	*War-related damage*	176	6.77
Mauritania	Several years of drought	140	4.37
Sierra Leone	*War-related damage*	179	5.00
Afghanistan	*Conflict and insecurity*, inadequate rainfall	181	7.07
Democratic People's Republic of Korea	*Economic constraints*	—	1.85
Severe Localized Food Insecurity			
Burundi	*Civil strife, IDPs, and returnees*	174	6.80
Central African Republic	*Refugees, insecurity in parts*	179	4.58
Chad	*Refugees, conflict*	175	5.31
Congo	*IDPs*	136	4.49
Côte d'Ivoire	*Conflict, related damage*	163	4.46
Democratic Republic of the Congo	*Civil strife, returnees*	176	6.20
Ethiopia	Adverse Weather, *insecurity in parts*	171	6.12
Guinea	*Refugees, conflicted related damage*	170	5.20
Guinea-Bissau	*Localized insecurity*	173	4.65
Sudan	*Civil strife (Darfur), insecurity (southern Sudan)*, localized crop failure	150	4.23
Uganda	Localized crop failure, *insecurity*	157	6.77
Bangladesh	Cyclones	146	2.74
Iran	Past drought	88	2.04
Myanmar	Past cyclone	138	2.07
Nepal	Poor market access and drought	144	2.64
Pakistan	*Conflict*	141	3.52
Sri Lanka	*Conflict, IDPs*	102	1.99
Timor-Leste	*IDPs*	162	6.53

Sources: http://www.fao.org/docrep/012/ai484e/ai484e02.htm; UN Human Development Index (HDI) from UNDP (*Human Development Report 2009*); total fertility rate from CIA (*World Factbook*).

TABLE 5.3. Countries in Crisis Likely to Require External Assistance, 2014

Nature of Food Insecurity	Main Reasons	HDI Ranking 2012	TFR 2014
	Exceptional Shortfall in Aggregate Food Production or Supplies		
Central African Republic	Crop production down due to "*prevailing civil insecurity*"	180	4.46
Zimbabwe	Tight maize supplies in 2014, following poor harvest, particularly in the south and west	172	3.56
Iraq	*Severe civil insecurity*	131	3.41
Syria	*Civil conflict*	116	2.68
	Widespread Lack of Access		
Burkina Faso	Extra pressure on local food supplies due to *large influx of refugees from Mali*	183	5.93
Chad	Additional pressure on local food supply due to *influx of refugees from Darfur, CAR, Nigeria*	184	4.68
Djibouti	Drought	164	2.47
Eritrea	Vulnerability to food insecurity due to *economic constraints*	181	4.14
Guinea	Assistance still needed to overcome effects of several years of high food prices and *general inflation*	179	4.93
Liberia	Slow recovery from *war related damages, refugees*	174	4.81
Malawi	Continuing increases in the price of maize and localized production shortfalls	170	5.66
Mali	*Insecurity and large population displacement* worsening already precarious food security situation	182	6.16
Mauritania	More than 67,000 Malian *refugees* registered in southeast	155	4.07
Niger	Successive severe food crises, below-average crop in 2013	186	6.89

Country	Description	HDI	Fertility
Sierra Leone	Lingering effects of several years of high food prices	177	4.83
Democratic People's Republic of Korea	*Food system in the DPRK remains highly vulnerable to shocks, and serious shortages exist*	188	
Yemen	*High levels of prolonged conflict, poverty, and high food and fuel prices*	160	4.09
Severe Localized Food Insecurity			
Cameroon	Climatic shocks, *returnees*	150	4.82
Congo	*Partly product of floods and explosion in capital in 2012*	142	4.73
Côte d'Ivoire	*Conflict, related damage*	168	3.63
Democratic Republic of the Congo	*Worst hit are conflict-affected Maniema, Oriental, and Katanga provinces*	186	4.80
Ethiopia	Assistance needed despite good harvest	173	5.23
Lesotho	Food security conditions remain stable, but assistance required April 2014	158	2.78
Madagascar	Impact of the locust plague and Cyclone Haruna	151	4.28
Mozambique	Overall satisfactory food security situation, but high prices continue to constrain food access	185	5.27
Senegal	2013 production 8% below average	154	4.52
Somalia	*IDPs*	193	6.08
South Sudan	*Following conflict*	194	5.43
Sudan	*IDPs in conflict-affected areas*	171	3.92
Uganda	Following two years of below-average crops	161	5.97
Afghanistan	*Conflict*	175	5.43
Kyrgyzstan	Lack of purchasing power; *socio-political tensions*	125	2.68
Philippines	Typhoons	114	3.06

Sources: http://www.fao.org/docrep/012/ai484e/ai484e02.htm; UN Human Development Index (HDI) from UNDP (Human Development Report 2012); total fertility rate from CIA (*World Factbook*).

Africa had recently been altered by the HIV/AIDS epidemic. In the future, they argued, new variant famines (NVFs) would be the product of the interaction between HIV infection, vulnerability to infectious disease, and malnutrition. De Waal and Whiteside proposed that NVFs would yield a new "Swiss cheese" pattern of vulnerability whereby susceptibility would turn on the incidence of the disease rather than on geography, with AIDS-affected households being less able to cope.[46] The presumption that HIV/AIDS would reduce agricultural productivity and increase food insecurity receives qualified support in two recent studies of Zambia by Nicole Mason et al. and by Antony Chapoto and T. S. Jayne, but a third Zambian study by Toman Omar Mahmoud and Rainer Thiele sounds a more skeptical note.[47]

In 2009 Scott Naysmith, de Waal, and Whiteside[48] tested the NVF hypothesis against conditions in Swaziland (population 1.2 million), which had as of 2012[49] the highest incidence of HIV/AIDS in the world. There is no denying the human cost of HIV/AIDS in Swaziland: according to the United Nations Development Programme (UNDP) data, the average lifespan of Swazis dropped from 56.8 years in 2000 to 48.7 years in 2011, and this drop is entirely attributable to HIV/AIDS.[50] Still, evidence that during this period HIV/AIDS was making Swazis more vulnerable to famine is lacking: for instance, the percentage of children who were seriously malnourished dropped during the 2000s. And even in Swaziland there are some grounds for hope: recent surveys of HIV incidence suggest that the epidemic may have begun to stabilize. The results of the Swaziland HIV Incidence Measurement Survey, released in 2012, revealed that the HIV prevalence among 20–24-year-old males fell from 28 to 21 per cent between 2007 and 2011, whereas the rate among women of the same age fell marginally from 49 to 47 percent.[51]

[46] De Waal and Whiteside 2003; see also Arrehag, de Waal, and Whiteside 2006.

[47] Mason et al. 2010; Chapoto and Jayne 2008; Omar Mahmoud and Thiele 2010.

[48] Naysmith, de Waal, and Whiteside 2009.

[49] UNAIDS Global Report 2013: A8 (http://www.unaids.org/en/media/unaids/contentassets /documents/epidemiology/2013/gr2013/unaids_global_report_2013_en.pdf).

[50] United Nations Development Programme, *Human Development Reports*, 1993 and 2011 (hdr.undp.org/).

[51] Swaziland HIV Incidence Measurement Survey (SHIMS), November 2012, https://www .k4health.org/sites/default/files/SHIMS_Report.pdf, 28.

The broader story about HIV/AIDS, like that about famine, is a mildly encouraging one, and one certainly not anticipated, say, a decade ago. According to the UNAIDS 2010 *Report on the Global Aids Epidemic*, fewer people worldwide were being infected with HIV and fewer people were dying from AIDS than previously. In recent years, as the proportion of the population infected has begun to fall in nearly all of the worst affected countries,[52] the risk posed by NVFs is also surely reduced. Is it too much to hope that we will never witness a New Variant Famine?

The Changing Role of NGOs

The food crisis in Niger was one of the major news stories of the summer of 2005. Just two days after Hilary Andersson's report from Zinder province on BBC1's nine o'clock news on 20 July 2005, John O'Shea, founder and former CEO of the Irish charity GOAL, predicted that "we are going to lose many, many thousands of lives." On the same day a United Nations spokesman castigated the international community for its slow response to the crisis; later he would declare that more donations had been received in the week following Andersson's broadcast from Zinder than during the previous six months. The same broadcast prompted O'Shea's boast that GOAL had "fed more people in its first week in Niger than the UN had this year."[53]

Even more than in the case of Malawi, apocalyptic accounts of the disaster in Niger followed. There were reports of rocketing prices, poor harvests, severe drought, and locust infestations. Estimates of 3.5 million people at imminent risk of starvation—almost invariably including 0.8 million children—were much recycled. According to Oxfam's regional director in West Africa, "families [were] feeding their children grass and leaves from the trees to keep them alive." After a briefing from MSF, Hilary Andersson reported from Zinder province, the epicenter of the crisis, on 15 September: "This is the

---

[52] UNAIDS, "Know your Epidemic," http://www.unaids.org/en/media/unaids/contentassets /documents/epidemiology/2012/gr2012/20121120_UNAIDS_Global_Report_2012_with _annexes_en.pdf; http://apps.who.int/gho/data/?vid=360.

[53] "UN Denies Inaction on Food Crisis in Niger," *Irish Times*, 15 August 2005.

only part of Niger where anyone has even tried to estimate how many people have starved to death. And the indications are that just in this town [Mirriah in Zinder province] and the villages immediately surrounding it, thousands of people have died in the last few months."[54]

Whether the Niger crisis of 2005 was really a "famine" became a controversial issue at several levels. For famine demographers the issue revolved around the appropriate definition of famine. For NGOs it reflected tensions between those interested in development aid and those focusing on emergency relief, with "the former commonly charging the latter with mobilizing disproportionate resources in a counterproductive way unable to address the deep-seated causes of primarily chronic crises."[55] In Niger the main protagonists were MSF and the World Food Programme (WFP). A key grievance concerned whether a highly emotive but effective famine warning signal was being used inappropriately: the Irish aid agency Concern Worldwide, for example, chose not to use the description "famine" at all. In Niger itself, the context was primarily political. President Mamadou Tandja was allergic to the word "famine" and "[flew] into a rage whenever it [was] used"; his denials prompted opposition leader Mahamadou Issoufou to ask whether "the head of state had a stone instead of a heart."[56] An added concern was whether the resultant inflow of food hurt competing local food producers, and thereby risked generating dependence on aid.

The controversy surrounding Niger in 2005 prompted Esther Garvi, a Norwegian activist based in Niger, to complain:

> As long as major institutions within the aid industry can continue to take credit for saving people from catastrophes that have never taken place, casting blame on those who say otherwise (often the local governments), the poor will be even poorer, as hasty relief campaigns built on untruthful events leave people and societies in lesser-known parts of the world worse off than before the intervention.

[54] The original BBC clip is no longer available, but the quote is available at http://esther garvi.com/2008/11/27/swedish-television-criticizes-bbc-niger-2005-report/.

[55] Crombé 2009: 59.

[56] Gazibo 2009: 39, 45.

There is something gone badly wrong when the world of aid—born out of a desire to help—has become an industry that in its desire for monetary growth is willing to tamper with the truth, not caring for the dignity and independence of the people whom they claim to assist.[57]

And the problem persists, with the result that sometimes it is hard to know whom to believe. In July 2011, Abdiweli Mohamed Ali, prime minister of Somalia, accused the al-Shahaab militia of "keeping out international aid workers despite a worsening famine."[58] At that time the UN had just declared a famine in two southern regions of Somalia. However, by mid-December in Ali's view the aid agencies had become an "entrenched interest group" who exaggerated suffering in order to increase donations. In his critique of NGOs Ali, who had been educated by George Mason University's libertarian economics department, even referred approvingly to Graham Hancock's controversial, fiercely anti-NGO *Lords of Poverty* (1989).[59]

The receding threat of major famine is well reflected in the changing character of international NGOs that owed their initial *raison d'être* to famines. Indeed, the history of disaster relief agencies tells us something about the incidence and changing intensity of famines. In Ireland the link between famines and such charities has been very close. Very soon after the publication of her classic *The Great Hunger* in 1962, Cecil Woodham-Smith obliged Muintir Mhuigheo (the County Mayo Association) by giving a lecture on behalf of the Irish Freedom from Hunger Campaign. During the sesquicentennial commemorations of the mid-1990s Irish aid agencies repeatedly linked their activities to the Great Famine, and popularized the notion of a particular Irish collective memory of famine. A century and a half earlier the Great Famine itself also prompted the creation of ad hoc bodies to relieve the poor, such as the Society of Friends Cen-

---

[57] Esther Garvi, "Inventing Famines" (http://www.esthergarvi.org/2009/11/20/inventing-famines/). The problem is not new: see Nathan 1965: 18.

[58] Somalia Central Government Condemns Militants' Famine Denial," *Voice of America*, 22 July 2011 (http://www.voanews.com/content/somalia-central-government-condemns-militants-famine-denial-126057038/142678.html).

[59] "We Have No Famine, Says Somali Prime Minister," *Daily Telegraph*, 13 December 2011. Hancock's tract was one of a series of right-wing anti–foreign aid tracts stretching from Peter Bauer's *Dissent on Development* (1972) through Michael Maren's *The Road to Hell* (2002) to Dambisa Moyo's *Dead Aid* (2009).

tral Relief Committee and the British Association for the Relief of
the Extreme Distress in Ireland and Scotland. But the Central Relief
Committee was wound up in 1852, and the British Association
closed its books in late 1848. Similarly, the Dublin Mansion House
Relief Committee, created to relieve distress in January 1880, was
disbanded in December of that year, in the wake of a relatively bountiful harvest.

Like those earlier organizations, the Irish development NGOs
Concern Worldwide and Trócaire owe their origins to famine. Concern Worldwide, Ireland's biggest development NGO, originated as
Africa Concern in response to a famine in the secessionist Nigerian
province of Biafra in the late 1960s. Trócaire, founded by the Irish
Catholic hierarchy in March 1973 to collect money for use in "the
areas of greatest need among the developing countries," took some
of its inspiration from the response to a special collection organized
by the Catholic Church in aid of famine victims in Bangladesh in
1972.[60]

Concern and Trócaire, unlike their nineteenth-century predecessors, are still with us. In 1970 Africa Concern became involved in relieving cyclone victims in Bangladesh, whereupon it changed its
name to Concern (now known as Concern Worldwide). For two decades or so it was identified primarily with emergency disaster relief,
notably, in the mid-1980s, in Ethiopia. But it is now nearly two decades since Concern's first strategic plan conceded in 1998 that famines were likely to be a thing of the past. And it must be said that, in
Ireland as elsewhere, there has always been a contradiction between
charities as disaster relief agencies relying on private charity in times
of emergency and NGOs as "institutions" or bureaucracies. Indeed,
that tension has also existed within NGOs. David Begg, who took
over as chief executive of Concern in July 1997, described the competing camps as "trads" and "mods." The chosen mission of the
"trads" was relief in emergency situations, while the "mods" were
more focused on the need to get people to help themselves. Whereas

[60] From the outset Trócaire had a dual function, however: humanitarian disaster relief and
"medium and long-term development programmes aimed at tackling the causes of underde-
velopment rather than treating the symptoms" ("L132,000 Trocaire Aid for 24 Projects," *Irish
Times*, 10 October 1974; see also "Hierarchy Stresses Third World Needs," *Irish Times*, 5 March
1973).

the "mods" were beginning to see aid as "tinkering" and to argue for advocacy and political change, the "trads" were less ambitious, convinced that saving or improving the lives of the poorest of the poor here and now was a gain. The "trads" could be politically naïve and, indeed, in Ethiopia in the mid-1980s and in Rwanda in the mid-1990s they were accused[61] of unwittingly sustaining tyrannical regimes—a charge they vehemently denied.[62]

The shift in the character of such NGOs was not limited to Ireland. In Great Britain too, the main aid-related NGOs began as responses to specific events. In 1921–23 Save the Children shifted its focus to famine relief in Russia, where it played an important and prominent role. It then became a permanent organization devoted to assisting children whenever they are "menaced by conditions of economic hardship and distress." Oxfam began life 1942 as the Oxford Committee for Famine Relief, an ad hoc group created to relieve famine in wartime Greece; it hired its first employee in 1949 to run its first gift shop. Great Britain's Save the Children Fund began in London in 1919 as an ad hoc effort at relieving starvation in Germany, still subject to a blockade during the armistice. CAFOD (the Catholic Agency for Overseas Development, an arm of the Catholic Church in England and Wales) also began life as an ad hoc body: its sole focus was a fast day organized by English Catholics in aid of a mother-and-child clinic in Dominica.

Further afield, an American Save the Children, modeled on its British namesake, was established during the Great Depression to help children in Appalachia: today Save the Children Federation Inc. is a major international organization with an annual budget of over $600 million. MSF, like Concern, has its origins in the famine caused by the Nigerian civil war of the late 1960s. It was founded by a group of French doctors led by Bernard Kouchner as a protest against what they deemed Red Cross complicity in atrocities committed by the Nigerian army against Biafran secessionists.

So how did the diminishing frequency and intensity of famine affect the NGOs? A glance at the annual financial statements of the leading Irish NGOs shows that private funds associated with disaster

[61] David Rieff, "Dangerous Pity," *Prospect*, July 2005, 112.
[62] Farmar 2002: 202–3.

relief come in unpredictable fits and starts: in the case of Concern, 1992 (Somalia), 1994 (Rwanda), and 2005 (Niger) stand out. But salaries and mobile phone bills must be paid week in, week out. This dilemma, of course, explains why charities such as Oxfam and Concern Worldwide have been transformed into development aid bureaucracies, heavily dependent on state funding. From the mid-1980s on, such charities faced a choice: either to disband at the end of their life cycle as famine relief agencies dependent on private philanthropy, or else to become corporate entities bent on survival by other means.

The switch to focusing on development was no panacea, because the public has always been more reluctant to contribute to campaigns supporting development than those supporting famine or disaster relief. That helps explain why the Irish agencies still spend a good deal of their income on what they call "emergencies" or "emergency and rehabilitation." And it explains why NGOs prefer regular fixed payments from a bank account to collecting with plastic buckets, since the former are more likely to yield a lasting dividend. Perhaps the recent history of famine also helps explain why agencies that become involved in a country for the first time during a crisis have been very slow to leave. The Irish aid agency GOAL entered Ethiopia in 1984, Malawi in 2002, and Niger in 2005, and never left.

The NGOs might have proved nonviable, and certainly they would be much smaller than they are, had they not in effect become semi-nationalized bureaucracies. All of Ireland's aid agencies began their existences as ad hoc groups or agencies dependent on private charity, but that is far from being the case today. Table 5.4 describes the evolution of funding of three Irish development NGOs between the 1990s and 2010s. It points to GOAL's greater reliance on the public purse, and suggests that Trócaire's efforts at maintaining a volunteering ethos have paid some dividends. By the 2010s Concern, the Goliath of Irish development NGOs, relied on government and international intergovernmental agencies for two-thirds of its income. Concern Worldwide, in its original form as Africa Concern, was born at the meeting of a small group of activists in a flat in an inner Dublin suburb in March 1968, and its first effort at fund-raising was a jumble sale; today, it handles a budget of over $200 million and its

TABLE 5.4. Revenue Sources of Three Irish Development Agencies (€1,000; percentages in parentheses)

Goal	2012	2011	2008	2007	1996	1995
Voluntary	2,999 (5)	7,229 (12)	10,942 (16)	11,614 (20)	1,686 (24)	1,386 (20)
Government	50,839(84)	48,952 (80)	38,426 (58)	35,984 (61)	5,083 (73)	5,173 (76)
In kind	5,421 (9)	3,046 (5)	14,185 (21)	7,611 (13)	—	—
Other	1220 (2)	1800 (3)	3,013 (4)	3,427 (6)	213 (3)	280 (4)
Total	60,479	61,027	66,566	58,636	6,982	6,839

Trócaire	2013	2012	2007	2006	1995	1994
Voluntary	25,311 (42)	34,794 (52)	31,702 (44)	26,481 (54)	5,731 (47)	13.283 (77)
Government	34,031 (56)	30,943 (46)	38,977 (54)	21,777 (44)	5,699(47)	3.413 (20)
Other	931 (2)	1,222 (2)	1,415 (2)	1,138 (2)	666 (5)	538 (3)
Total	60,273	66,965	72,129	49,396	12,098	17,234

Concern	2012	2011	2003	2002	1992	1991
Voluntary	41,765 (29)	50,377 (32)	42,215 (43)	38,324 (51)	16,434 (45)	7,368 (22)
Government	93,807 (66)	104,007 (65)	31,762 (32)	29,426 (39)	9,830 (27)	11,686 (35)
In kind	7,190 (5)	5,444 (3)	23,973 (24)	8,136 (11)	9,048 (25)	13,800 (41)
Other	662 (0)	403 (0)	—	—	860 (2)	440 (1)
Total	143,424	160,231	98,828	74,700	36,172	33,294

Source: Annual reports.

focus has shifted radically in a developmental and global direction. Concern is just one example of a more general pattern, whereby ad hoc, local charities are transformed into bureaucracies bent on self-preservation and expansion. The gradual shift from idealistic volunteers "shaking tins in pubs and workplaces and on street corners"[63] to paid collectors[64] and corporate offices characterized these organizations' survival strategy.

Across the Irish Sea, in the financial year ended 31 March 2012 only £377 million of Oxfam's £918 million revenue came from fundraising in the community; £345 million came from state institutions. CAFOD, perhaps, has remained truest to its origins in terms of ethos:

[63] Gill 2010: 180.

[64] Compare "Call for Tighter Regulations to Curtail Rise of 'Chuggers,'" *Irish Examiner*, 24 February 2012; "Chuggers, Chuggers Everywhere: Is Street Fundraising Crossing the Line?" *thejournal.ie*, 6 October 2013 (http://www.thejournal.ie/readme/huggers-chuggers-everywhere---is-street-fundraising-crossing-the-line-1107864-Oct2013/). A "chugger" is a street fundraiser who approaches passers-by soliciting donations for a charity.

in the financial year 2010/11 two-thirds of its receipts of £56 million came from supporters, the remaining third mostly from government. In the United States about two-fifths of Save the Children's revenue in 2012 and 2013 came from the government, while less than half came from contributions and private grants.[65]

The historical decline of famine has also coincided with NGOs becoming important vehicles for the distribution of state aid. Today well over one-quarter of Irish foreign aid is dispensed through NGOs. This raises further questions: has the ready availability of state funding compromised the activism and idealism of NGOs? Has it dented or crowded out the private charity that used to be their wellspring? If not, has it influenced their direction and energies? Have the links between the NGOs and government become too close for comfort? For the public to continue believing that the NGOs are on the side of the angels requires clear commitments to transparency and efficiency on the part of the NGOs.

Finally, international NGOs have a double reason for highlighting the risks of excess mortality during food crises. Firstly, their warnings act as a spur to action on the part of international agencies such as the UN and the WFP. Secondly, crises prompt a generous response from private donors. Understandably, in the past this has sometimes prompted NGOs to exploit particular crises as vehicles for funding broader, unrelated ventures. Thus in 1997 Trócaire used the high-profile crisis in North Korea—where it had no presence but claimed "direct access" through the Catholic-run Caritas Network—as a means of generating revenues towards "Trócaire's fight against famine in North *and throughout Asia*" (emphasis added). In 2002 GOAL used the crisis in southern Africa to solicit funds for its work in Angola, Malawi, the Democratic Republic of the Congo, Ethiopia, and Sudan. And again during Lent 2003 Trócaire invoked the receding crisis in southern Africa in its church-gate appeals for support towards its broader mission.[66]

[65] Save the Children Consolidated Financial Statements, 31 December 2013 (http://www.savethechildren.org/atf/cf/%7B9def2ebe-10ae-432c-9bd0-df91d2eba74a%7D/SAVE-THE-CHILDREN-AUDITED-FINANCIALS-2013.PDF).

[66] "When Famine Stalked the West," *Irish Times*, 7 June 1997; "Africa Is in Crisis" (GOAL advertisement), *Irish Times*, 31 July 2002; "Crisis in Africa: Church Collections for Africa" (Trocaire advertisement), *Irish Times*, 1 February 2003.

Popular understanding of famine nowadays depends very much on images relayed by the media and by aid agencies. That poses its own problems, not least that first-world journalists are not good at distinguishing between ordinary, everyday misery and famine. Another danger is what human rights expert David Rieff dubs "disaster hype": exaggerating the danger and the incidence of famine. Alex de Waal has claimed that in Africa people "never, never die in the numbers predicted by the aid agencies."[67]

The distinction between malnutrition as a steady state and famine as a crisis is important for another reason, mentioned earlier in connection with Malawi after 2002. Food aid in a crisis situation may avert famine; granted continuously in "normal" times, it may simply injure or destroy an already vulnerable domestic agricultural sector. Thus the U.S. Agency for International Development (USAID) dispensed "Food for Peace" to as many as 53 low-income countries under its Title II program during the fiscal year 2010. This program, nowadays the main vehicle of American food aid and implemented mostly by the WFP with some help from NGOs, is geared towards addressing "emergency needs and for developmental programs that reduce vulnerability to crises and improve the nutrition and food security of poor, malnourished populations." Recent research on one of the countries included in USAID's Title II list, Ethiopia, suggests that in that case cash funding that would encourage or even, for a time, subsidize domestic food production would be preferable to in-kind food transfers.[68]

Meanwhile, Back in Pyongyang

Another prominent recent example of politically charged debate on a famine's demographic toll is the Democratic People's Republic of Korea (North Korea) since the mid-1990s. Nobody doubts that

---

[67] As cited in Rieff 1997; see also Rieff 2011.

[68] US FoodAid website (http://foodaid.org/food-aid-programs/food-for-peace/). On evidence from Ethiopia, compare Levinsohn and McMillan 2007; Gelan 2007. See also Laura Freschi, "US Food Aid Policies Create 561 Jobs in Kansas, Risk Millions of Lives around the World," http://aidwatchers.com/2010/06/us-food-aid-creates/, 24 June 2010.

North Korea faced a severe crisis at the time—dubbed a "famine in slow motion" by the World Food Programme. Hard data are lacking;[69] nonetheless, an estimate of three million deaths gained widespread credence and traction. It underpins the 1999 analysis of the North Korean economy by U.S.-based Marcus Noland, Sherman Robinson, and Tao Tang:

> As well as can be ascertained, North Korea is ... experiencing a famine of unknown severity. US Congressional staffers who visited the country concluded that from 1995 to 1998 between 900,000 and 2.4 million people had died from starvation or hunger-related illnesses with deaths peaking in 1997.... Non-governmental organizations, extrapolating from interviews with refugees in China and observations on the ground, have produced estimates of famine-related deaths on the order of 2.8–3.5 million.... [T]he number of delegates at the 1998 Supreme People's Assembly implied a mid-1998 population more than three million fewer than demographic projections made on the basis of the 1989 census. If these estimates are accurate, they imply that a double-digit share of the pre-crisis population of roughly 22 million has succumbed.[70]

The figure of three million was given a wider currency by Jasper Becker in *Rogue Regime: Kim Jong Il and the Looming Threat of North Korea* (2005), even though UN officials were highly skeptical of that number from the outset, and the scholarly case for a much lower estimate of "600,000 to 1 million people" had already been made by Daniel Goodkind and Lorraine West three years earlier. Becker's numerical "sputnik," a toll of three million out of a population of about 22 million, entailed "more victims than in Pol Pot's Cambodia," or indeed "in proportion to the country ... any comparable disaster in the twentieth century"; perhaps that is why he clung to it.[71] In a

---

[69] Compare Philippe Pons, "Un demi-million de Coréens du Nord seraient menacés de famine," *Le Monde*, 15 December 1995; Philippe Pons, "La Corée du Nord vit a l'heure de la famine 'au ralenti' et du marché noir," *Le Monde*, 21 May 1997; Yves Mamou, "La Corée du Nord souffre d'une famine aujourd'hui structurelle," *Le Monde*, 14 October 1997.

[70] Noland, Robinson, and Tang 1999.

[71] Becker 2005: 211–12; see also Joshua Kurlantzick, "Rogue Regime: A Marxist Sun King," *New York Times*, 7 August 2005. In fact the estimated death toll in Cambodia—1.5–2.5 million out of 8 million—was proportionately higher. See Heuveline 1998.

2007 study coauthored with Stephen Haggard, Noland worked with Goodkind and West's lower figure of 0.6 million to 1 million.[72] However, a further downward revision by Goodkind, West, and Johnson in 2011 caused Noland to blog:

> So why does it matter? Perhaps this paper does not quite measure up to Nick Eberstadt's initial characterization "oops, I guess you and Haggard will have to re-write that book on the famine ... oops, I guess you'll have to re-write that refugee book .." But if you took some of the figures in this paper seriously, including one estimate of famine deaths of 330,000, the analysis would suggest that collectively we way overestimated the magnitude of the North Korean famine.
>
> This reconsideration would quite naturally inform our views of the severity of the current situation—if we were that wrong about the past, then could we be once again making the same mistake?[73]

But it doesn't end there. A recent reappraisal of demographic trends in North Korea in the 1990s by Thomas Spoorenberg and Daniel Schwekendiek (2012) proposes an even lower estimate of excess famine mortality—between 240,000 and 420,000.[74] Spreading the average of this range over a five-year period would imply an annual excess death rate of about 3 per 1,000 or 1.5 percent in toto. This is about one-tenth of the apocalyptic three million given wide currency by Becker and initially by Noland and his coauthors.

Spoorenberg and Schwekendiek note that "while the new estimates proposed here indicate a substantially lower number of deaths, they still point to a high number of deaths that could have been avoided."[75] Another key feature of their analysis is that there were more deaths in the wake of the famine than during the famine itself. In other words, North Korea has been suffering the effects of a slow-burning but intense economic crisis since the mid-1990s.

---

[72] Haggard and Noland 2007; Goodkind and West 2001; Goodkind, West, and Johnson 2011.

[73] http://www.piie.com/blogs/nk/?p=2871.

[74] Spoorenberg and Schwekendiek (2012) prompted another blog from Noland: http://www.piie.com/blogs/nk/?p=5587.

[75] Spoorenberg and Schwekendiek 2012: 154.

Table 5.5. Weight-for-Age (0–5 Years) in North and South Korea and a Range of Developing Countries

Percentages >3SDs below median					
North Korea		South Korea		Cuba	
1987	3	2009	0.0	1990	13
1997	14			2000	8
2002	6–7			2011	6
2009	3.9				
India		Bangladesh		Afghanistan	
1992/3	24.3 (0–4)	1991	26.8 [Rural]	2004	12.2 (0.5–5)
1998/9	20.0 (0–4)	1999	14.4		
2005/6	17.4	2004	14.1		
		2007	12.1		
Niger		Swaziland		Ethiopia	
1992	18.0	2000	3.1	2000	17.5
2000	16.1	2006/7	1.5	2005	13.7
2006	16.5	2008	1.1	2010/11	9.5

Sources: http://www.who.int/nutgrowthdb/database/countries/en/index.html#I; Schweken-diek 2011: 60.

Spoorenberg and Schwekendiek's understated criticism carries more conviction than the loaded claims of Becker or Noland.

What of measures of malnutrition in North Korea? Schwekendiek reckons that about 3 percent of North Korean children were "severely underweight" (i.e., their weight-for-age was three standard deviations below the UN reference population) in 1987. By 1997 that percentage had jumped to 14 percent, but it had fallen back to 6–7 percent by 2002.[76] And a 2009 survey conducted by the Central Bureau of Statistics of North Korea with UNICEF support found that "19 percent of children under age five were moderately underweight and 4 percent were severely underweight . . . [and] that 32 percent of children are moderately stunted, or too short for their age, and 5 percent are moderately wasted, or too thin for their age."[77] Even

---

[76] Schwekendiek 2011: 59–61.

[77] Immigration and Refugee Board of Canada, *Democratic People's Republic of Korea: Starva-*

TABLE 5.6. Child Mortality Rates in North Korea and Selected
Developing Countries c. 1990–2012 *(per 1,000)*

Year	North Korea	India	Bangladesh
1900	44	126	144
2000	60	92	88
2011	29	56	41
	Mongolia	*Bangladesh*	*Cambodia*
1990	107	144	116
2000	63	88	111
2011	28	41	40
	Afghanistan	*Egypt*	*Somalia*
1990	176	86	177
2000	134	45	171
2011	99	21	147
	Swaziland	*Mozambique*	*Cuba*
1990	71	233	13
2000	121	166	8
2011	80	90	6

Source: http://www.childinfo.org/files/Child_Mortality_Report_2013.pdf.

these depressing data may not tell the whole truth, but a comparative perspective is always useful, and so table 5.5 presents World Health Organization data on child malnutrition for a selection of countries (based on WHO child growth standards). By this reckoning the situation in North Korea in the mid-1990s was certainly worrying, but hardly more worrying than that obtaining in India or in Bangladesh in the early 2010s. Child mortality data tell a similar story (table 5.6).

Figure 5.1, based on FAO data, offers another perspective on North Korea. It suggests that since the early 1990s the malnourished proportion of North Korea's population has failed to fall, whereas in three other impoverished countries—Niger, Bangladesh, and Malawi—the malnourished share changed from being higher than

tion and Malnutrition, Including Periods of Food Shortages from 1990 to 2012, 19 July 2012, PRK104137.E, http://www.unhcr.org/ref/docid/507566232.html.

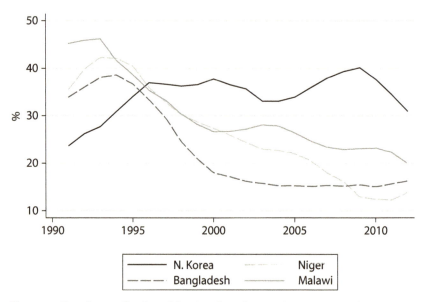

Figure 5.1 Prevalence of malnutrition in selected countries, 1991–2012 (3-year average). Source: FAO (http://faostat3.fao.org/faostat-gateway/go/to/browse/D/FS/E).

North Korea's in the early 1990s to considerably lower in the early 2010s. Again, these data are more easily squared with a chronically underperforming economy than one subject to a one-off shock like a famine.[78]

What does the controversy about North Korean numbers tell us? First, it serves as a warning against highly charged analyses that employ phantom famine deaths in a campaign for "regime change."[79] Second, it may tell us something about the resilience of the masses even in a brutal political climate such as that in the People's Democratic Republic of Korea. The history of famines, after all, is also a history of poor people trying to cope in adverse circumstances. Third, part of the answer is relief: between 1996 and 2004 North

[78] Compare Valérie Brunschwig, "Polémique sur l'étendue de la famine en Corée du Nord," *Le Monde*, 2 October 1998.

[79] Noland (2004) "quantitatively analyze[d] the probability of regime change and examines the character of possible successor regimes" (http://books.google.ie/books/about/Korea_After_Kim_Jong_Il.html?id=4pu0AAAAIAAJ&redir_esc=y).

Korea received about 7.5 million metric tons of food in humanitarian assistance. The food aid was significant: enough to provide every man, woman, and child in North Korea over 300 kcal daily for ten years.[80]

Concluding Comments

In accounting for hunger-related deaths, it is important to distinguish the extraordinary from the ordinary. For decades now, steady-state non-famine malnutrition has been responsible for far more deaths and much more damage to physical and cognitive development than the extraordinary deaths from famine. While the FAO reckons that the number of malnourished people in the world has hardly fallen—an estimated 880 million in 1970, 842 million in 2011–13—the malnourished *share* of the developing world's population has dropped quite dramatically from 37 percent in 1970 to 20 percent in 1990 and 12 percent today. The World Bank likes to highlight how "3 million fewer under-5 children died from diseases such as diarrhea, malnutrition, pneumonia, AIDS, malaria, and tuberculosis in 2006 than in 1990."[81] In 2011 David Lam sounded a reassuring note, pointing out that all the doomsday warnings of the 1960s and 1970s had proven incorrect, and that global food output expanded faster than population in every decade between the 1960s and the 2000s.[82]

How fragile are these gains? On the one hand, the virtual doubling of grain prices in 2008 did not lead to famine—or indeed a significant increase in the death rate (at least as reflected in the *UN Demographic Yearbook*)—anywhere in the world in 2008–9. On the other, it increased the number of malnourished people worldwide by about 100 million to about one billion, and led to widespread riots and unrest.[83]

---

[80] Haggard and Noland 2005: 32. The calculation assumes that an ounce of food was worth 100 kcal.

[81] World Bank 2014.

[82] Lam 2011.

[83] Schneider 2008.

Moreover, forecasts of future food output are unreliable and conflicting. In 1996 demographer Tim Dyson ended a careful analysis on the struggle between population and food on a rather optimistic note:

> We find the pessimistic neo-Malthusian view seriously wanting; several of its fundamental claims are demonstrably unsound.... There is fair reason to expect that in the year 2020 world agriculture will be feeding the larger global population no worse—and probably a little better—than it manages to do today. This all adds up to tempered hope.[84]

Dyson's focus then was on the period up to 2020, and within that time-horizon he found it hard to foresee "drought, by itself, causing famine ... unless the global climate really does go awry during the period to 2020." Less than a decade later Dyson was taking a longer view, sounding a much more pessimistic note and worrying in particular about the dangers of "an abrupt change in climate" at some point in the present century.[85]

Recent analyses of climate change leave no room for doubt about the severity of the threat posed by global warming in the medium term. The contours of warming may be rather imprecise and unpredictable, but the extreme vulnerability to higher temperatures of certain "climate hotspots" such as the Sahel, where malnutrition already kills over 0.2 million children annually, is clear.[86] Given the likely cost of alternative strategies for sustaining human life in such areas—it has been reckoned that to pump water one hundred kilometers uphill from a tributary of the Congo River to the Chari River in the Central African Republic and then on to Lake Chad would cost $14.5 billion[87]—large-scale migration to "cooler" and more adaptable regions may be both the most humane and cost-effective—if not, to some, the most politically appealing—solution to environmental degradation.[88]

[84] Dyson 1996: 201, 208.

[85] Dyson 2005.

[86] Boko et al. 2007; *The Economist* 2010; Barnett and Webber 2010.

[87] Chimtom 2013. That sum is about one-third of the combined GDPs of Chad, Niger, and Burkina Faso.

[88] Compare International Organization for Migration 2012.

Some economists highlight evidence of the ability of communities in the past to adapt to climate change. Economic historians Alan Olmstead and Paul Rhode draw mildly optimistic inferences from the capacity of nineteenth-century U.S. farmers and agricultural scientists to adapt to colder climates, as the cultivation of wheat spread further west:

> [T]he historical record does show that farmers were able to develop technologies to push crop production into areas previously thought unsuitable for agriculture because of the harsh climatic conditions. There is little reason to think that future technological advances and crop substitutions will not partially offset some of the problems created by global warming.[89]

And Richard Sutch, another skilled practitioner of what is sometimes called the "dismal science," has drawn similarly positive implications from how American farmers adapted to the challenge of temperature change in the 1930s:

> [F]armers (even those of rural America in the 1930s) are remarkably resilient and adaptive. Sudden and dramatic climate change induced a prompt and prudent response. An unexpected consequence was that an otherwise more gradual process of technological development and adoption was given a kick start by the drought and the farmers' response. That pushed the technology beyond a tipping point and propelled the major Corn Belt states to the universal adoption of hybrid corn by 1943. The country as a whole reached universal adoption by 1960. While this process was driven by individual farmers and privately owned seed companies, there was also a role played by the government.[90]

Technology's capacity to adapt to climate change must not be overlooked. Barreca et al. show how the spread of domestic air conditioning in the United States since the mid-twentieth century greatly reduced the impact of extremely hot weather on mortality. Yet the irony is that the same solution is available to poor countries

---

[89] Olmstead and Rhode 2011: 191; see also Olmstead and Rhode 2002.
[90] Sutch 2011: 220–21.

today only at the cost of an acceleration in the rate of climate change and attendant damage to agricultural productivity.[91] Other economists who have studied the link between climate and agriculture are much gloomier regarding the impact of climate change in the medium term. Relying again on evidence from the past, Dell, Jones, and Olken find that higher temperatures reduce economic growth in poor countries, and have and adverse impact on "agricultural output, industrial output, and political stability,"; Barrios, Ouattara, and Strobl claim that much of the growing gap in agricultural productivity since the 1960s between sub-Saharan Africa and the rest of the developing world is due to global warming; and Urban and his coauthors sound an equally bleak note regarding the impact of global warming on the future variability of maize yields in the United States.[92]

Finally, "making famine history" is not the same thing as "making hunger history." Amartya Sen famously claimed in the 1990s that eliminating famine (in the traditional meaning of the term) nowadays is "easy." He was right. In recent decades, much has also been achieved in alleviating hunger. But eliminating hunger is not at all as straightforward as the marketing agencies and street canvassers employed by some NGOs imply. In the past some development agencies had a tendency, understandable and well intentioned, to exaggerate the risk and dimensions of famine; today they risk a similar mistake by exaggerating the benefits of foreign aid and making conquering hunger seem "easy." The NGOs have the major advantage of being for the most part corruption-free, and they have a lot of experience. But their efforts are constrained by vested interests, by power politics, by geography, by poverty, by ignorance, by cynicism, and by false analysis. The goals we have set ourselves may not be unachievable, but we must not pretend that they are easier to achieve than they really are.

[91] For an interesting application, see Barreca et al. 2012.
[92] Dell, Jones, and Olken 2012; Barrios, Ouattara, and Strobl 2008; Urban et al 2012. See also Blanc and Strobl 2013.

Bibliography

Aker, Jenny C. 2010a. "Droughts, Grain Markets and Food Crisis in Niger." *Revue d'économie de développement* 24(1): 71–108.

———. 2010b. "Information from Markets Near and Far: The Impact of Mobile Phones on Grain Markets in Niger." *American Economic Journal: Applied Economics* 2: 46–69.

Alfani, Guido. 2011. "The Famine of the 1590s in Northern Italy: An Analysis of the Greatest 'System Shock' of Sixteenth Century." *Histoire et mésure* 26(1): 17–50.

———. 2013. *Calamities and the Economy in Renaissance Italy: The Grand Tour of the Horsemen of the Apocalypse*. London: Palgrave Macmillan.

Allen, Robert C. 2000. "Economic Structure and Agricultural Productivity in Europe." *European Review of Economic History* 4(1): 1–26.

Allen, Robert C., and Roman Studer. 2009. "Indian Wages and Prices 1595–1930." gpih.ucdavis.edu/files/India_Allen-Studer_v2,pl.xls.

Alogoskoufis, George, and Ron Smith. 1995. "On Error Correction Models: Specification, Interpretation, Estimation." In Les Oxley, Donald A.R. George, Colin J. Roberts, and Stuart Sayer, eds., *Surveys in Econometrics*, Oxford: Blackwell, pp. 139–70.

Alsop, Joseph. 1962. "China's Descending Spiral." *China Quarterly* 11: 21–37.

Amery, Leopold S. 1988. *The Empire at Bay: The Leo Amery Diaries, 1929–1945*, ed. J. Barnes and D. Nicholson. London: Hutchinson.

Araujo, Claudio, Catherine Araujo Bonjean, and Stéphanie Brunelin. 2012. "Alert at Maradi: Preventing Food Crises by Using Price Signals." *World Development* 40(9): 1882–94.

Araujo Bonjean, Catherine, and Catherine Simonet. 2014. "Are Grain Markets in Niger Driven by Speculation?" http://www.imf.org/external/np/seminars/eng/2014/food/pdf/araujo.pdf.

Arens, W. 1979. *The Man-eating Myth: Anthropology and Anthropophagy*. Oxford: Oxford University Press.

Arnold, David. 1988. *Famine: Social Crisis and Historical Change*. Oxford: Blackwell.

Arrehag, Lisa, Alex de Waal, and Alan Whiteside. 2006. "'New Variant Famine' Revisited: Chronic Vulnerability in Rural Africa." *Humanitarian Exchange* 33: 7–10.

Arrow, Kenneth. 1982. "Why People Go Hungry." *New York Review of Books*, 15 July.

Ashton, Basil, Kenneth Hill, Alan Piazza, and Robin Zeitz. 1984. "Famine in China, 1958–61." *Population and Development Review* 10(4): 613–45.

Asian People's Anti-Communist League. 1962. *Famine As Told by Letters from the Chinese Mainland*. Taipei.

Avramescu, Cătălin. 2009. *An Intellectual History of Cannibalism*. Princeton: Princeton University Press.

Aykroyd, W. R. 1974. *The Conquest of Famine*. London: Chatto & Windus.

Banik, Dan. 2002. "*Democracy, Drought and Starvation in India: Testing Sen in Theory and Practice*." Doctoral dissertation, Dept. of Political Science, University of Oslo.

Banister, Judith. 1984. "An Analysis of Recent Data on the Population of China." *Population and Development Review* 10(2): 241–71.

———. 1987. *China's Changing Population*. Stanford, CA: Stanford University Press.

Barber, John, and Andrei Dzeniskevich, eds. 2005. *Life and Death in Besieged Leningrad, 1941–44*. London: Palgrave Macmillan.

Barnett, Jon, and Michael Webber. 2010. "Accommodating Migration to Promote Adaptation to Climate Change." World Bank Policy Research Paper No. 5270. Washington, DC: World Bank.

Barnouin, Barbara, and Yu Changgen. 2007. *Zhou Enlai: A Political Life*. Hong Kong: Chinese University Press.

Barreca, Alan I., Karen Clay, Olivier Deschenes, Michael Greenstone, and Joseph S. Shapiro. 2012. "Adapting to Climate Change: The Remarkable Decline in the U.S. Temperature-Mortality Relationship Over the 20th Century." http://ssrn.com/abstract=2192245.

Barrington, Sir Jonah. 1827–32. *Personal Sketches of His Own Times*. London: Henry Colburn.

Barrios, Salvador, Bazoumana Ouattara, and Eric Strobl. 2008. "The Impact of Climatic Change on Agricultural Production: Is It Different for Africa?" *Food Policy* 33(4): 287–98.

Bassino, Jean-Pascal. 2007. "Market Integration and Famines in Early Modern Japan, 1717–1857." http://federation.ens.fr/ydepot/semin/texte0708/BAS2007MAR.pdf.

Batabyal, Rakesh. 2005. *Communalism in Bengal: From Famine to Noakhali, 1943–47*. New Delhi: Sage.

Bauer, Peter. 1972. *Dissent on Development*. Cambridge, MA: Harvard University Press.

Bayley, W. B. 1818. "Bengal: Statistical Account of the Population of Burdwan." *Transactions of the Society Instituted in Bengal for Inquiring into the History and Antiquities . . . of Asia* 12: 549–74.

Bayly, Christopher, and Tim Harper. 2004. *Forgotten Armies: Britain's Asian Empire and the War with Japan*. London: Allen Lane.

Becker, Jasper. 1996. *Hungry Ghosts: Mao's Secret Famine*. New York: Free Press.

———. 2005. *Rogue Regime: Kim Jong Il and the Looming Threat of North Korea*. New York: Oxford University Press.

Belozerov, Boris. 2005. "Crime during the Siege." In Barber and Dzeniskevich 2005, pp. 213–26.

Bence-Jones, Mark. 1982. *The Viceroys of India*. London: Constable.

Bernstein, Thomas P. 1983. "Starving to Death in China." *New York Review of Books*, June 16.

———. 2006. "Mao Zedong and the Famine of 1959–1960: A Study in Willfulness." *China Quarterly* 186: 421–45.

Besley, Timothy, and Robin Burgess. 2002. "The Political Economy of Government Responsiveness: Theory and Evidence from India." *Quarterly Journal of Economics* 117(4): 1415–51.

Bhatia, B. M. 1967. *Famines in India 1860–1965: A Study in Some Aspects of the Economic History of India*. Delhi: Asia Publishing House.

Bhattacharya, Sanjoy. 1995. "The Colonial State and the Communist Party of India, 1942–45: A Reappraisal." South Asia Research 15(1): 48–77.

Bhattacharya, Sanjoy. 1997. "Wartime Policies of State Censorship and the Civilian Population: Eastern India, 1939–45." *South Asia Research* 17(2): 140–77.

Bianco, Lucien. 2001. *Peasants without the Party: Grass-roots Movements in Twentieth-Century China*. New York: M. E. Sharpe.

Blackwood, Frederick T. [Lord Dufferin], and George F. Boyle [Earl of Glasgow]. 1847. *Narrative of a Journey from Oxford to Skibbereen during the Year of the Irish Famine*. Oxford.

Blanc, Elodie, and Eric Strobl, 2013. "The Impact of Climate Change on Cropland Productivity: Evidence from Satellite Based Products at the River Basin Scale in Africa." *Climatic Change* 117(4): 873–90.

Blunt, Sir Edward. 1937. *The I.C.S.: the Indian Civil Service*. London: Faber & Faber.

Bohstedt, John. 2010. *The Politics of Provisions: Food Riots, Moral Economy, and Market Transition in England, c. 1500–1850*. Farnham, Surrey: Ashgate Books.

Boko, Michel, Isabelle Nyang, Anthony Niong, Coleen Vogel, et al. 2007. "Africa." In M. L. Parry et al., eds., *Climate Change 2007: Impacts, Adaptation and Vulnerability*, Cambridge: Cambridge University Press, pp. 433–67; http://www.ipcc.ch/pdf /assessment-report/ar4/wg2/ar4-wg2-chapter9.pdf.

Borsje, Jacqueline. 2007. "Human Sacrifice in Medieval Irish Literature." In Jan N. Bremmers, ed., *The Strange World of Human Sacrifice*, Leuven: Peeters, pp. 31–54.

Bose, Sugata. 2011. *His Majesty's Opponent: Subhas Chandra Bose and India's Struggle against Empire*. Cambridge, MA: Harvard University Press.

Bourke, Angela. 1993. "Irish Women's Lament Poetry." In Joan Newton Rader, ed., *Feminist Messages: Coding in Women's Folk Culture* (Publications of the American Folklore Society), Champaign: University of Illinois Press, pp. 160–82.

Bourke, Austin 1993. *The Visitation of God? The Potato and the Great Irish Famine*. Dublin: Lilliput.

Bowbrick, Peter. 1986. "The Causes of Famines: A Refutation of Professor Sen's Theory." *Food Policy* 11(2): 105–24.

Bowen, Huw V. 1991. *Revenue and Reform: The Indian Problem in British Politics 1757–1773*. Cambridge: Cambridge University Press.

Boyce, James K. 1987. *Agrarian Impasse in Bengal: Institutional Constraints to Technological Change*. Oxford: Oxford University Press.

Boyle, Phelim P., and Cormac Ó Gráda. 1986. "Fertility Trends, Excess Mortality, and the Great Irish Famine." *Demography* 23(4): 543–62.

BPP (British Parliamentary Papers). 1831–32. "East India Company Affairs, Report and General Appendix." vol. 8. http://books.google.ie/books?id=6bUIAAAAQAAJ &pg=RA1-PA11&lpg=RA1-PA11&dq=i#v=onepage&q=i&f=false.

Bramall, Chris. 2011. "Agency and Famine in China's Sichuan Province, 1958–1962." *China Quarterly* 208: 990–1008.

Brandt, Loren, and Barbara Sands. 1992. "Land Concentration and Income Distribution in Republican China." In Thomas G. Rawski and Lillian M. Li, eds., *Chinese History in Economic Perspective*, Berkeley: University of California Press, pp. 179–206.

Braund, Henry B. 1944. "Famine in Bengal." Unpublished typescript. June 30 (deposited in British Library, Oriental and India Office Library, Mss. Eur. D792/2).

Breschi, Marco, and Lucia Pozzi, eds. 2004. *The Determinants of Infant and Child Mortality in Past European Populations*. Udine: Forum.

Brennan, Lance. 1984. "The Development of the Indian Famine Codes." In B. Currey and G. Hugo, eds., *Famine as a Geographical Phenomenon*, Dordrecht: Reidel, pp. 91–111.

———. 1988. "Government Famine Relief in Bengal, 1943." *Journal of Asian Studies* 47(3): 541–66.

Brewster, David. 1830. "India." In *The Edinburgh Encyclopedia*, Edinburgh: Blackwood, vol. 12, pp. 1–115.

A Brief History of the Statesman. 1948. Calcutta: Statesman.

Brittlebank, William. 1873. *Persia during the Famine: A Narrative of a Tour in the East and of the Journey Out and Home*. London: Basil Montague Pickering.

Brown, Jeremy. 2011. "Great Leap City: Surviving the Famine in Tianjin." In Manning and Wemheuer (2011), pp. 226–50.

Brun, Thierry. 1980. Comment on Robert Dirks, "Social Responses during Severe Food Shortages and Famine." *Current Anthropology* 21(1): 34.

Burgess, Robin, and Dave Donaldson. 2010. "Can Openness Mitigate the Effects of Weather Shocks? Evidence from India's Famine Era." *American Economic Review Papers & Proceedings* 100: 449–53.

Buttimer, Cornelius G. 1997. "*Pláig fhollasach, pláig choimhtheach*: Obvious Plague, Strange Plague." *Journal of the Cork Historical and Archaeological Society*, 102: 41–69.

Cabourdin, Guy, Jean-Noel Biraben, and Alain Blum. 1988. "Les crises démographiques." In Jacques Dupâquier, ed., *Histoire de la population française*, Paris: Presses Universitaires de France, vol. 2, 175–219.

Cai, Yong, and Wang Feng. 2005. "Famine, Social Disruption, and Involuntary Fetal Loss: Evidence from Chinese Survey Data." *Demography* 42(2): 301–22.

Cai, Yong, and Wang Feng. 2010. "Reproductive Consequences of China's Great Leap Forward Famine." In Satomi Kurosu, Tommy Bengtsson, and Cameron Campbell, eds., *Demographic Responses to Sudden Economic and Environmental Change*, Tokyo: Reitaku University Press, pp. 133–49.

Campbell, Sir George. 1874. "Memoir by Mr [Sir] George Campbell on the Famines which affected Bengal in the Last Century." In J. C. Geddes, *Administrative Experience Recorded in Former Famines*, Calcutta.

Camporesi, Piero. 1989. *Bread of Dreams*. Oxford: Polity Press.

Canny, Nicholas P. 1973. "The Ideology of English Colonization: From Ireland to America." *William and Mary Quarterly* 30(4): 575–98.

Cantillon, Richard. 1997 [1755]. *Essai sur la nature du commerce en general*. Paris: INED.

Cao, Shuji. 2005. *Dajihuang—1959–1961 nian de Zhongguo renkou*. Hong Kong: Dangdai guoji chubanshe gongsi.

———. 2010. "The Politics of the Age of Famine in Wuwei County." Paper presented at the International Workshop on Famines of the Twentieth Century, University of Melbourne, 8–11 June.

Carleton, William. 1852a. *Red Hall: Or, the Baronet's Daughter*. London: Saunders & Otley.

———. 1852b. *The Squanders of Castle Squander*. London: Office of the Illustrated London Library.

———. 1979 [1847]. *The Black Prophet: A Tale of Famine*. New York: Garland.

Carlyle, Thomas. 1882. *Reminiscences of My Irish Journey in 1849*. New York: Harper.

Caşu, Igor. 2010. "Stalinist Terror in Soviet Moldavia, 1940–1953." In Kevin McDermott and Matthew Stibbe, eds., *Stalinist Terror in Eastern Europe: Elite Purges and Mass Repression*, Manchester: Manchester University Press, pp. 39–56.

Chakrabarti, Malabika. 2004. *The Famine of 1896–1897 in Bengal: Availability or Entitlement Crisis?* New Delhi: Orient Longman.

Chakraborty, Ratan Lal. 1997. *Rural Indebtedness in Bengal*. Calcutta: Progressive Publishers.

Chang, Gordon. 1988. "To the Nuclear Brink: Eisenhower, Dulles, and the Quemoy-Matsu Crisis." *International Security* 12(4): 96–123.

Chang, Jung. 1991. *Wild Swans*. London, Simon & Schuster.

Chang, Jung, and Jon Halliday. 2005. *Mao: The Unknown Story*. New York: Alfred A. Knopf.

Chapoto, Antony, and T. S. Jayne. 2008. "Impact of AIDS-related Mortality on Farm Household Welfare in Zambia." *Economic Development and Cultural Change* 56(2): 327–74.

Charnock, Richard Stephen. 1866. "Cannibalism in Europe." *Journal of the Anthropological Society of London* 4: xxii–xxxi.

Chatterji, Joya. 1994. *Bengal Divided: Hindu Communalism and Partition, 1932–1947: Hindu Communalism and Partition, 1932–1947*. Cambridge University Press.

———. 2001. "The Decline, Revival and Fall of Bhadralok Influence in the 1940s." In S. Bandopadhyay, ed., *Bengal: Rethinking History: Essays on Historiography*, Manohar Publishers, pp. 29–315.

Chattopadhyay, Kshitis Prasad, and R. K. Mukherjee. 1946. *A Plan for Rehabilitation*. Calcutta: Statistical Publishing Society.

Checchi, Francesco, and W. Courtland Robinson. 2013. *Mortality among Populations of Southern and Central Somalia Affected by Severe Food Insecurity and Famine during 2010–12*. Washington, DC: FewsNet.

Chen, Yixin. 2009. "Cold War Competition and Food Production in China, 1957–1962." *Agricultural History* 83(1): 51–78.

———. 2010. "Politicization of Sickness: Diseases and the Failure of Public Health Response during China's Great Leap Forward Famine." Paper presented at the International Workshop on Famines of the Twentieth Century, University of Melbourne, 8–11 June.

———. 2011. "Under the Same Maoist Sky: Accounting for Death Discrepancies in Anhui and Jiangsi." In Manning and Wemheuer (2011), pp. 197–225.

Chevet, Jean-Michel, and Alain Guery. 1985. "Consommation et approvisionnement de Paris en céréales de 1725 à 1733." *Les techniques de conservation des grains à long terme 3*, fasc. 2: 463–77.

Chimtom, Ngala Killian. 2013. "Saving a Shrinking Lake." *Intel Press Service*, February 9 (http://www.ipsnews.net/2013/02/saving-a-shrinking-lake/).

China Population Information Centre. 1988. *Female Fertility in China: A [One-per-thousand] Population Survey*. 5 vols. Beijing: New World Press.

Chu, Valentin. 1964. *Ta, Ta, Tan, Tan: The Inside Story of Communist China*. New York: Norton.

Ci, Longun, and Xiaohui Yang. 2010. *Desertification and Its Control in China*. Beijing and Heidelberg: Springer.

Coale, Ansley J. 1984. *Rapid Population Growth in China, 1952–1982*. Washington, DC: National Academy Press.

Collins, William J. 1999. "Labor Mobility, Market Integration, and Wage Convergence in Late 19th Century India." *Explorations in Economic History* 36: 246–77.

Cornia, Giovanni Andrea, and Laura Deotti. 2008. "Niger's 2005 Food Crisis: Extend, Causes, and Nutritional Impact." University of Florence European Development Research Network Working Paper 2008/15.

Costa, Dora L., and Matthew E. Kahn. 2009. *Heroes and Cowards: The Social Face of War*. Princeton, NJ: Princeton University Press.

Crombé, Xavier. 2009. "Building the Case for Emergency: MSF and the Malnutrition Factor." In Crombé and Jézéquel (2009), pp. 59–81.

Crombé, Xavier, and Jean-Hervé Jézéquel, eds. 2009. *Not-So-Natural Disaster: Niger 2005*. London: Hurst & Company.

Crowley, John, William Smyth, and Michael Murphy. 2012. *Atlas of the Great Irish Famine*. Cork: Cork University Press.

Curtis, Perry. 1999. "The Edible Complex: Images of Cannibalism in Ireland." Unpublished paper.

Daly, Mary E. 1981. *Social and Economic History of Ireland since 1800*. Dublin: Educational Company.

Dando, William. 1980. *The Geography of Famine*. London: Edward Arnold.

Das, Debarshi. 2008. "A Relook at the Bengal Famine." *Economic and Political Weekly*, August 2, 59–64.

Das, S. C. 2000. *The Biography of Bharat Kesri Dr. Syama Prasad Mookerjee, with Modern Implications*. New Delhi: Abhinav Publications.

Das, Tarakchandra. 1949. *Bengal Famine (1943) as Revealed in a Survey of the Destitutes in Calcutta*. Calcutta: University of Calcutta.

Dasgupta, M. K. 1984. "The Bengal Famine, 1943 and the Brown Spot of Rice: An Inquiry into Their Relations." *History of Agriculture* 2(3): 1–18.

Datta, Rajat. 1990. "Rural Bengal: Social Structure and Agrarian Economy in the Late Eighteenth Century." PhD dissertation, University of London. https://kclpure.kcl.ac.uk/portal/files/2926683/241693.pdf.

Davies, R. W., and Stephen G. Wheatcroft. 2004. *The Years of Hunger: Soviet Agriculture, 1931–33*. London: Palgrave Macmillan.

De, Bikramjit. 2006. "Imperial Governance and the Challenges of War: Management of Food Supplies in Bengal, 1943–44." *Studies in History* 22: 1–43.

Dell, Melissa, Benjamin Jones, and Ben Olken. 2012. "Temperature Shocks and Economic Growth: Evidence from the Last Half Century." *American Economic Journal: Macroeconomics* 4(3): 66–95.

Devereux, Stephen. 2002. *State of Disaster: Causes, Consequences and Policy Lessons from Malawi*. http://www.actionaid.org.uk/sites/default/files/doc_lib/113_1_state_of_disaster.pdf, p. 18.

De Waal, Alex, and Alan Whiteside. 2003. "New Variant Famine: AIDS and Food Crisis in Southern Africa." *The Lancet* 362(9391, 11 October): 1234–37.Diamond, Jared. 2000. "Archaeology: Talk of Cannibalism." *Nature* 407 (7 September): 25–26.

Dickson, David. 1997. *Arctic Ireland: The Extraordinary Story of the Great Frost and Forgotten Famine of 1740–41*. Belfast: White Row Press.

Dikötter, Frank. 2010. *Mao's Great Famine: The History of China's Most Devastating Catastrophe, 1958–1962*. New York: Walker & Co.

———. 2013. "Response to 'Hard Facts and Half-truths: The New Archival History of China's Great Famine.'" *China Information* 27: 371–78.

Dillon, Charles. 2000. "Cín lae Uí Mhealláin: Friar Ó Meallan Journal." In Charles Dillon and Henry A. Jeffries, eds., *Tyrone: History and Society*, Dublin: Geography Publications, pp. 327–402.

Drèze, Jean, and Amartya Sen. 1989. *Hunger and Public Action*. Oxford: Oxford University Press.

Dronin, Nikolai M., and Edward G. Bellinger. 2005. *Climate Dependence and Food Problems in Russia 1900–1990*. Budapest and New York: Central European University Press.

Dwyer, D. J. 1962. "China's Natural Calamities and Their Consequences." *Geography* 47: 301–6.

Dyson, T. 1991. "On the Demography of South Asian Famines, part 2." *Population Studies* 45: 279–97.

———. 1996. *Population and Food: Global Trends and Future Prospects*. London: Routledge.

———. 2005. "On Development, Demography and Climate Change: The End of the World As We Know It?" *Population and Environment* 27(2): 117–49.

Dyson, T., and A. Maharatna. 1991. "Excess Mortality during the Bengal Famine: A Re-evaluation." *Indian Economic and Social Review* 28: 281–97.

Dyson, T., and A. Maharatna. 1992. "Bihar Famine, 1966–67 and Maharashtra Drought, 1970–73." *Economic and Political Weekly*, 27 June: 1331.

Dyson, T. and C. Ó Gráda. 2002. *Famine Demography*. Oxford: Oxford University Press.

The Economist. 2010. "Survival in the Sahel: It's Getting Harder all the Time: Climatic Extremes, from Drought to Flood, Threaten Survival." December 2.

———. 2013. "New (Approved) Assessments: The Great Famine." 9 September 2013 (http://www.economist.com/blogs/analects/2013/09/new-approved-assessments).

Edgerton-Tarpley, Kathryn. 2008. *Tears from Iron: Cultural Responses to Famine in Nineteenth-Century China*. Berkeley: University of California Press.

Egg, J., F. Lerin, and M. Venin. 1975. *Analyse déscriptive de la famine des années 1931 au Niger, et implications méthodologiques.* Paris: INRA, Groupe d'étude des relations économiques internationales.

Ehrlich, Paul R. 1968. *The Population Bomb.* Cuthogue, NY: Bucaneer.

Elias, Norbert. 2007. "Involvement and Detachment." *Collected Works,* vol. 8. Dublin: UCD Press.

Ellman, Michael. 2000. "The 1947 Soviet Famine and the Entitlement Approach to Famines." *Cambridge Journal of Economics* 24(5): 603–30.

Fabel, Robin F. A., ed. 1990. *Shipwreck and Adventure of Monsieur Pierre Viaud.* Gainesville: University of West Florida Press.

Farmar, Tony. 2002. *Believing in Action: Concern, the First Thirty Years 1968–1998.* Dublin: A. & A. Farmar.

Federico, G. 2005. *Feeding the World: An Economic History of Agriculture, 1800–2000.* Princeton, NJ: Princeton University Press.

Feenstra, Robert C., Robert Inklaar, and Marcel P. Timmer. 2013. "The Next Generation of the Penn World Table." http://www.ggdc.net/pwt.

Fegan, Melissa. 2002. *Literature and the Irish Famine.* Oxford: Oxford University Press.

Fennell, Barbara. 2011. "Dodgy Dossiers? Hearsay and the 1641 Depositions." *History Ireland* 19(3): 26–29.

Fiske, John. 1876. *The Unseen World and Other Essays.* Boston: Houghton, Mifflin.

Fitzpatrick, Thomas. 1904. "The Wars of 1641 in County Down: The Deposition of High Sheriff Peter Hill." *Ulster Journal of Archaeology* 2nd ser. 10(2): 73–90.

Flower, John, and Pamela Leonard. 2006. "Moral Landscape in a Sichuan Mountain Village: A Digital Ethnography of Place." http://xiakou.uncc.edu/index.htm.

Fogel, Robert W. 1992. "Second Thoughts on the European Escape from Hunger: Famines, Chronic Malnutrition, and Mortality Rates." In Siddiq Osmani, ed., *Nutrition and Poverty,* Oxford: Oxford University Press, pp. 243–86.

Freeman, A. Martin, ed. 1944. *Annala Connacht: The Annals of Connacht A.D. 1224–1544.* Dublin: Dublin Institute of Advanced Studies.

Fuglestad, F. 1974. "La Grande Famine de 1931 dans l'ouest Nigérien: Réflexions autour d'une catastrophe naturelle." *Revue française d'histoire d'outre-mer* 61(222): 18–33.

Fuller, Pierre. 2011. "'Barren Soil, Fertile Minds': North China Famine and Visions of the 'Callous Chinese' *circa* 1920." *International History Review* 33(3): 453–72.

Gallagher, Thomas. 1982. *Paddy's Lament, Ireland, 1846–1847: Prelude to Hatred.* New York: Harcourt Brace Jovanovich.

Gamble, John. 2011. *Society and Manners in Early Nineteenth-Century Ireland.* Ed. Breandán Mac Suibhne. Dublin: Field Day.

Gao Hua. 2011. "Food Augmentation Methods and Food Substitutes during the Great Famine." In Manning and Wemheuer (2011), pp. 171–96.

Garnaut, Anthony. 2009. "What Role Has Bad Weather Played in Modern Chinese Famines?" Paper delivered at the World Economic History Congress, Utrecht, August.

———. 2013a. "Hard Facts and Half-truths: The New Archival History of China's Great Famine." *China Information* 27(2): 223–46.

———. 2013b. "A Quantitative Description of the Henan Famine of 1942." *Modern Asia Studies*. 47(6): 2007–45.

———. 2014a. "The Geography of the Great Leap Famine." *Modern China*, 40(3): pp. 315–48.

———. 2014b. "Large, Unacknowledged Debts: A Note on Frank Dikötter Sources." Unpublished paper.

Gazibo, Mamadou. 2009. "Famine or Food Crisis? Views from Niger's Political Scene." In Crombé and Jézéquel (2009), pp. 37–57.

Gazley, John G. 1973. *The Life of Arthur Young 1741–1820*. Philadelphia: American Philosophical Society.

Gelan, Ayele Ulfata. 2007. "Does Food Aid Have Disincentive Effects on Local Production? A General Equilibrium Perspective on Food Aid in Ethiopia." *Food Policy* 32: 436–58.

Ghose, A. K. 1982. "Food Supply and Starvation: A Study of Famines with Reference to the Indian Subcontinent." *Oxford Economic Papers* 34: 368–89.

Ghosh, Kali Charan. 1944. *Famine in Bengal 1770–1943*. Calcutta: Indian Associated Publishing Company.

Ghosh, Tushar Kanti. 1944. *The Bengal Tragedy*. Lahore: Hero Publications.

Gill, Peter. 2010. *Famine and Foreigners: Ethiopia Since Live Aid*. Oxford: Oxford University Press.

Glendevon, John. 1971. *The Viceroy at Bay: Lord Linlithgow in India 1936–1943*. London: Collins.

Goodkind, Daniel, and Loraine West. 2001. "The North Korean Famine and Its Demographic Impact." *Population and Development Review* 27(2): 219–38.

Goodkind, Daniel, Loraine West, and Peter Johnson. 2011. "A Reassessment of Mortality in North Korea, 1993–2008." Paper presented to the Population Association of America meetings, Washington, DC.

Goodman, David S. G. 1980. "Li Jingquan and the South-west Region, 1958–66: The Life and 'Crimes' of a 'Local Emperor.'" *China Quarterly* 81: 66–96.

Goswami, O. 1990. "The Bengal Famine of 1943: Re-examining the Data." *Indian Economic and Social History Review* 27: 445–63.

Graves, Ralph A. 1917. "Fearful Famines of the Past." *National Geographic Magazine* 32(1): 69–90 (http://en.wikisource.org/wiki/National_Geographic_Magazine/Volume_32/Number_1/Fearful_Famines_of_the_Past).

Grayson, Donald K. 1990. "Donner Party Deaths: A Demographic Assessment." *Journal of Anthropological Research* 46(3): 223–42.

Green, E.R.R. 1956. "Agriculture." In R. D. Edwards and T. D. Williams, eds., *The Great Famine: Essays in Irish History*, Dublin: Browne & Nolan, pp. 88–128.

Greenough, Paul R. 1982. *Prosperity and Misery in Rural Bengal: The Famine of 1943–44*. Oxford: Oxford University Press.

Gupta, P. S. 1997. "Food Situation." In P. S. Gupta, ed., *Towards Freedom: Documents on the Movement for Independence in India, 1943–1944*, Delhi: Oxford University Press, vol. 2, pp. 1817–2065.

Haan, Nicholas, Stephen Devereux, and Daniel Maxwell. 2012. "Implications of Somalia 2011 for Famine Prevention, Mitigation and Responses." *Global Food Security* 1: 54–59.

Haggard, Stephen, and Marcus Noland. 2005. *Hunger and Human Rights: The Politics of Famine in North Korea.* Washington, DC: U.S. Committee for Human Rights in North Korea.

Haggard, Stephen, and Marcus Noland. 2007. *Famine in North Korea: Markets, Aid, and Reform.* New York: Columbia University Press.

Häkkinen, Anti, Vappu Ikonen, Kari Pitkänen, and Hannu Soikkanen. 1991. *Kun Hallen nälän tuskan toi. Miten Suomalaiset kokivat 1860-luvun nälkävuodet.* Helsinki: WSOY.

Hall-Matthews, David.1998. "The Historical Roots of Famine Relief Paradigms." In Helen O'Neill and John Toye, eds. *A World without Famine? New Approaches to Aid and Development.* London: Macmillan, pp. 107–27.

Hamilton, Walter. 1820. *Geographical, Statistical and Historical Description of Hindoostan.* London: John Murray.

Hansch, S., S. Lillibridge, G. Egeland, C. Teller, and M. Toole. 1994. *Lives Lost, Lives Saved: Excess Mortality and the Impact of Health Intervention in the Somali Emergency.* Washington, DC: Refugee Policy Group.

Hara, Kazuo. 1987. *The Emperor's Naked Army Marches On.* Facets video, 2007.

Hastrup, Kirsten. 1973. "Hunger and the Hardness of Facts." *Man* n.s. 28(4): 727–39.

Herbert, Claude-Jacques. 1759. *Observations sur la liberté du commerce des grains.* Amsterdam.

Henderson, W. O. 1984. *The Zollverein.* 3rd ed. London: Cass.

Herrmann, Rachel B. 2011. "The 'Tragicall Historie': Cannibalism and Abundance in Colonial Jamestown." *William & Mary Quarterly* 68(1): 47–74.

Hershatter, Gail. 2011. *The Gender of Memory: Rural Women and China's Collective Past.* Berkeley: University of California Press.

Heston, Alan, Robert Summers, and Bettina Aten. 2012. Penn World Table Version 7.1, Center for International Comparisons of Production, Income and Prices at the University of Pennsylvania July.

Heuveline, Patrick. 1998. "L'insoutenable incertitude du nombre: Estimations des décès de la période Khmer rouge." *Population* 53(6): 1103–17.

Hionidou, Violetta. 2006. *Famine and Death in Occupied Greece.* Cambridge: Cambridge University Press.

———. 2011. "What Do Starving People Eat? The Case of Greece through Oral History." *Continuity and Change* 2011 26(1): 113–34.

Hoffman, Elizabeth, and Joel Mokyr. 1984. "Peasants, Potatoes and Poverty: Transactions Costs in Prefamine Ireland." In Gary Saxonhouse and Gavin Wright, eds., *Technique, Spirit and Form in the Making of the Modern Economy: Essays in Honor of William N. Parker,* Greenwich, CT: JAI Press, pp. 115–45.

Holliday, Paul. 1998. *A Dictionary of Plant Pathology.* 2nd ed. Cambridge: Cambridge University Press.

Howe, Paul, and Stephen Devereux. 2004. "Famine Intensity and Magnitude Scales: A Proposal for an Instrumental Definition of Famine." *Disasters* 28(4): 353–72.

Hulme, Peter. 1986. *Colonial Encounters: Europe and the Native Caribbean, 1492–1797.* London: Methuen.

Hunter, W. W. 1868. *The Annals of Rural Bengal.* Edinburgh: Murray and Gibb.

———. 1874. *Famine Aspects of Bengal Districts*. London: Trübner.

Hurd, John. 1975. "Railways and the Expansion of Markets in India, 1861–1921." *Explorations in Economic History* 12: 263–88.

Islam, M. Mufakharul. 1978. *Bengal Agriculture 1920–1946, a Quantitative Study*. Cambridge: Cambridge University Press.

———. 2007. "The Great Bengal Famine and the Question of FAD Yet Again." *Modern Asian Studies* 41(2): 421–40.

International Organization for Migration. 2012. *Climate Change, Environmental Degradation, and Migration*. Geneva: IOM.

Jin, Xiaoding. 2009. "A critique of Jung Chang and Jon Halliday, *Mao: The Unknown Story*." In Gregor Benton and Lin Chun, eds., *Was Mao Really a Monster?* London: Routledge, pp.135–62.

Johnson, Ian. 2010. "Finding the Facts about Mao's Victims." *New York Review of Books Blog*, http://www.nybooks.com/blogs/nyrblog/2010/dec/20/finding-facts-about-maos-victims/.

Jordan, William Chester. 1996. *The Great Famine: Northern Europe in the Early Fourteenth Century*. Princeton, NJ: Princeton University Press.

Kaplan, Steven L. 1984. *Provisioning Paris: Merchants and Millers in the Grain and Flour Trade in the Eighteenth Century*. Ithaca, NY: Cornell University Press.

Kaukiainen, Yrjö. 1984. "Harvest Fluctuations and Mortality in Agrarian Finland (1810–1870)." In Tommy Bengtsson, Gunnar Fridlizius, and Rolf Ohlsson, eds., *Pre-industrial Population Change: the Mortality Decline and Short-term Population Movements*, Stockholm: Almqvist and Wiksell, pp. 235–54.

Keenleyside, Anne, Margaret Bertully, and Henry C. Fricke. 1997. "The Final Days of the Franklin Expedition: New Skeletal Evidence." *Arctic* 50(1): 36–46.

Kelly, Morgan, and C. Ó Gráda. 2013. *Numerare est errare*: Agricultural Output and Food Supply in England before and during the Industrial Revolution." *Journal of Economic History* 73(4): 1125–56.

Kenneally, Thomas. 2010. *Three Famines*. North Sydney: Knopf.

Keys, Ancel, Josef Boržek, Austin Henschel, Olaf Michelsen, and Henry Longstreet Taylor. 1950. *The Biology of Human Starvation*. Minneapolis: University of Minnesota Press.

Kiiskinen, Auvo. 1961. "Regional Economic Growth in Finland, 1880–1952." *Scandinavian Economic History Review* 9: 83–104.

Killeen, J. F. 1976. "Ireland in the Greek and Roman Writers." *Proceedings of the Royal Irish Academy, Section C* 76: 207–15.

Kindler, Robert. 2011. "Die Starken und die Schwachen: Zur Bedeutung physischer Gewalt während der Hungersnot in Kasachstan (1930–1934)." *Jahrbücher für Geschichte Osteuropas* 59(1): 51–78.

———. 2014. *Stalins Nomaden: Herrschaft und Hunger in Kasachstan*. Hamburg: Hamburger Edition.

Kirschen, Lisa A. 2006. *The Legacy of the Siege of Leningrad, 1941–1995: Myth, Memories, and Monuments*. Cambridge: Cambridge University Press.

Knight, Sir Henry. 1954. *Food Administration in India 1939–47*. Stanford, CA: Stanford University Press.

Kochina, Elena. 1990. *Blockade Diary*. Ann Arbor, MI: Ardis.

Kueh, Y. Y. 1984. "A Weather Index for Analysing Grain Yield Instability in China, 1952–81." *China Quarterly* 97: 68–83.

———. 1995. *Agricultural Instability in China, 1931–1990: Weather, Technology, and Institutions*. Oxford: Clarendon Press.

Kung, James Kai-sing, and Justin Yifu Lin. 2003. "The Causes of China's Great Leap Famine." *Economic Development and Cultural Change* 52(1): 51–73.

Kung, James Kai-sing, and Shuo Chen. 2011. "The Tragedy of the Nomenklatura: Career Incentives and Political Radicalism during China's Great Leap Famine." *American Political Science Review* 105(1): 27–45.

Lachiver, Marcel. 1991. *Les années de misère: La famine au temps du Grand Roi*. Paris: Fayard.

Lam, David. 2011. "How the World Survived the Population Bomb: Lessons from 50 Years of Extraordinary Demographic History." *Demography* 48(4): 1231–62.

Lamb, Hubert. 1982. *Climate, History and the Modern World*. London: Routledge.

Langan-Egan, Maureen. 1999. "Some Aspects of the Great Famine in Galway." *Journal of the Galway Historical and Archaeological Society* 51: 120–39.

Lavin, Deborah. 2004. "Amery, Leopold Charles Maurice Stennett (1873–1955)." *Oxford Dictionary of National Biography*, Oxford: Oxford University Press.

Law-Smith, Auriol. 1989. "Response and Responsibility: The Government of India's Role in the Bengal Famine, 1943." *South Asia* 12(1): 49–65.

Lawrence, Richard. 1682. *The Interest of Ireland in Its Trade and Wealth Stated*. Dublin.

Lee, Joseph. 1997. "The Famine As History." In C. Ó Gráda, ed., *Famine 150: Commemorative Lecture Series*, Dublin: Teagasc, pp. 159–75.

Lefgren, John. 1973. "Famine in Finland 1867–8." *Intermountain Economic Review* 4(2): 17–31.

Legge, James. 1978. *The Famine in China: Illustrations by a Native Artist with a Translation of the Chinese Text*. London: Kegan Paul.

Lenihan, Pádraig. 1997. "War and Population, 1649–52." *Irish Economic and Social History* 24: 1–21.

Levi, Primo. 1988. *The Drowned and the Saved*. New York: Vintage International.

Levinsohn, James, and Margaret McMillan. 2007. "Does Food Aid Harm the Poor? Household Evidence from Ethiopia." In Ann Harrison, ed., *Globalization and Poverty*, Chicago: University of Chicago Press, pp. 561–92.

Leys, Simon. 1990. "The Art of Interpreting Nonexistent Inscriptions Written in Invisible Ink on a Blank Page." *New York Review of Books*, 11 October.

Li, Lillian. 2007. *Fighting Famine in North China: State, Market and Environmental Decline, 1690s–1990s*. Stanford, CA: Stanford University Press.

Li, Wei, and Dennis Tao Yang. 2005. "The Great Leap Forward: Anatomy of a Central Planning Disaster." *Journal of Political Economy* 113(4): 840–77.

Li, Zhisui. 1994. *The Private Life of Chairman Mao*. London: Chatto & Windus.

Lin, Chun. 2013. *China and Global Capitalism: Reflections on Marxism, History, and Contemporary Politics*. London: Palgrave Macmillan.

Longfield, Mountifort. 1834. *Lectures on Political Economy delivered in Trinity and Michaelmas Terms, 1833*. Dublin: Milliken.

Luo, Sheng. 1988. "Reconstruction of Life Tables and Age Distributions for the

Population of China, by Year, from 1953 to 1982." PhD dissertation, University of Pennsylvania.

Lynch, Katherine A. 1992. "History and the Pursuit of Interdisciplinary Research in the Human Sciences." In Peter K. Karsten and John Modell, eds., *Theory, Method, and Practice in Social and Cultural History*, New York: New York University Press, pp. 57–77.

Macbeth, Helen, Wulf Schiefenhövel, and Paul Collinson. 2007. "Cannibalism: No Myth, but Why So Rare?' in Jeremy MacClancy, Jeya Henry, and Helen Macbeth, eds., *Consuming the Inedible: Neglected Dimensions of Food Choice*. New York: Berghahn, pp. 163–76.

MacFarquhar, Roderick. 1983. *The Origins of the Cultural Revolution: The Great Leap Forward 1958–1960*. New York: Columbia University Press.

———. 1995. "The Founding of the *China Quarterly*." *China Quarterly* 143: 692–96.

Mac Suibhne, Breandán. 2013. "A Jig in the Poorhouse." *Dublin Review of Books*, Issue 32, 8 April, http://www.drb.ie/essays/a-jig-in-the-poorhouse.

Maddison, Angus. 2009. *Statistics on World Population, GDP and Per Capita GDP, 1–2008 AD*. http://www.ggdc.net/MADDISON/oriindex.htm.

Mahalanobis, P. C., Ramkrishna Mukherjea, and Ambica Ghose. 1946. *A Sample Survey of After Effects of the Bengal Famine of 1943*. Calcutta: Statistical Publishing Society.

Maharatna, Arup. 1996. *The Demography of Famines: An Indian Historical Perspective*. Delhi: Oxford University Press.

Mallory, Walter H. 1926. *China: Land of Famine*. New York: National Geographic Society.

Malthus, Thomas R. 1800. *An Investigation of the Cause of the Present High Price of Provisions*. 3rd ed. London: Johnston.

Manning, Kimberley E., and Felix Wemheuer. 2011. *Eating Bitterness: New Perspectives on China's Great Leap Forward and Famine*. Vancouver: University of British Columbia Press.

Mansergh, Nicholas. 1971. *The Transfer of Power*, vol. 3: *Reassertion of Authority, Gandhi's Fast and the Succession to the Viceroyalty, 21 September 1942–12 June 1943*. London: HMSO.

Mansergh, Nicholas. 1973. *The Transfer of Power*, vol. 4: *The Bengal Famine and the New Viceroyalty, 15 June 1943–31 August 1944*. London: HMSO.

Maren, Michael. 2002. *The Road to Hell*. New York: Free Press.

Marr, David. 1997. *Vietnam 1945: The Quest for Power*. Berkeley: University of California Press.

Marshall, Alfred. 1920. *Principles of Economics*. 8th ed. London: Macmillan.

Martines, Lauro. 2013. *Furies: War in Europe, 1450–1700*. London: Bloomsbury.

Marvin, J. 1998. "Cannibalism as an Aspect of Famine in two English Chronicles." In M. Carlin and J. T. Rosenthal, eds., *Food and Eating in Medieval Europe*, London: Hambledon Press, pp. 73–86.

Mason, Nicole, T. S. Mason, Antony Chapoto, and Robert J. Myers. 2010. "A Test of the New Variant Famine Hypothesis: Panel Survey Evidence from Zambia." *World Development* 38(3): 356–68.

McAlpine, Michelle B. 1983. *Subject to Famine: Food Crises and Economic Change in Western India, 1860–1920*, Princeton, NJ: Princeton University Press.

McCloskey, D. N., and J. Nash. 1984. "Corn at Interest: The Extent and Cost of Corn Storage in Medieval England." *American Economic Review* 74(1): 174–87.

McGregor, P. 1989. "Demographic Pressure and the Irish Famine: Malthus after Mokyr." *Land Economics* 65(3): 228–38.

McGregor, Richard. 2010. "The Man Who Exposed Mao's Secret Famine." *Financial Times*, June 12.

Meadows, Donella H., Jorgen Randers, and Dennis L. Meadows. 1972. *The Limits to Growth*. New York: Universe Books.

Meng, Xin, Nancy Qian, and Pierre Yared. 2010. "The Institutional Causes of China's Great Famine, 1959–61." NBER Working Paper No. 16361.

Merewether, F.H.S. 1985 [1898]. *A Tour through the Famine Districts of India.* New Delhi: Usha.

Mirsky, Jonathan. 2010. "Livelihood Issues." *Literary Review*, September.

Mitchel, John. 1873. *The Last Conquest of Ireland (Perhaps)*. New York: Lynch, Cole, and Meehan.

Mitchell, Brian R. 1975. *European Historical Statistics*. London: Macmillan.

Mitra, Asok. 1989. "Famine of 1943 in Vikrampur Dacca." *Economic and Political Weekly*, February 4.

Mitra, Rajarji. 2012. "The Famine in British India: Quantification Rhetoric and Colonial Disaster Management." *Journal of Creative Communications* 7(1–2): 153–74.

Mokyr, Joel. 1980. "The Deadly Fungus: An Econometric Investigation into the Short Term Demographic Impact of the Irish Famine." *Research in Population Economics*, 2: 237–77.

———. 1985. *Why Ireland Starved: A Quantitative and Analytical History of the Irish Economy 1800–1850.* 2nd ed. London: Allen & Unwin.

Mokyr, Joel, and Cormac Ó Gráda. 2002. "What Do People Die of during Famines? The Great Irish Famine in Comparative Perspective." *European Review of Economic History* 6(3): 339–64.

Mookerjee, S. P. 1993. *Leaves from a Diary*. Calcutta: Oxford University Press.

Morash, Chris. 1989. *The Hungry Voice: The Poetry of the Irish Famine.* Dublin: Irish Academic Press.

Moriceau, Jean-Marc, and Gilles Postel-Vinay. 1992. *Ferme, entreprise, famille: Grande exploitation et changements agricoles, XVIIe–XIXe siècles*. Paris: EHESS.

Moyo, Dambisa. 2009. *Dead Aid: Why Aid Is Not Working and How There Is Another Way for Africa*. New York: Farrar, Straus and Giroux.

Mukerjee, Madhusree. 2010. *Churchill's Secret War: the British Empire and the Ravaging of India during World War II*. New York: Perseus Books.

———. 2014. "The Bengal Famine of 1943." *Economic and Political Weekly* 49(11): 71–75.

Mukerji, Karuna Moy. 1965. *Agriculture, Famine and Rehabilitation in South Asia*. Santiniketan: Visva-Bharati.

Murphey, Rhoads. 1967. "Man and Nature in China." *Modern Asian Studies* 1(4): 313–33.

Nakam, Géralde. 1975. *Au lendemain de la Saint-Barthélemy: Guerre civile et famine.* Paris: Éditions Anthropos.

Nathan, Andrew J. 1965. *A History of the China International Famine Relief Commission.* Cambridge, MA: Harvard East Asian Monographs.

Naysmith, Scott, Alex de Waal, and Alan Whiteside. 2009. "Revisiting New Variant Famine: The Case of Swaziland." *Food Security* 1(3): 251–60.

Nicholson, Asenath. 1851. *Annals of the Famine in Ireland in 1847, 1848 and 1849.* New York: E. French.

Noland, Marcus. 2004. *Korea after Kim Jong-Il.* Washington, DC: Institute for International Economics.

Noland, Marcus, Sherman Robinson, and Tao Tang. 1999. "Famine in North Korea: Causes and Cures." Peterson Institute of International Economics Working Paper 1999, no. 2.

Ó Ciosáin, Niall. 2004. "Approaching a Folklore Archive: The Irish Folklore Commission and the Memory of the Great Famine." *Folklore* 115: 222–32.

Ó Donnchadha, Tadhg. 1931. "Cín lae Ó Mealláin." *Annalecta Hibernica* 3: 1–61.

Ó Drisceoil, Proinsias. 2001. "Lucht feola daoine d'ithe agus míle milliún aineamh eile." *Bliainiris* 2: 11–26.

Ó Gráda, Cormac. 1993. *Ireland before and after the Great Famine: Explorations in Economic History.* 2nd ed. Manchester: Manchester University Press.

———. 1994. *An Drochshaol: Béaloideas agus Amhráin.* Dublin: Coiscéim.

———. 1997. "Markets and Famines: A Simple Test with Indian Data." *Economic Letters* 57: 241–44.

———. 1999. *Black '47 and Beyond: the Great Irish Famine in History, Economy and Memory.* Princeton, NJ: Princeton University Press.

———. 2001. "Markets and Famines: Evidence from Nineteenth-century Finland." *Economic Development and Cultural Change* 49(3): 575–90.

———. 2002. "The Dublin Potato Market during the Famine." In Ó Gráda (2006), pp. 106–20.

———. 2005. "Markets and Famines in Pre-industrial Europe." *Journal of Interdisciplinary History* 36(2): 143–66.

———. 2006. *Ireland's Great Famine: Interdisciplinary Perspectives.* Dublin: UCD Press.

———. 2008. "The Ripple That Drowns? Two Twentieth-century Famines as Economic History." *Economic History Review* 61 (supplement): 5–37.

———. 2009. *Famine: A Short History.* Princeton, NJ: Princeton University Press.

———. 2010. "Sufficiency and Sufficiency and Sufficiency': Revisiting the Bengal Famine of 1943–44." http://papers.ssrn.com/sol3/papers.cfm?abstract_id=1664571.

———. 2011. "Great Leap into Famine." *Population and Development Review* 37(1): 191–202.

———. 2013a. "Great Leap, Great Famine: A Review Essay." *Population and Development Review* 39(2): 333–47.

———. 2013b. "Varieties of Irish Famine Death." In James Kelly and Mary Ann Lyons, eds. *Death and Dying in Ireland, Britain, and Europe: Historical Perspective.* Dublin: Irish Academic Press, pp. 203–20.

Ó Gráda, Cormac, and Jean-Michel Chevet. 2002. "Market Segmentation and Famine in *ancien régime* France." *Journal of Economic History* 62(3): 706–33.

Ó Gráda, Cormac, Richard Paping, and Eric Vanhaute, eds. 2007. *When the Potato Failed: Causes and Effects of the Last European Subsistence Crisis, 1845–1850.* Turnhout: Brepols.

Ó Gráda, Cormac, and Diarmaid Ó Muirithe. 2010. "The Famine of 1740–41: Representations in Gaelic Poetry." *Eire-Ireland* 45(3–4): 41–62.

O'Brien, Robert Viking. 2001. "Cannibalism in Edmund Spenser's *Faerie Queene*, Ireland, and the Americas." In Kirsten Guest, ed., *Eating Their Words: Cannibalism and the Boundaries of Cultural Identity*, Albany: State University of New York Press, pp. 35–56.

Ohayon, Isabelle. 2013. "The Kazakh Famine: The Beginnings of Sedenterization." http://www.massviolence.org/IMG/article_PDF/The-Kazakh-Famine-The-Beginnings.pdf.

Olmstead, A. L., and P. W. Rhode. 2002. "The Red Queen and the Hard Reds: Productivity Growth in American Wheat, 1800–1940." *Journal of Economic History* 62(4): 929–66.

Olmstead, A. L., and P. W. Rhode. 2011. "Responding to Climatic Challenges: Lessons from U.S. Agricultural Development." In Gary D. Libecap and Richard H. Steckel, eds., *The Economics of Climate Change: Adaptations Past and Present*, Chicago: University of Chicago Press, pp. 169–94.

Omar Mahmoud, Toman, and Rainer Thiele. 2010. "Does AIDS-Related Mortality Reduce Per-Capita Household Income? Evidence from Rural Zambia." Kiel Institute for the World Economy, Working Paper 1530.

Padmanabhan, S. Y. 1973. "The Great Bengal Famine." *Annual Review of Phytopathology* 2: 11–26.

Paddock, William, and Paul Paddock. 1967. *Famine 1975! America's Decision: Who Will Survive?* Boston, MA: Little Brown.

Pankhurst, Richard K. 1986. *The History of Famine and Epidemics in Ethiopia Prior to the Twentieth Century*. Addis Ababa: Relief and Rehabilitation Commission.

Patenaude, Bruce. 2002. *The Big Show in Bololand: The American Relief Expedition to Soviet Russia in the Famine of 1921*. Stanford, CA: Stanford University Press.

Pearce, F. 2010. *Peoplequake: Mass Migration, Ageing Nations and the Coming Population Crash*. London: Eden Project.

Peng, Xizhe. 1987. "Demographic Consequences of the Great Leap Forward in China's Provinces." *Population and Development Review* 13(4): 639–70.

Perkins, D. H. 1969. *Agricultural Development in China, 1368–1968*. Edinburgh: Edinburgh University Press.

Perry, E. 1980. *Rebels and Revolutionaries in North China, 1845–1945*. Stanford, CA: Stanford University Press.

Persson, Karl-Gunnar. 1999. *Grain Markets in Europe 1500–1900, Integration and Regulation*. Cambridge: Cambridge University Press.

Petty, Sir William. 1899. *Economic Writings*, ed. C. H. Hull. 2 vols. Cambridge: Cambridge University Press.

Philbrick, Nathaniel. 2001. *In the Heart of the Sea: The Tragedy of the Whaleship Essex*. New York: Penguin.

Piancola, Niccolò. 2004. "Famine in the Steppe: The Collectivization of Agriculture and the Kazak Herdsmen 1928–1934." *Cahiers du monde russe* 45(1–2): 137–92.

Pinnell, Leonard G. 2002. *With the Sanction of Government: The Memoirs of L. G. Pinnell*. Perth: M. C. Pinnell (copies in the Centre for South Asian Studies, Cambridge and in the British Library).

Póirtéir, Cathal. 1995. *Famine Echoes*. Dublin: Gill & Macmillan.

———. 1996. *Glórtha ón Ghorta*. Dublin: Coiscéim.

Post, John D. 1977. *The Last Great Subsistence Crisis in the Western World*. Baltimore: Johns Hopkins University Press.

———. 1984. "Climatic Variability and the European Mortality Wave of the Early 1740s." *Journal of Interdisciplinary History* 15(1): 1–30.

Prasad, Bishewar, ed. 1960. *Indian Records Series: Fort William-India House Correspondence and Other Contemporary Papers Relating Thereto*, vol. 6: *Public, Select, and Secret 1770–1772*. Delhi: Government of India.

Purcell, Andrew. 2011. "How the UN Defines a Famine." *New Scientist*, 20 July.

Quddus, Munir, and Charles Becker. 2000. "Speculative Price Bubbles in the Rice Market and the 1974 Bangladesh Famine." *Journal of Economic Development* 25(2): 155–75.

Quesnay, François. 1958. *François Quesnay et la Physiocratie*, vol. 2: *Textes annotés*. Paris: INED.

Quinn, David B. 1966. *The Elizabethans and the Irish*. Ithaca, NY: Cornell University Press.

Rahmato, Dessalegn. 1991. *Famine and Survival Strategies: A Case Study from Northeast Ethiopia*. Uddevala: Bohus Läningens Boktrykeri.

Rashid, Salim. 1980. "The Policy of Laissez-faire during Scarcities." *Economic Journal* 90: 493–503.

Ravallion, Martin. 1987a. *Markets and Famines*. Oxford: Oxford University Press.

———. 1987b. "Trade and Stabilization: Another Look at British India's Controversial Foodgrain Exports." *Explorations in Economic History* 24(4): 354–70.

———. 1997. "Famines and Economics." *Journal of Economic Literature* 35(3): 1205–42.

Read, Piers Paul. 1974. *Alive: The Story of the Andes Survivors*. New York: Harper.

Reid, Anna. 2011. *Leningrad: The Epic Siege of World War II, 1941–1944*. London: Bloomsbury.

Ricardo, David. 1951. *The Works and Correspondence of David Ricardo*. Piero Sraffa, ed. Vol. 9. Cambridge University Press.

Ricker-Gilbert, J., T. S. Jayne, and E. Chirwa. 2010. "Subsidies and Crowding Out: A Double Hurdle Model of Fertilizer Demand in Malawi." *American Journal of Agricultural Economics* 93(1): 26–42.

Rieff, David. 1997. "Without Rules or Pity." *Foreign Affairs* March/April.

———. 2011. "Millions May Die . . . or Maybe Not: How Disaster Hype Became Big Business." *Foreign Policy*, 22 August.

Riskin, Carl. 1996. "Hidden Hunger, Shameful Secrets." *Times Higher Education Supplement*, 2 December.

———. 1998. "Seven Questions about the Chinese Famine of 1959–61." Special issue of *Chinese Economic Studies* 9(2): 111–24.

Robinson, F. N. 1913. "Human Sacrifice among the Irish Celts." In *Anniversary Papers by Colleagues and Pupils of George Lyman Kittredge*, Boston and London: Ginn, pp. 185–97.

Rosen, Sherwin. 1999. "Potato Paradoxes." *Journal of Political Economy* 107(S6): S294–S313.

Rothschild, Emma. 2001. *Economic Sentiments: Adam Smith, Condorcet and the Enlightenment*. Cambridge, MA: Harvard University Press.

Rousseau, Jean-Jacques. 2000 [1782]. *Confessions*. Translated by Angela Scholar. New York: Oxford University Press.

Roy, Thirtankar. 2012. *Natural Disasters and Indian History*. Oxford: Oxford University Press.

Samuelson, Paul. 1957. "Intertemporal Price Equilibrium: A Prologue to a Theory of Speculation." *Weltwirtschaftliches Archiv* 79: 181–219.

Santhanam, K. 1944. *The Cry of Distress: A First-hand Description and an Objective Study of the Indian Famine of 1943*. New Delhi: Hindustan Times.

Sauvy, Alfred. 1958. *De Malthus à Mao-Tsé-Toung*. Paris: Editions Denoël.

Sayles, G. O. 1956. "The Siege of Carrickfergus Castle, 1315–16." *Irish Historical Studies* 10(37): 94–100.

Schwekendiek, Daniel. 2011. *A Socioeconomic History of North Korea*. Jefferson, NC: McFarland.

Schneider, Mindi. 2008. *"We Are Hungry!" A Summary of Food Riots, Government Responses, and States of Democracy in 2008*. http://www.corpethics.org/downloads/Hungry_rpt2008.pdf.

Schram, Stuart. 1974. *Mao Tse-Tung Unrehearsed: Talks and Letters 1956–71*. Harmondsworth: Penguin.

Scott, Sir Walter. 1830. *The History of Scotland*, vol. 1. Zwickau: Schumann.

Sen, Amartya. 1981. *Poverty and Famines: An Essay on Entitlement and Deprivation*. Oxford: Clarendon Press.

———. 1999. *Development as Freedom*. Oxford: Oxford University Press.

———. 2009. *The Idea of Justice*. London: Penguin.

Sen, Ela. 1944. *Darkening Days: Being a Narrative of Famine-stricken Bengal*. Calcutta: Susil Gupta.

Sharma, Sanjay. 2001. *Famine, Philanthropy and the Colonial State*. New Delhi: Oxford University Press.

Shapiro, Judith 2001. *Mao's War Against Nature: Politics and the Environment in Revolutionary China*. Cambridge: Cambridge University Press.

Sheng, Michael M. 2008. "Mao and China's Relations with the Superpowers in the 1950s: A New Look at the Taiwan Strait Crises and the Sino–Soviet Split." *Modern China* 34(4): 477–507.

Simpson, A.W.B. 1984. *Cannibalism and the Common Law: The Story of the Tragic Last Voyage of the Mignonette and the Strange Legal Proceedings to Which it Gave Rise*. Chicago: University of Chicago Press.

Skouras F., A. Hatzedemos, A. Kaloutses, and G. Papademetriou. 1947. *E psuhopathologia tes peinas, Η ψυχοπαθολογία της πείνας, του φόβου και του άγχους*. Athens: Odusseas.

Smart, Robert. 2010. "Mapping the Imperial Body: Body Image and Representation in Famine Reporting." In David Valone, ed. *Ireland's Great Hunger: Relief, Representation and Remembrance*, Lanham, MD: University Press of America.

Smart, Robert, and Michael Hutcheson. 2007. "Suspect Grounds: Temporal and Spatial Paradoxes in Bram Stoker's *Dracula:* A Postcolonial Reading." *Postcolonial Text* 3(3): 1–22.

Smith, Adam. 1976 [1776]. *An Inquiry into the Nature and Causes of the Wealth of Nations*. Oxford: Oxford University Press.

Smith, William J. 2006. *Map-making, Landscapes and Memory: A Geography of Colonial and Early Modern Ireland c. 1530–1750*. Cork: Cork University Press.

Somerville, Alexander. 1994. *Letters from Ireland during the Famine of 1847*, ed. Keith D. M. Snell. Dublin: Irish Academic Press.

Sorokin, Pitirim A. 1975. *Hunger as a Factor in Human Affairs*. Gainesville: University of Florida Press.

Spenser, Edmund. 1970 [1596]. *A View of the Present State of Ireland*, ed. W. L. Renwick. Oxford: Oxford University Press.

Spoorenberg, Thomas, and Daniel Schwekendiek. 2012. "Demographic changes in North Korea: 1993–2008." *Population and Development Review* 38(1): 133–58.

Stathakopoulos, Dionysios. 2004. *Famine and Pestilence in the Late Roman and Early Byzantine Empire: A Systematic Survey of Subsistence Crises and Epidemics*. Aldershot: Ashgate.

Stephens, Chuck. 2007. "Both Ends Burning." Essay accompanying the 2007 Criterion Collection edition of Kon Ichikawa's film *Fires on the Plain*.

Stephens, Ian. 1966. *Monsoon Morning*. London: Benn.

Stromberg, Joseph. 2013. "Starving Settlers in Jamestown Colony Resorted to Cannibalism." *Smithsonian Magazine*, May 1. http://www.smithsonianmag.com /history/starving-settlers-in-jamestown-colony-resorted-to-cannibalism-46000815.

Studer, Roman. 2008. "India and the Great Divergence: Assessing the Efficiency of Grain Markets in Eighteenth- and Nineteenth-Century India." *Journal of Economic History* 68(2): 393–437.

Sutch, Richard. 2011. "The Impact of the 1936 Corn-belt Drought on American Farmers' Adoption of Hybrid Corn." In Gary D. Libecap and Richard H. Steckel, eds., *The Economics of Climate Change*, Chicago: University of Chicago Press, pp. 195–223.

Sweeney, Stuart. 2008. "Indian Railways and Famine 1875–1914: Magic Wheels and Empty Stomachs." *Essays in Economic and Business History* 26: 147–57.

Taaffe, Dennis. 1801. *An Impartial History of Ireland from the Period of the English Invasion to the Present Time*. 2 vols. Dublin: Christie.

Tahk, Kathleen. 2013. "The Biopolitics of Photography in the Soviet Famine, 1920–22." *Fuse Magazine*, 18 June, http://fusemagazine.org/2013/06/36–3_tahk.

Taithe, Bertrand. 2009. "Humanitarianism and Colonialism: Religious Responses to the Algerian Drought and Famine of 1866–1870." In Christoph Mauch and Christian Pfister, eds., *Natural Disasters, Cultural Responses: Case Studies toward a Global Environmental History*, Lanham, MD: Lexington Books, pp. 137–63.

Tannehill, Ray. 1975. *Flesh and Blood: A History of the Cannibal Complex*. New York: Stein & Day.

Tauger, Mark B. 2004. "Entitlement, Shortage, and the 1943 Bengal Famine: Another Look." Journal *of Peasant Studies* 31: 45–72.

———. 2009. "The Indian Famine Crises of World War II." *British Scholar* 1(2): 18–48.

Tawney, R. H. 1966 [1932]. *Land and Labour in China*. Boston: Beacon Press.

Terrill, Ross. 1973. *R. H. Tawney and his Times: Socialism as Fellowship*. Cambridge, MA: Harvard University Press.

Thaxton, Ralph A., Jr. 2008. *Catastrophe and Contention in Rural China: Mao's Great Leap Forward Famine and the Origins of Righteous Resistance in Da Fo Village*. Cambridge: Cambridge University Press.

UNDP Somalia. 1997. *Population Statistics of Somalia*. www.somali-jna.org/downloads/ACFA9.pdf.

Urban, Daniel, Michael J. Roberts, Wolfram Schlenker, and David B. Lobell. 2012. "Projected Temperature Changes Indicate Significant Increase in Interannual Variability of U.S. Maize Yields." *Climate Change* 112(2): 525–44.

Vandenberg, Vincent. 2008. "Fames facta est ut homo hominem comederet: l'Occident mediéval face au cannibalisme de survie (Ve–XIe siècle)." *Revue belge de philologie et d'histoire* 86(2): 217–72.

Vaughan, Megan. 2007. *The Story of an African Famine: Gender and Famine in Twentieth-century Malawi*. Cambridge: Cambridge University Press.

Villiers-Tuthill, Kathleen. 1997. *Patient Endurance: The Famine in Connemara*. Clifden: Connemara Publications.

von Braun, Joachim, Tesfaye Teklu, and Patrick Webb. 1999. *Famine in Africa: Causes, Responses, and Prevention*. Baltimore: Johns Hopkins Press.

Walker, Kenneth R. 1984. *Food Grain Procurement and Consumption in China*. Cambridge: Cambridge University Press.

Webb, Patrick, and Joachim von Braun. 1994. *Famine and Food Security in Ethiopia: Lessons for Africa*. New York: John Wiley.

Weigold, Auriol. 1999. "Famine Management: The Bengal Famine (1942–1944) Revisited." *South Asia* 22(1): 63–77.

Weir, David N. 1989. "Markets and Mortality in France, 1600–1789." In John Walter and Roger Schofield, eds., *Famine, Disease and the Social Order in Early Modern Society*, Cambridge: Cambridge University Press, pp. 201–34.

Wemheuer, Felix. 2010. "Dealing with Responsibility for the Great Leap Famine in the People's Republic of China." *China Quarterly* No. 201: 176–94.

———. "Sites of Horror: Mao's Great Famine." With response by Frank Dikötter. *China Journal* (66): 155–64.

———. *Famine Politics in Maoist China and the Soviet Union*. New Haven: Yale University Press.

Werth, Nicholas. 2007. *Cannibal Island: Death in a Siberian Gulag*. Princeton, NJ: Princeton University Press.

Wheatcroft, Stephen G. 1997. "Soviet Statistics of Nutrition and Mortality during Times of Famine: 1917–1922 and 1931–1933." *Cahiers du monde russe* 38(4): 525–57.

———. 2001. "Current Knowledge of the Level and Nature of Mortality in the

Ukrainian Famine of 1931–3." http://www.melgrosh.unimelb.edu.au/documents /SGW-UkranianFamine_mortality.pdf.

———. 2008. "Famines in Russia and China in Historical Perspective." Paper presented to the Harvard Economic History Workshop, March 7. http://isites .harvard.edu/fs/docs/icb.topic240844.files/Wheatcroft%20paper.pdf.

———. 2011. "Die sowjetische und die chinesische Hungersnot in historischer Perspektive." In Mathias Middell and Felix Wemheuer, eds., *Hunger, Ernährung und Rationierungssysteme unter dem Staatssozialismus (1917–2006)*, Bern: Peter Lang.

———. 2012. "The Soviet Famine of 1946–1947, the Weather and Human Agency in Historical Perspective." *Europe-Asia Studies* 64(6): 987–1005.

Whelan, Kevin. 1987. "The Catholic Priest in the 1798 Rebellion in County Wexford." In Kevin Whelan, ed., *Wexford: History and Society*, Dublin: Geography Publications, pp. 296–315.

White, Theodore H. 1978. *In Search of History: A Personal Adventure*. New York.

White, Theodore H., and Annalee Jacoby. 1946. *Thunder out of China*. New York: William Sloane.

Will, Pierre-Étienne. 1990. *Bureaucracy and Famine in Eighteenth-Century China*. Stanford, CA: Stanford University Press.

Williams, Rob. 2013. "North Korean Cannibalism Fears amid Claims Starving People Forced to Desperate Measures." *The Independent*, 28 January.

Witherow, Thomas. 1879. *Derry and Enniskillen in the Year 1689*. Belfast: Mullan & Sons, p. 184. http://www.archive.org/stream/derryenniskillen00withrich/derryenniskillen00withrich_djvu.txt.

Wittkowsky, George. 1943. "Swift's Modest Proposal: The Biography of an Early Georgian Pamphlet." *Journal of the History of Ideas* 4(1): 75–104.

World Bank. 2014. "Millennium Development Goals, Goal 4: Reduce Child Mortality by 2015." http://www.worldbank.org/mdgs/child_mortality.html.

World Food Programme Somalia. 2012. *Trend Analysis of Food and Nutrition Security in Somalia 2007–2012*. Nairobi: WFPS.

Wright, T. 2000. "Distant Thunder: The Regional Economies of Southwest China and the Impact of the Great Depression." *Modern Asian Studies* 34: 697–738.

Wright, William. 1882. *The Chronicle of Joshua the Stylite*. Cambridge: Cambridge University Press.

Yang, Jisheng. 2008. *Mubei: Zhongguo liu shi nian dai da jihuang ji shi [Tombstone: A Record of the Great Chinese Famine of the 1960s]*. Hong Kong: Cosmos Books.

———. 2010. "The Fatal Politics of the PRC's Great Leap Famine: The Preface to Tombstone." *Journal of Contemporary China* 19(66): 755–76.

———. 2011. "In Response to Mr. Dikötter's Comments on *Tombstone*." *Independent Chinese Pen Center*, November 16, http://insideoutchina.blogspot.ie/2011/12/ yang-rebuts-dikotter-on-famine-research.html.

———. 2012. *Tombstone: The Great Chinese Famine 1958–1962*. New York: Farrar, Strauss and Giroux.

Yao, S. 1999. "A Note on the Causal Factors of China's Famine in 1959–1961." *Journal of Political Economy* 107: 1365–69.

Young, Arthur. 1793. *Travels in France*. Dublin: Cross.

———. 1801. *The Question of Scarcity Plainly Stated, and Remedies Considered.* London.

Yu Xiguang. 2006. *Dayuejin, Kurizi Shanghuji [A Collection of the Petitions Made during the Hard Times of the Great Leap Forward].* Hong Kong: Shidai Chaoliu Chubanshe.

Zhao, Zhongwei, and Anna Reimondos. 2012. "The Demography of China's 1958–61 Famine: A Closer Examination." *Population* 67(2): 281–308.

Zhongguo zaiqing baogao 1949–1995 [China Calamity Report 1949–1995]. 1996. Beijing: Zhongguo tongji chubanshe.

Zhou Xun, ed. 2012. *The Great Famine in China, 1958–1962: A Documentary History.* New Haven: Yale University Press.

———. 2013. *Forgotten Voices of Mao's Great Famine, 1958–1962.* New Haven, CT: Yale University Press.

Zima, V. F. 1999. *The Famine of 1946–47 in the USSR.* Lewiston, NY: Edwin Mellen Press.

Zinn, Howard. 2003. *A People's History of the United States.* 3rd ed. Harrow: Pearson.

Index

Lightning Source UK Ltd.
Milton Keynes UK
UKHW010624180920
370055UK00001B/1